The Southwestern Grill

Other Books by Michael McLaughlin

All on the Grill
Good Mornings
The Little Book of Big Sandwiches
The Mushroom Book
More Back of the Box Gourmet
Cooking for the Weekend
Fifty-Two Meat Loaves
The Back of the Box Gourmet
The New American Kitchen
The Manhattan Chili Co.'s Southwest American Cookbook

by W. Park Kerr and Michael McLaughlin

The El Paso Chile Company's Burning Desires
The El Paso Chile Company's Texas Border Cookbook

by Susan Wyler and Michael McLaughlin

Great Books for Cooks

by Pamela Morgan and Michael McLaughlin

Pamela Morgan's Flavors

by Julee Rosso and Sheila Lukins in collaboration with Michael McLaughlin

The Silver Palate Cookbook

The Southwestern Grill

200 Terrific Recipes for Big and Bold Backyard Barbecue

MICHAEL McLAUGHLIN

THE HARVARD COMMON PRESS
Boston, Massachusetts

The Harvard Common Press
535 Albany Street
Boston, Massachusetts 02118

Printed in the United States of America
Printed on acid-free paper

Library of Congress Cataloging-in-Publication Data
McLaughlin, Michael.
  The Southwestern grill : 200 terrific recipes for big and bold backyard barbecue / Michael McLaughlin ; illustrations by Sandra Bruce.
       p. cm.
  Includes index.
  ISBN 1-55832-163-2 (cloth : alk. paper) — ISBN 1-55832-164-0 (pbk. : alk. paper)
    1. Barbecue cookery. 2. Cookery, American—Southwestern style. I. Title.
  TX840.B3 M438 2000
  641.5'784–dc21

                                                00-025754

Special bulk-order discounts are available on this and other Harvard Common Press books. Companies and organizations may purchase books for premiums or for resale, or may arrange a custom edition, by contacting the Marketing Director at the address above.

Cover photograph by Martin Jacobs Photography, Inc.
Cover design by Suzanne Noli
Text illustrations by Sandra Bruce
Book design by Kathleen Herlihy-Paoli, Inkstone Design

10 9 8 7 6 5 4 3 2 1

For Joan and Howard

Contents

Preface

Among the many very good things that have happened to American cooking over the last twenty years, two of the most important have also happened to be personally significant to me. First, grilling, formerly a casual backyard art form, evolved into an accepted and respected cooking method, far exceeding anything several generations of "Kiss the Cook" apron-wearers could have predicted. Second, the food of the Southwest escaped from its regional confines and swept like a mesquite brushfire across the country. Like grilling, southwestern ingredients and dishes found a warm welcome in the kitchens of fine restaurants from coast to coast, transforming previously European-derived menus with heat, spice, and savory smoke. In the hands of serious chefs, the two grew far beyond their weenie-and-burgers, taco-and-salsa origins, and frequently traveled in tandem. Now, home cooks are adventurous enough to grill almost anything edible (and have increasingly sophisticated equipment for doing so). And, thanks to a booming Latino population, grocery stores far from San Antonio, Albuquerque, and Tucson are well stocked with the ingredients necessary for reproducing the authentic flavors of the Southwest. For those who like it spicy, smoky, and fresh off of the grill, it's a very good time to be cooking.

I'm happy to have been along for most of the ride. Leaving college, I was fortunate enough to get a job, my first real one, waiting tables in a popular Tex-Mex restaurant. Some years later, following a stint at the seminal 1980s New York City gourmet shop, The Silver Palate, I again found myself working in a Tex-Mex restaurant, The Manhattan Chili Co., this time as chef and an owner. My co-authorship of _The Silver Palate Cookbook_ soon led to my first solo writing project, based on my restaurant's menu, celebrating chili (the dish) as well as chile (the ingredient). Together, those first two cookbooks launched a writing career that got me out of the restaurant kitchen's heat for good, and brought about many opportunities to celebrate gourmet cooking—grilling included—and southwestern cuisine.

Six years ago I made a move as significant as the one that originally took me from Colorado to New York, heading back west this time to settle in the 400-year-old city of Santa Fe, historically and culturally the most significant in the Southwest. For _Food & Wine_, I wrote the lead story in an entire issue devoted to the Southwest. For _Bon Appétit_, I wrote—still write—about grilling in all its many mouthwatering, not exclusively southwestern, forms. Among the twenty-plus books I've written or co-written over the years, seven have dealt with southwestern cookery, one winning an award for the advancement of the cultural heritage of the Southwest. Two have covered grilling and smoking exclusively, while several more have featured grilling prominently among their coverage of how we cook and eat today.

All of which is why this book, when it was proposed to me, seemed like such a natural and necessary one to undertake. Grilling has grown up, while I have matured alongside it, liberally seasoned with a dose of the special magic that is the unique culinary contribution of the American Southwest. Here you will find authentic dishes of the region as well as more "evolved" fare—the food of the modern Southwest—authentic, too, now that the winds of change have moved through the area, but fresh, lively, and appealing, also.

Not so long ago, grilling was simple, even primitive, and the southwestern kitchen was represented by greasy imitations of the real thing. Those times are gone forever, as I think you will come to appreciate as you cook your way through this book. Join me in a celebration of the new and exciting southwestern grill.

Santa Fe, New Mexico
January 2000

Acknowledgments

First and foremost I thank my agent, Deborah Krasner, who is as passionate about my food and writing as she is tireless on my behalf.

At The Harvard Common Press, I thank everyone (literally everyone—they are a small but dedicated bunch), most especially my editor, Dan Rosenberg, who remained calm and patient as well as keenly insightful throughout the process of producing this book. I also thank Publisher Bruce Shaw and Marketing Director Christine Alaimo, both of whom have worked and continue to work to get this book into as many hands as possible.

Andrea Chesman copyedited the manuscript with an attention to detail and an understanding of grilling that were inspiring, while Patricia Jalbert-Levine skillfully shepherded the book through its final editing stages.

I also thank Martin Jacobs for his vivid cover photograph and Sandra Bruce for her evocative illustrations.

At *Bon Appétit*, Bill Garry, Barbara Fairchild, and Kristine Kidd have long encouraged my interest in grilling, as did Barbara Fine at the late, lamented *On the Grill* magazine. My thanks to them all.

Thanks and gratitude also go to Marsh Heckel, who did the shopping for this book with good humor and a fierce determination to find the right ingredient in the best condition for the lowest price.

Finally, many tasters shared their opinions of my grill food with me. Among them I especially thank Joan and Howard Ellis, of course, my brother, David McLaughlin, and his wife, Dianne, Sandy MacGregor, Marilyn Abraham, Steve Lange, Michael Honstein, Martina Lorey, Park Kerr, Pamela Morgan, who doesn't come to Santa Fe often enough, and Anne Lower and Jack Gantos, who left Santa Fe all too soon.

Introduction:
The Southwestern Grill

No region of the United States, especially in these days of mesquite madness, is more closely identified with grilling than the Southwest. Year-round, indoors or out—but outdoors whenever possible, to take advantage of our abundance of dry, sunny days—southwesterners embrace the grill with a passion. Not only do we prefer the kind of casual entertaining that most grill meals seem automatically to inspire, we also love big, bold flavors and are never happier than when the seasoning smoke of an open flame blends successfully and vibrantly with the Southwest's other assertive seasonings. Factor in a tradition of outdoor cookery that goes back centuries, and southwestern grilling begins to seem as natural and logical as salt and pepper on a T-bone steak.

Perhaps we should define our terms. Because the Southwest is so fashionable these days, it is fashionable to say the Southwest is a state of mind. In fact—and especially when it comes to food rather than paint colors, furniture, or clothing— the Southwest is a fairly specific geographical region whose borders can nevertheless be determined in several ways. Good enchiladas and burritos may be had, for example, in Oklahoma and in southern Colorado, but few would include those states on their idealized southwestern map. Taking the latitude line of San Francisco as the Southwest's northern border, as one writer has done, includes chunks of Nevada and Utah—again, not quite the Southwest of our dreams.

Texas, on the other hand, despite its melting pot cuisine (up to twenty-five separate ethnic influences, according to pioneering Dallas restaurant chef Stephan Pyles), belongs, of course, while the heart of the Southwest lies indisputably within the relatively recent state boundaries of New Mexico and Arizona. Finally, California—the lower third of it at any rate—often seems to be a veritable extension of Mexico proper and must also be included.

What these three-and-one-third states that make up this vast chunk of the U.S. have in common is both a lengthy, modern international border, as well as a long, mingled political and cultural history with Mexico, the 500-pound gorilla to our immediate south. Indeed, southwestern cooking authority James Peyton has said that rather than Mexican food traveling north with immigrants, it is the border that has headed south, co-opting the cuisine as it went. (And, in fact, Santa Fe, the spiritual capital of the modern southwest, established as the actual capital of the Territory of New Spain by the Mexican Spanish some four hundred years ago, now lies nearly 325 miles north of Juarez, the closest Mexican border city.)

The cross-cultural cuisine that has evolved here and continues to evolve ever more quickly is a wonder, certainly not Mexican, definitely not "American," but a hybrid stew of both. Enriched by the curiosity of regional chefs who range deep into Mexico and Central America for "southwestern" ingredients and inspiration, and dispersed across the country and around the world through their restaurants, writings, and teachings, a cuisine that was once simple, even stark, has become dazzling, bold, and beautiful. And at its heart lies the southwestern grill.

For many cooks, grilling means beef and beef means Texas, which is as good a place as any to begin our smoky odyssey, although some adjustment of expectations may be in order. Cowboys, longhorns, and hearty chuckwagon feasts are the inaccurate mental legacy of too many idealized movie westerns. In fact, driving cattle was dangerous, dusty, grueling work, and the food, while it was surely cooked over an open fire—probably of burning cow chips—was most often simmered in Dutch ovens or fried in cast-iron skillets and could hardly be called grilled. In fact, trail drive fare often consisted of the same, monotonous Three B's—bacon, beans, and biscuits—meal after meal. The fourth potential B—beef—was far too valuable to be served often to trail hands, and far too tough (until recent times, at least), for grilling, even if the fuel in question had been more palatable.

Today, while beef is still frequently on the Texas menu, and a big old T-bone or a succulent burger can be readily enjoyed, the grill scene is considerably changed. Three of the country's best-known and most highly regarded chefs—Stephan Pyles and Dean Fearing in Dallas and Robert Del Grande in Houston—have elevated grilling and southwestern food in general to a high art. In their footsteps, chefs like Jay McCarthy from San Antonio, Grady Spears in Fort Worth, and the Austin-based duo of Jeff Blank and Jay Moore continue to refine what southwestern grilling means right now. Ever more frequently, these creative incubators produce a fusion of cuisines—part southwestern, part Mexican, part Texas home cooking, part Asian, and part modern restaurant overkill of the best kind.

Fearing, for example, may team grilled Gulf snapper with a chile and tomatillo salsa for a fairly classic dish, or may garnish orange- and horseradish-crusted halibut with a Thai shrimp salad. Jamaica-born McCarthy loves to work with such inherently southwestern ingredients as tequila and prickly pear cactus, but the menu at his Zuni Grill might also include grilled cider-cured pork with an adobo sauce. If much of what turns up on the plate in these restaurants has very little to do with what the chefs' grandmothers cooked, not to mention what their fathers "barbecued," well, welcome to the new southwestern grill.

Of course, if you've barely switched from cheddar to jalapeño Jack on your cheeseburgers, this may all strike you as too fancy to bear. Relax. There's still plenty of casual grilled grub in Texas to satisfy the heartiest two-fisted eater. Consider the fajita. By now a coast-to-coast Tex-Mex restaurant standard (and plenty easy to grill up at home as well), fajitas may have begun their rise to fame in Austin, the Texas state capital. Located in the beautiful Hill Country, Austin is the home of Sonny Falcon, the "Fajita King," and the man many authorities credit with originally popularizing this addictively messy dish. Other experts mention Ninfa Rodriquez Laurenzo, whose Houston restaurants are famed for the dish. All agree, however, that fajitas are directly descended from the traditional Mexican dish *arracheras*, and were being grilled across the border long before anyone in Texas caught on. Fajitas means "little sashes" or perhaps "little belts" and refers to the cummerbundlike piece of meat—skirt steak or diaphragm—from which they are made. (*Arracherra* is just another name for the same cut of beef.) Such is the popularity of fajitas these days that the price of this once-rejected cut (butchers used to grind it into burger meat or take it home for their own dinners) has climbed steeply, each cow supplying only about eight pounds of steak. At their most basic, *arracheras* get little more than a squeeze of lime and a rubbing with garlic and jalapeño, letting the flavor of meat and mesquite dominate. Elsewhere, in Mexico, raw cucumbers and radishes (also with a squeeze of fresh lime) are the equally simple accompaniments, particularly at street food stands, where the dish may simply be called *tacos de carne*.

More-is-more Tex-Mex fajitas, on the other hand, are frequently marinated in everything from soy sauce, Worcestershire sauce, and pineapple juice (producing a teriyakilike result) to pico de gallo salsa blended with beer and tequila, a combo favored by one colorful Texas television food personality, Park Kerr, who then flings the marinade onto the coals for a sizzling cloud of savory steam. Slivers of grilled onions and sweet and hot peppers are traditional accompaniments, with the meat and vegetables swaddled together into warmed flour tortillas, along with lashings of guacamole, sour cream, or salsa—or all three. Elemental or fabulous, only the drastically uninitiated try to eat this food any way other than by hand.

Fajita-lovers seeking alternatives to beef have led to the creation of such novelties as chicken, lamb, shrimp, pork, and even vegetable variations. Purists grumble that chicken fajitas ("chicken breast beef skirt steaks") is a contradiction in terms, and so it is, but no one denies the simple pleasure of grilled whatever-you-callits, rolled into taco-like creations, and devoured in the fragrant haze of mesquite smoke.

Speaking of mesquite, the wood or charcoal of this thorny, fast-growing tree (actually a legume) is considered by many to be a requirement for successful fajita-making—and indeed, for all southwestern grilling. In fact, so popular now is mesquite as a grill fuel, there is some worry that this once invasive plant may actually become endangered. For those interested in renewable resources, the beans of the mesquite are now gathered and sold to toss onto your grill fire, in lieu of wood chips, and are said to impart the same flavorful smoke without requiring the destruction of a living plant.

Also to be found sizzling over an open Texas flame, especially in the southern part of the state, is *cabrito asado al pastor*, or milk-fed kid (baby goat), spit-roasted shepherd's style. Butterflied onto a metal rack angled over a bed of coals, the kid may be cooked au naturel or spice-rubbed, mopped, even glazed with a fairly traditional barbecue sauce. Chopped or thinly sliced, the smoky meat is rolled up taco-style in soft corn or flour tortillas, and served with salsa. Normally a seasonal specialty (spring is the time for baby goats), cabrito can regularly be found on the menus of El Azteca, in Austin, and Los Barrios Mexican Restaurant, in San Antonio, among others.

Other Texas specialties also entice. Look for *parrillada*, a manly Mexican mixed grill of sausages and other meats, variously accompanied by chiles rellenos (deep-fried cheese-stuffed green chiles), enchiladas, beans, rice, etc. In the same excessive spirit, and perhaps best enjoyed at Martino, an elegant restaurant in Juarez, Mexico, just across the border from El Paso, is *carne asada a la Tampequena*. The dish—a tender grilled steak, topped with strips of roasted poblano chiles and melted cheese, accompanied by an enchilada, rich refried beans, and guacamole—migrated north from Mexico City. Enjoy one after your dashing Martino waiter shakes up a martini for you at tableside.

Freshwater bass and tiny game birds, such as quail, are also grilled in this border region, although neither can be considered common. You are much likelier to run across *tacos al carbon* (fajitas in all but name, the diced charcoal-grilled Mexican beef in each tortilla bundle is garnished with a whole grilled green onion and dolloped with salsa and guacamole) or *hamburguesas con queso*—cheeseburgers to Anglos—grilled and served in flour tortillas instead of on buns.

El Paso is just a taco's throw from New Mexico, a state famed for its chile-based cuisine, but not necessarily the first place one thinks of as a source of traditional grilled food. Though Native Americans obviously cooked over open fires for centuries (as did the Spanish and Anglos who settled the region), grilling is a recent phenomenon, one just as likely to be found in the backyard of an Albuquerque home or on the tables of the many trendy new southwestern restaurants. Fresh green and dried red chiles, which are the state's largest cash crop, inevitably season the smoky fare. In fact, for those who stock up on gunny sacks full of the green pods when the harvest hits its stride in late summer, a hot grill fire—augmented by mesquite chips if desired—is the best place to char the peels prior to stashing them in the freezer for a year of spicy eating.

Santa Fe, at least during the colder months, typically smells of piñon wood smoke from the fireplaces that heat the adobe homes, but lately mesquite, pecan, hickory, and apple wood smoke have also been sniffed, a sure sign that any number of eateries are grilling a goodly portion of their menus. (Piñon, like other soft, resinous woods, is not suitable for grilling.)

Among chefs who have transformed southwestern cooking, none is better known than Mark Miller. At his internationally-famed Coyote Café, the chile-rubbed prime rib steak is first pan-seared, then finished over a pecan wood fire and served with a small mountain of chile-dusted shoestring potatoes. At Café Pasqual's, just off the Santa Fe plaza, chef Katherine Kagel acknowledges vegetarian concerns by offering fire-roasted squash and red onion enchiladas with a sauce of guajillo, ancho, and de árbol chiles, garnished with a grilled banana. Located farther out from the heart of the city is The Old Mexico Grill, an anomaly among regional restaurants in that its cuisine is that of Mexico proper. Here the hickory-grilled skirt steaks are indeed called *arracheras*, and the picante house-made salsa of fierce red chiles de árbol is exactly the right lively condiment.

Arizona's culture, despite the proximity of Mexico, is more Indian and Anglo than that of its neighbors to the east, and so the food is milder and less chile-driven. It is also a state with more cacti than trees, and thus its grilling tradition is newer. In Tucson, home of many dude ranches, the cowboy influence holds sway at Li'l Abner's. The steaks, beef short ribs, and chicken that make up the entire menu are cooked outdoors over mesquite coals on a huge rack, cranked up and down according to the whims of the grillmaster and the cooking requirements of the proteins in question.

At The Rancher's Club, also in Tucson, diners may select the cut of meat, the grill wood to be used (sassafras is popular), and the sauce or relish they want on their meat after cooking. At Café Terra Cotta, Tucson chef Donna Nordin, one of the earliest exponents of new southwestern cooking, serves up a smoky grilled pork tenderloin, marinated in an adobo barbecue sauce and accompanied by tender black beans and a jalapeño-spiked apricot chutney. Or, visit La Parrilla Suiza, the Phoenix and Tucson branches of a Mexico City chain, where charcoal-grilled fajitas are the specialty (*parrilla* is Spanish for grill). And at the several Chuy's Mesquite Broilers, shrimp, chicken, and beef tri-tip are grilled over glowing mesquite logs and served with rice, beans, salsa, and tortillas in a funky, laid-back atmosphere reminiscent of college spring breaks in Mexico.

The Baja influence is naturally felt in California, San Diego especially, where the rage these days is all for fish (sometimes shrimp) tacos—popular street (and beach) fare along the Baja. Though the seafood is traditionally battered and deep-fried, grilled versions are also turning up. Plainly seasoned fish like swordfish, snapper, and especially the grouper/sea bass relative known as cabrilla, is worth seeking out. Such fish, grilled over mesquite, shredded, moistened with fresh salsa, mounded into a semi-crisp corn tortilla shell and topped with shredded lettuce or cabbage, tomatoes, avocado, and a creamy sauce, tastes best eaten barefoot, and with a beer in the other hand.

California is the same sort of magnificent melting pot as Texas, and the home, probably, of both traditional backyard "barbecue" and modern restaurant grilling as we know them. Just as likely to consist of Korean beef, Thai chicken (both plenty spicy), or wild mushroom pizza as it is to be derived from the old Southwest, California grilling celebrates low-fat, high-flavor, and cutting-edge creativity with typically sunny enthusiasm. Among the state's finest contributions to the smoky arts is Santa Maria–style oak-barbecued beef. This unique preparation is a specialty of the Santa Maria area, northwest of Santa Barbara, a very Texas-like part of California, in which oil wells and cattle ranching play a substantial part. The meat is tri-tip, and it is more accurately slow-grilled, rather than barbecue-smoked, over fragrant oak logs. The meat is sometimes rubbed, sometimes left plain for cooking, then thinly sliced when done and served with pinto beans, garlic bread, and a mild salsa that, virtually by definition, must be made with canned green Ortega brand chiles.

New, old, or new again, from Texas to east L.A., the tastes and smells of the grilled food of the Southwest are as mouthwatering and satisfying as any regional cuisine this very large country has to offer. That's worth another margarita and a second helping of everything.

Grilling, Southwestern or Otherwise

Fuels, Tools, Techniques, and Tips

What gets grilled may well be southwestern, but how it gets grilled is more universal: Good grilling is good grilling. Perhaps I should make clear what I mean by *grilling*, that frequently misunderstood word. Grilling is a fairly fast, high-heat, open-flame method of cooking, suitable for relatively small or thin cuts of meat and other foods. Ideally, grilled foods are prepared and eaten outdoors.

As a cooking process, grilling is relatively low-tech and rather imprecise. In other words, there are a lot of different ways to arrive at a plate of skillfully grilled food, none of them overly complicated. Advice helps (mine follows), but experience is the best teacher. Sooner or later you're going to have to fire up the grill and get cooking. If you're hungry enough and dedicated enough, you'll soon be a backyard expert.

Fuels

Nearly all grills fall into one of two categories, those fueled by charcoal and those fueled by gas. You can make great food on either type of grill, but the two are not interchangeable. There are reasons for choosing (or avoiding) each, and most people heading out to buy a grill already have, for whatever reason, one fuel or other in mind. Still, it never hurts to review your options.

Charcoal

Charcoal is produced by partially burning wood in a low-oxygen environment. The result is lighter and longer-burning than wood. Briquettes, the most common American form of charcoal, were invented by Henry Ford—reportedly to use up wood left over from the manufacture of Model T's—and usually consist of pulverized charcoal, glue, and some kind of petroleum product pressed into a uniform cake. Charcoal briquettes are cheap and widely available, and they do their job well. The alternative, natural charcoal, comes in solid chunks that look just like burned wood, which they are. Free of the additives required to form briquettes, increasingly available natural charcoal retains some of the fragrance and flavor of the wood itself. Although more expensive than briquettes, it can be extinguished and reused. Natural charcoal is the first choice of many professional chefs and serious home grillers.

Gas

"Gas" is usually liquid propane. Stored under pressure in tanks attached to the grill's burners, propane is also affordable and convenient, and it gets the job done. Grills can also be purchased or retrofitted to burn natural gas. Hooked up to a gas line, they are obviously not portable, but, unless you forget to pay your utility bill, they never run out of fuel.

Other Fuels

In the interest of thoroughness, I should point out that there are also electric grills to be found. In addition to the awkward need to plug them into an outlet, the models I've tried don't do the job for me that charcoal and gas grills have done for years. They have all been on the small side and none has produced sufficient heat. I occasionally hear from a reader who has had good luck with this or that brand of electric grill, but, for now, I remain skeptical.

Grills

Charcoal grills come in several forms. Hibachis, originally of Japanese design, are small, uncovered (or brazier-style) grills. Larger inexpensive braziers, usually purchased at discount stores, often come set on rickety legs. Kettle grills, with their distinctively domed covers, and rectangular cousins to the kettle grill set the industry's standards, while table grills, actually very large braziers, are commonly seen under dozens of burgers, hot dogs, and chicken parts at charity barbecues and other catered public events. There are also drum or barrel smokers—factory-manufactured look-alikes of those rustic smokers home-fashioned out of fifty-gallon barrels split in half—that can do double-duty as grills. Charcoal grills (as well as ones that use propane or natural gas) can also be found as built-ins, surrounded by attractive suburban brickwork, in backyards from coast to coast.

Gas grills are most commonly rectangular and covered. Most stand on legs or a post in the ground, but there are tabletop models as well. The common rectangular gas grills come with or without side work tables and burners. Some are filled with briquette-like lava stones (actually a ceramic product), while others have inverted V-shaped bars between the heat elements and the rack. Both the stones and the bars are designed to some degree to replicate the flavorsome smoke of fats and juices dripping onto live coals.

There are several advantages to charcoal grills. Most of them are cheaper than most gas grills, the low price making them a good choice for the hesitant beginner. In case it doesn't work out, little has been ventured. Most of them are lighter than most gas grills and thus more portable, letting you take them on the road. Fans of the charcoal grill also say charcoal gives a better, more distinctive flavor—caused by fats and juices falling onto the coals—than gas. Charcoal grills also burn hotter than gas, say supporters, searing meat for maximum flavor and sealing in juices for maximum succulence. It may well be a guy thing, but those who swear by charcoal actually enjoy determining the temperature of a fire by the amount of time they can stand to hold their hands above the coals before the pain becomes overwhelming. They also like the fact that no two fires are ever quite the same and love the problem-solving inherent in working with a fire that, once it reaches its peak heat, is already beginning to die down. Such grills are, the charcoal guys say, "more fun."

Gas grills, with their built-in fuel supply and stove-control knobs, offer steady, reliable, adjustable heat—features that, despite the cost of the equipment, can also seem attractive to inexperienced grillers. Gas grills can be hot and ready to go in ten minutes, rather than the thirty or forty minutes a charcoal unit takes, making them great for spontaneous meals and ideal for those who are cooking only for one or two and for anyone who wants dinner on the table fast. V-shaped bars may help boost the flavor of food grilled over gas (some cooks don't find them very successful at this), while lava stones do a somewhat better job, although they are increasingly less common. (The stones are also more prone to flare-ups than the bars are.) In any case, using southwestern-style rubs and zesty marinades and supplementing your fire with wood smoking chips—more on these later—can easily compensate for any perceived lack of "grill flavor" (a lack I've never noticed, by the way). Although some people say gas grills provide insufficient heat, the one I use gets quite hot enough, thank you, heading well past 550°F, at which point the in-hood thermometer stops counting.

Gas does have drawbacks, though. On the esoteric side, it is said by serious cooks to be a "wet" heat, producing moisture as a byproduct of its burning and thus preventing food from getting truly crusty. On the all-too-obvious side, running out of propane before the pork chops are cooked is truly inconvenient.

Fuel determined, what defines a grill worth buying? First, look for solid, high-quality construction and, as is often the case in life, be willing to spend a little more money to get a better product. Legs and side shelves should be sturdy, and the grill should be of the heaviest gauge metal offered. Extend the lifespan of your investment by always buying a suitable weather-protective cover.

The best charcoal grills have holders for the lid, built-in ash collectors, hinged racks (nice for refueling the fire during a long smoke-cooking session), slotted coal baskets (which make it easier to set up hot and cool zones), and in-hood thermometers (especially useful if you'll be doing any low-temperature smoking). Choose a large grill—a 22- to 30-inch diameter is a nice size—so that you don't have to crowd food on the rack. Charcoal grills increasingly come with shelves alongside and below, giving the cook room for sauces, brushes, dishes, and so on—a huge improvement over the classic "where-do-I-put-it?" design.

Look for a gas grill that features three burners, not two, for greater flexibility. Three burners are especially useful if you want to do any indirect-heat grilling or smoke-cooking. Choose a grill with the largest rack area you can afford. It's easier to grill for one or two on a large grill than it is to cook for a crowd on a small one. My current gas grill provides about 360 square inches, and I wouldn't want one any smaller. Select a grill that promises at least 33,000 BTUs of heat, for maximum searing potential. You'll also want an in-hood thermometer and plenty of side shelving and storage. A side burner is great for heating a sauce or for cooking corn on the cob or other side dishes.

If you want to use wood smoking chips when grilling by direct heat, or if you think you will want to do some low-and-slow smoking, select a grill with a special side compartment designed to help wood chips or chunks smolder and flavor your food, rather than quickly burn up.

Gas grills typically come with only one propane tank, but you should buy a second one at the earliest opportunity and always keep the extra filled and handy. Expect to get an average of fifteen hours of grilling out of a standard twenty-pound tank. Even with good planning, you may run out of fuel from time to time; with a spare at hand, modern quick-change couplers let you replace an empty tank without significant heat loss, so you can keep on grilling. (Yes, your new grill may very well come with a gas gauge, but that gauge will, in my experience, be of dubious reliability. Buy the extra tank.)

Techniques

Gentlemen (and Ladies): Light your grills. Once the worst part of acquiring a new grill—putting it together—is over, you are ready to fire it up. If your grill is charcoal, you have essentially three choices of how to get the fire started.

Traditional but nasty-smelling starter or lighter fluid will do the job, but I urge you to avoid it. While the odor may not linger in the grill or on the food, it still lingers in the yard, and it can ruin a meal.

There are also electric starters. Like a large version of those little coils designed to heat a cup of water for tea or coffee, the starter will slowly ignite a grill full of briquettes. You will naturally need an outlet to plug it into, and you should remove it from the coals as soon as things get going or it will burn up. Electric starters can be cumbersome, but they do the job.

The best choice by far, however, is the chimney starter. Less odorous and much more environmentally friendly than starter fluid, quicker and more portable than electric starters, this brilliantly simple device consists of a twelve-inch-tall metal cylinder with a handle and an open bottom grate. A few wadded-up sheets of newspaper quickly ignite up to fifty briquettes. Once lit, the chimney is set on a heatproof surface (the grill rack is ideal) for about twenty minutes. When covered with white ash and glowing red-orange within, the briquettes are transferred (tongs work best) from the chimney to the grill, which is then covered and which will be hot and ready to go in about ten minutes.

Lighting a gas grill is simpler. Turn on the tank at its valve, set the burners to the desired temperature, and ignite the burners according to the manufacturer's directions (most modern gas grills have ignition clickers built-in).

Direct-Heat Grilling

Direct-heat grilling is the most common way to grill. You put the food on the rack directly above the coals or propane flame, close the hood on the grill, and cook.

The most basic direct-heat charcoal grilling requires a solid two-coals-deep bed of white, ash-covered briquettes. The bed of coals should be about one inch larger in diameter than the area occupied by the foods you will be grilling. In determining the size of the fire bed you need, remember that individual foods like burgers or chicken pieces should be well-spaced in order to brown and cook evenly. Charcoal is cheap: Don't skimp. This kind of fire will produce hot, direct heat for twenty minutes, maybe more, perfect for quickly cooking small or relatively thin pieces of food (most of what you will grill, in other words). Set the rack in place, ideally about six inches above the coals, and let it get hot before laying the food on it.

To determine the temperature level of a direct-heat charcoal fire, use the "ouch" technique: hold your hand about six inches above the coals. If it becomes painful enough to jerk your hand away in 3 seconds, your fire is hot; painful in 5 seconds, medium-hot; and painful in 7 to 8 seconds, medium.

For direct-heat cooking on a gas grill, ignite all the burners, set the temperature controls at the desired level, and preheat thoroughly. The food goes on the rack, the hood is closed, and the food is grilled.

Not every grill expert would agree, but I always (always!) grill covered. The windy New Mexico weather probably has a lot to do with this, but even on calm and mild days I get better and more consistent results with a covered grill. The fire maintains its heat, the flavor of the wood chips I like to use infuses the food more deeply, and, since there is less oxygen present, flare-ups are fewer.

Indirect-Heat Grilling

For indirect-heat grilling of dishes like satays and pizzas, a cool zone must be created to prevent the foods from burning. For this method, bank the chimney-ignited coals on one side of your charcoal grill. If your grill comes with coal baskets, use one here to collect and concentrate the coals. Place the food on the section of the grill rack not over the coals, and cover the grill. Monitor to make certain the food is not burning, and turn and rotate the food to promote even cooking. Use the air intake vent on the bottom and the exhaust vent in the hood to regulate the temperature.

For indirect-heat grilling on a gas grill, preheat to the desired setting (350° to 400°F is ideal). After the burners have heated, shut off the middle one of three or one of two (depending on the grill configuration). Adjust the temperature controls for the burner(s) left on to maintain the desired heat level. Watch food closely and rotate it or turn it on the rack, always taking advantage of the cool zone to prevent burning.

Smoke-Cooking

For even lower and slower smoke-cooking, which is the method for a handful of recipes in this book, the ideal temperature range is 230° to 250°F.

In a charcoal grill, use fewer coals than for other methods—about 36 briquettes. Bank the coals on two sides of the grill with a cool zone in the middle. (I actually have the best luck setting the two coal baskets that came with my grill at 45-degree angles to each other, creating a fairly generous cool zone.) Set the soaked and drained smoking wood chunks atop the coals as directed in the recipe. My standard kettle grill with a fire built this way maintains an amazingly steady 250°F for at least two hours without refueling, but be prepared to add freshly ignited coals from the chimney if the heat begins to drop.

For smoke-cooking in a gas grill, turn on only one burner of a three-burner grill to produce the desired heat level of 230° to 250°F. If you have only two burners, you will need to turn the remaining lighted one very low; this is more successful on some models of grill than others.

Gas grills vary in how well suited they are for smoke-cooking. On models with lava stones, follow the directions given above for charcoal smoking, treating the lava stones just like live coals. Models with V-shaped bars can be more of a challenge. Some offer the option of a smoking wood compartment that fits in alongside the grill rack; these models may also have a water compartment, for creating a moister smoky environment. (This is the same compartment that holds wood chips for flavoring grilled foods. The compartment is not really designed for the larger wood chunks used for smoked foods. For smoking, simply use more chips and refill the compartment as often as they burn up.) You may also find, in grill accessory catalogs and shops, a vented box of fairly heavy metal that is designed to hold small wood chunks or chips and to sit across the V-shaped bars. It's not an easy alliance but it can be made to work. In all cases, read and follow the manufacturer's directions for getting the maximum smoke out of your particular model of grill.

When I smoke-cook in a charcoal or gas grill, I put the food in a disposable foil pan on the rack, over the cool zone. The grill is covered, of course, forcing the smoke to penetrate the food, and opening or closing the lower and upper vents regulates the temperature. For convenience (eventually maintaining the fire becomes tedious) and to prevent the food from becoming overly smoky and bitter, some long-cooking items like beef brisket and pork shoulder are smoked and partially cooked on the grill, then finished in the oven.

These are the basics of grilling, which will get you equipped, lit, and knowledgeable enough not to ruin too much food. Beyond the general, however, are a whole host of tips that will add real finesse to your grilling and transform you from a merely serviceable griller to a real master of the art. Briefly, but essentially, here they are.

Tips

Light a Two-Tier Charcoal Fire

Rather than make one level bed of coals, you may wish to arrange one-third of the coals on one side of the grill and two-thirds on the other side, creating a hot and a less-hot side of the grill. This will allow you to sear food on the hot side, then move it to the less-hot side, or to move the food back and forth. This gives a charcoal grill some of the temperature variety of a gas unit.

Use Wood Chips with Finesse

If you want to use smoky wood chips to add extra flavor to your grilled food, you will find that I have included a recommended chip type with each recipe in this book. Suit the wood to the food: Mesquite is of medium intensity and traditional in the southwest, and can be used on almost any grilled food. Hickory is stronger in taste and great on red meats like beef and on some poultry and seafood. Oak is classic for barbecue, and also complements red meat. Both hickory and oak are good for flavoring foods, like quesadillas, that don't spend much time on the fire. Pecan smoke is similar to hickory, though a little lighter; it's nice with lamb and poultry. Fruit woods like apple, cherry, and peach have a sweet smoke, and particularly complement seafood—especially shellfish—and poultry. The same applies to the larger wood chunks needed for low and slow smoke-cooking.

Whichever chips you use, soak them in water and drain them, or use them dry, following the grill manufacturer's directions. Scatter the chips directly on the coals or lava stones (they will smoke and burn up rather quickly this way) or enclose the chips in a partially open foil packet or in a clean tuna can (they will smolder a bit longer this way, before they ultimately burst into flame and burn up). Foods that are over the grill for only eight to ten minutes or so need the maximum amount of smoke if the flavor is to be evident. Use at least two good handfuls of chips, or more if you want a really smoky taste, and lay the food on the rack and cover the grill when the chips just start to smoke.

Start with a Clean Grill Rack

Food sticks to dirty racks and can acquire off flavors. It takes extra discipline when all you really want to do is sit down and eat, but the best and easiest time to clean a grill rack is right after you have taken the last of the food off it. Turn the heat to high if you have that option, use a specially designed metal-bristle grill brush to thoroughly scrape built-up residue off the rack, and let the high heat finish burning it clean.

Oil the Grill Rack

I nearly always oil the rack, unless there is oil in a marinade or the food has its own natural lubrication built in (as with sausages, skin-on poultry, or burgers). The food is less likely to stick and will be more likely to acquire attractive grill markings. To use a nonstick cooking spray, lift the preheated rack off the grill and away from the flame before spritzing. (Never aim an aerosol can of anything at a grill fire.) Alternatively, fold several paper towels into a thick pad, dip the pad into vegetable oil, and lightly rub it over the grill. As soon as the rack is oiled, add the food you are grilling.

Choose Utensils That Make Life Easier

All grill utensils should be long-handled, to keep your fingers as far away from the heat as possible. You'll need tongs (the spring-loaded kind that snap open are preferred); a large, off-set spatula (the kind with an angled blade, like diner cooks use); a carving fork (but only for carving—poking food on the grill can let juices escape); and a basting brush with natural, not nylon, bristles. Serious grillers will probably want to have more than one of each of these, thus avoiding the need to dash to the sink to wash something. (You may also need to change utensils to avoid bacterial cross-contamination, which can happen when you use the same utensil with both raw and cooked foods.) Oven mitts look silly but do the job. A good kitchen timer, preferably one that times more than one process, is essential.

Be Organized

Imitate cooking schools; they set up the ingredients and utensils for each dish to be demonstrated on large jellyroll sheet pans. The pans are great for ferrying food to the grill and for hauling used dishes and utensils back to the kitchen. I own several.

Use Rubs, Marinades, and Mops

I rarely put food on the grill without using one or more of these easy flavor-makers. Go bold and you and your guests will be glad you did.

Create Attractive Grill Marks

Do what restaurant chefs do and rotate foods 45 degrees on the rack about halfway through the grilling process on each side. The brown cross-hatching created by this simple step is attractive and professional-looking.

Be Sure the Food Is Done

"Burnt offering" is the usual grill disaster joke, but in fact, more grilled food is underdone than overdone. Throughout this book, methods for determining the doneness of poultry, seafood, and red meat are given. It won't help in every instance, but an instant-read thermometer, which is briefly inserted into food, then removed and read, can be an invaluable aid to determining doneness. When in doubt, cut into the food in question to be certain.

Pay Attention

Don't wander off. Let the answering machine pick up. Let someone else tend bar. Grill disasters are not common but they usually spring up quickly and while you are meandering back to the grill, an expensive dinner can be incinerated.

Avoid Flare-Ups

Flare-ups of open flame are caused by fat dripping onto coals, lava stones, or V-shaped bars. A little fire is a good thing, and a little char is part of the essential grill flavor. Large spots that look burnt or taste bitter, however, are grilling faux pas to be avoided. Trim as much visible fat off the food as possible. Use the minimum amount of oil in marinades. Keep an extra-close eye on things when grilling fatty foods and move them around on the rack to avoid charring. Keep the grill covered; less oxygen in the grill means fewer flare-ups. Keep a spritzer bottle (or a squirt gun!) of water handy and gently douse flames that get out of hand. Be conservative; too much water can cool off or extinguish a charcoal fire, and too vigorous a squirt can toss ashes up onto the food.

Have a Water Source Nearby

Try to locate the grill within reach of the garden hose. Or at least keep a bucket of water handy. You never know.

Final Advice

Every cookbook I write teaches me at least one new thing. When I wrote a previous book on grilling, I learned to position an umbrella over the grill; even in the Southwest, rain happens. This time around, my most useful new insight was even more prosaic but no less important to enriching my grilling life: You should have a trash can close at hand. The deck where I do my grilling has a view of the magnificent mountain range called the Sandias, and the last thing I want marring its splendor is to have the wads of paper towels I use for oiling the grill rack blowing around my yard.

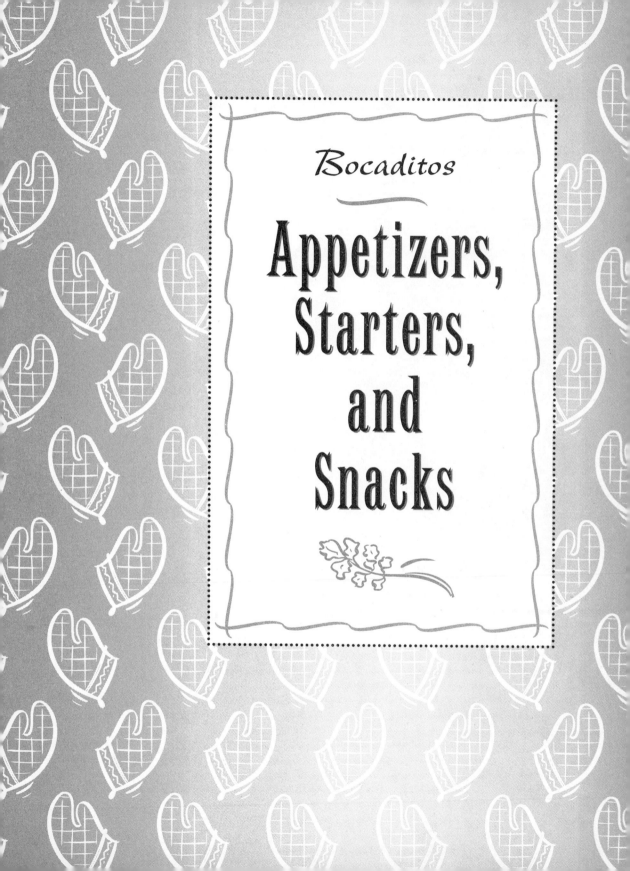

Bocaditos

Appetizers, Starters, and Snacks

Bocaditos
APPETIZERS, STARTERS, AND SNACKS

*Grill-Opened Clams on the Half Shell with
Quick Rosemary-Bacon Salsa 45*

Grilled Mini Crab Cakes with Mango Pico de Gallo 46

Santa Fe Chicken Satays with Red Chile–Peanut Sauce 47

Cumin-Oregano Chicken Wings 48

Steak and Grilled Green Onion Quesadilla 49

*Small Grilled Pizzas with Chorizo, Goat Cheese, and
Green Chile "Jam" 50*

Chili Meatballs with Hot Pepper Jelly Dipping Sauce 52

*Grilled Beef Heart Skewers with
Cascabel–Roasted Garlic Salsa 53*

Spiced Pepitas

Pepitas are pumpkin seeds. They are commonly ground and used in Mexico to thicken sauces. They can also be spiced and oven-roasted whole, as they are here, making a crunchy, zippy, and completely habit-forming nibble. Locate shiny green, raw pumpkin seeds in health food stores. Stored in a cool, dark place, they will keep for a month or two; once roasted, they are more perishable and should be consumed within a week or so (this won't be a problem). The recipe is a forgiving one; adjust the seasonings to suit your mood and what you find in the spice rack.

1. Position a rack in the middle of the oven and preheat to 375°F. Lightly spray a large jellyroll pan with nonstick cooking spray.

2. In a small bowl, thoroughly stir together the red chile powder, cumin, salt, jalapeño powder, chipotle powder, oregano, pepper, and garlic powder.

3. In a large bowl, whisk the egg whites until smooth but not beginning to stiffen. Add the pumpkin seeds and stir to coat them evenly with the egg whites. Working quickly, before the egg whites can dry, transfer the spice mixture to a coarse sieve. Stir the pumpkin seeds while sprinkling the spice mixture from the sieve over them. When they are evenly coated with spices, transfer them immediately to the prepared pan and spread them to its edges.

4. Bake for 5 minutes. Stir the pumpkin seeds, breaking up any clumps. Return the pan to the oven and continue to bake the pumpkin seeds, stirring them often, until they have puffed (you will hear a popping sound) and are crisp, another 10 to 12 minutes.

5. Remove from the oven and cool. Store the pumpkin seeds in an airtight container at room temperature.

MAKES ABOUT 1 POUND

4 teaspoons medium-hot pure red chile powder
1 tablespoon freshly ground cumin (preferably from toasted seeds)
1½ teaspoons coarse or kosher salt
1¼ teaspoons jalapeño powder
1¼ teaspoons chipotle powder
½ teaspoon dried oregano, crumbled
½ teaspoon freshly ground black pepper
¼ teaspoon garlic powder
2 egg whites
1 pound raw pumpkin seeds

Appetizers, Starters, and Snacks

Tostaditas

SERVES 6

24 (6-inch) yellow or blue
  corn tortillas
About 3 cups corn oil
2 teaspoons coarse or
  kosher salt

Snack corn chips are made from batters, extruded from nozzles into the frying medium, which gives a texture completely different from that of chips made from corn tortillas. This will be evident to you as you find yourself munching on these about as quickly as you can make them. Of course good salsa and guacamole from scratch will not be harmed if commercial chips are used for eating them. On the other hand, when homemade tostaditas, still warm, are the scoop of choice, everything gets elevated to a new level, which justifies the use of the phrase "southwestern cuisine."

1. Stack several tortillas on a cutting board. With a long sharp knife, cut the stack into 6 equal wedges. Repeat with the remaining tortillas. Spread the cut-up tortillas on the work surface for a few minutes to dry them slightly.

2. Meanwhile, in a large skillet over medium heat, warm the oil. When it is hot, add half the tortilla pieces and cook, stirring once or twice, until crisp but not browned, about 1 minute. With a slotted spoon transfer to a paper towel-lined baking sheet. Sprinkle with half the salt. Repeat with the remaining tortilla pieces and salt.

3. Ideally, serve the tostaditas warm. Or, cool and store airtight at room temperature, and use within a day or two.

Guacamole with Tostaditas and Chile-Dusted Jicama Slices

Prepared guacamole now comes in pump-handled tubes, like grout for bathroom tile, and in far too many restaurants these days, that is the guacamole you get. At home, however, freshness prevails, and guacamole less than 15 minutes old can be enjoyed for the lively yet delicate triumph that it is. The combined flavors of corn tortilla chips and guacamole are divinely greater than the sum of the parts, but crisp, sweet slices of red chile-dusted jicama are tasty, too, and much lower in fat.

1. First, make the guacamole. In a food processor or blender, combine ¾ cup of the cilantro, ½ cup of the onion, the jalapeño, garlic, and ½ teaspoon of the salt. Process until fairly smooth. (The cilantro puree can be prepared up to 30 minutes in advance. Cover and hold at room temperature.)

2. Halve the avocados and remove the pits. With a spoon, scoop the flesh of two of the avocados into a bowl. With a fork or the edge of a wooden spoon, coarsely mash the avocados. With a table knife, score the flesh of the remaining avocado into ½-inch cubes. With a large spoon, scoop the cubes out of the peel into the bowl. Stir in the cilantro puree and all but ¼ cup of the tomato. Adjust the seasoning (avocados take a lot of salt) and transfer to a serving bowl.

3. Pour a small mound of the chile powder onto a plate. Dip one edge of each of the jicama slices in the chile powder to generously coat. Arrange on a plate.

SERVES 4 TO 6

GUACAMOLE

1 cup chopped cilantro
¾ cup diced red or yellow onion
1 to 2 fresh jalapeños, stemmed and chopped
1 garlic clove, chopped (optional)
Salt
3 large, perfectly ripe, black-skinned (Hass) avocados
2 ripe plum tomatoes, stemmed, seeded, and diced

Medium-hot unblended red chile powder
½ jicama, peeled and cut into thin, tortilla chip-sized slices
Tostaditas (page 20) or best-quality purchased corn tortilla chips

4. Scatter the remaining ¼ cup cilantro, ¼ cup onion, and ¼ cup tomato over the guacamole and serve immediately, accompanied by the jicama slices and the tostaditas.

Note: Several recipes call for guacamole as a sauce or topping. For those recipes, make the guacamole as above, omitting the chile-dusted jicama slices and the tostaditas.

Guac Talk

Functioning variously as salad, dip, or sauce, guacamole ("avocado concoction" in the ancient Nahuatl Indian language) is, at its best, one of the world's great dishes. It is also one of the world's simplest, or ought to be. When it comes to guacamole, less is more, and such additions as sour cream, salsa, chile powder, and lime juice, which obscure the sweet, nutty flavor of a properly ripened avocado, really should be avoided. Cilantro, tomatoes, chiles, and onions are the acceptable supporting players. Garlic also occurs, but it is optional (though popular in northern New Mexico, among other places); use fresh garlic, at least, not powdered. It is the avocados that are the stars, however, and ideally they should be the bumpy-black-skinned, high-fat types grown in Mexico and California. (Hass is the preferred variety, though you may not see it so labeled at the store.)

Buy the avocados green and hard and let them ripen at cool room temperature; typically they reach perfection in four to five days. The high seasons for tomatoes and avocados do not overlap, a frustrating prospect. Look for really red-ripe and flavorful tomatoes (plum or cherry tomatoes are good, off-season alternatives), and thoroughly seed them, to prevent their juices from thinning the guacamole. Adjust the levels of cilantro and jalapeño to suit your taste. Above all, do not puree the avocados. Guacamole, says Mexican cooking doyen Diana Kennedy, "should be lumpy, not smooth." You may or may not want to make your guacamole in the rustic volcanic stone mortar-and-pestle *(molcajete y tejolote)* that is traditional in Mexico, but at least consider using one for serving the dip. And by all means add an avocado pit or two to the finished guacamole. Not because it prevents discoloration (it doesn't) but, as Mrs. Kennedy says, it makes "a nice effect."

Raw Vegetables with Cool Green Dipping Sauce

The modern Southwest has all the vegetables any other part of the country does, but with a primarily desert climate, its traditional vegetable dishes are somewhat limited and raw vegetables are rarely served. Certainly fresh fennel, pencil-thin asparagus, and sweet red and yellow bell peppers were uncommon even fifteen years ago. So, this appetizer is purely fanciful, and quite obviously a southwestern take on the French vegetable starter, crudités. Regardless of origin, it's light, crisp, and perfect before a chile- and smoke-seasoned main course. The line-up of vegetables given here (not all of them actually raw) is one I like; potential substitutions or additions include blanched baby artichokes, broccoli, sugar snap peas, green beans, and cauliflower; grilled zucchini and yellow squash; roasted beets; and raw celery, button mushrooms, and green onions. Alternative dips include Lime Caesar Dressing (page 297), Roasted Garlic Aioli (page 294), and Goat Cheese Cream (page 296).

1. Bring a medium pan of well-salted water to a boil. Add the asparagus and cook uncovered, stirring once or twice, until the asparagus is crisp/tender, about 4 minutes. Drain, transfer to iced water, and, when cool, drain immediately and pat dry.

2. Set a bowl on a large platter. Arrange the asparagus, carrots, Belgian endive, tomatoes, fennel, bell pepper, and radishes on the platter. Spoon the dipping sauce into the bowl and serve immediately.

SERVES 6 TO 8

16 medium-thick asparagus, woody ends trimmed

Salt

3 medium carrots, cut into long, thin strips

1 head Belgian endive, cored and separated into leaves

About 18 ripe cherry tomatoes, stemmed

1 small fennel bulb, trimmed, separated in layers, layers cut into ½-inch strips

1 large bell pepper, preferably orange or yellow, stemmed, cored, and cut into ½-inch strips

About 12 firm, crisp, unblemished red radishes, trimmed

Cool Green Dipping Sauce (page 291)

Soft Tacos of Grilled Cactus and Green Chiles with Goat Cheese

SERVES 6

4 prickly pear cactus pads (about 1 pound)

4 tablespoons olive oil

5 long green chiles, such as Anaheim or New Mexico

1 tomato (about 6 ounces), cored, seeded, and chopped

3 green onions, tender tops included, sliced

1 to 2 fresh jalapeños, stemmed and minced

2 tablespoons fresh lime juice

1 garlic clove, crushed through a press

Salt

⅓ cup finely chopped cilantro

¼ pound fresh mild goat cheese, crumbled

8 to 12 (10-inch) flour tortillas

SMOKING CHIP OPTION: MESQUITE

The title alone (never mind the main ingredient) marks this starter as unconventional, though it's based on a similar cactus salad preparation I've enjoyed from stalls in the Mercado Cuauhtemoc, in Juarez, Mexico. The salad ends up looking rather like salsa (and I've spooned it over grilled chicken breasts with terrific results), but it's at its best scooped onto torn pieces of grill-warmed flour tortillas and rolled into soft tacos—informal, rustic, and delicious.

1. Wearing gloves if necessary, lay a cactus pad on the work surface. With a long serrated knife, cutting parallel to the work surface and leaving as much of the cactus pad's skin intact as possible, gently saw off any remaining bumps or stickers. Trim off the tough edges and the stem end. Repeat with the remaining pads. Brush the pads all over with 2 tablespoons of the oil.

2. Meanwhile, light a direct-heat charcoal fire and let it burn down to medium-hot (5 seconds to "ouch") or preheat a gas grill to medium-high. Position the rack about 6 inches above the heat source.

3. When the grill is ready, lay the pads and the green chiles on the rack. Cover and grill, turning once, until the cactus pads are lightly browned and tender and the chile peels are lightly charred, about 10 minutes total. Transfer the cactus pads to a cutting board and cool. Transfer the chiles to a paper bag, close the bag, and steam the chiles until cool.

4. Chop the cactus pads. Peel, stem, and core the chiles and chop the flesh.

5. In a medium bowl, combine the cactus, chiles, tomato, onions, jalapeño, lime juice, the remaining 2 tablespoons olive oil, the garlic, and ½ teaspoon of salt. Let stand for 30 minutes. Stir in the cilantro and adjust the seasoning. Transfer the salad to a shallow serving dish. Scatter the cheese over the salad.

6. Divide the tortillas into batches of four and wrap each batch in foil. On the grill or in a 400°F oven, warm the tortillas just until soft and flexible, about 10 minutes. Transfer them to a napkin-lined basket to keep them warm and serve immediately, accompanied by the cactus salad.

Cozying Up to Cactus

Both the pads *(nopales)* and fruits (see page 252) of the prickly pear cactus have their charms and uses, and now that south-of-the-border ingredients are increasingly available, they turn up frequently in supermarkets with Latino customers and in specialty produce stores. The store-bought pads are thinner, smaller, and more uniform than ones I see growing wild in my yard, leading me to believe they are raised commercially for food or at least harvested very young. (You can also find *nopalitos*, cactus pads that are cut into strips, in cans or jars, but these are not suitable for the recipes in this book.)

There are relatively few stickers on the cactus pads, and they tend to be rather harmless, though you may want to handle the pads with gloves, just in case. The pads are always cooked—typically boiled—though grilling works well, too. The flavor is green and vegetal, rather like zucchini or asparagus, and, even when thoroughly cooked, the pads exude slippery juices (warning's fair) that will remind you of okra. The pads keep a week, maybe even two, in the vegetable crisper of your refrigerator, so you'll have plenty of time to schedule them into a grill meal of one sort or another. The best thing about serving grilled cactus? You can be fairly sure no one had it for lunch.

Grilled Eggplant Dip
with
Sweet and Smoky Flavors

SERVES 6 TO 8
(MAKES ABOUT 2 CUPS)

3 tablespoons pine nuts
2 eggplants (about 1½
   pounds total), trimmed
   and cut lengthwise into
   ½-inch slices (do not
   peel)
5 tablespoons roasted
   garlic-flavored olive oil
   (available in gourmet
   shops and some super-
   markets) or plain olive
   oil
⅓ cup chopped oil-packed
   sun-dried tomatoes
3 tablespoons balsamic
   vinegar
3 tablespoons minced
   canned chipotle chiles
   en adobo
3 garlic cloves, chopped
1 teaspoon salt
¼ cup finely chopped
   cilantro (optional)
Corn tortilla chips

SMOKING CHIP OPTION: MESQUITE

Rich and spicy-sweet, tinged with the smoke of
the grill as well as smoldering heat of chipotle
chiles, this easy dip is about as good as eggplant gets. Serve it with corn tortilla chips for
scooping, or with warm flour tortillas and encourage guests to tear off sections and create small roll-
ups. When I have leftover dip, I grill lamb burgers,
and spread it on the buns in place of mayonnaise.

1. Position a rack in the middle of the oven and
preheat to 375°F. Spread the pine nuts in a shallow metal pan, like a cake tin, and toast them, stirring often, until they are crisp and lightly browned,
about 8 minutes. Remove from the pan and cool.

2. Meanwhile, light a direct-heat charcoal fire
and let it burn down to medium-hot (5 seconds to
"ouch"), or preheat a gas grill to medium-high.
Position the rack about 6 inches above the heat
source.

3. Brush the eggplant slices on both sides with
4 tablespoons of the oil. When the grill is ready, lay
the eggplant slices on the rack. Cover and grill,
turning once, until the eggplant slices are tender
and well-browned, about 9 minutes total. Transfer
to a cutting board and let cool. Coarsely chop the
eggplant.

4. In a food processor, combine the eggplant,
sun-dried tomatoes, vinegar, chipotles, garlic,
remaining 1 tablespoon oil, and salt. Process, stopping several times to scrape down the sides of the
work bowl, until the mixture is almost pureed
(leave a bit of texture). Adjust the seasoning. (The

dip can be prepared up to this point 2 days ahead. Cover tightly and refrigerate, returning it to room temperature for serving.)

5. Transfer the dip to a serving dish. Sprinkle the pine nuts and the cilantro over the dip. Serve, accompanied by the corn chips, for scooping.

Bean, Guajillo Chile, and Cheese Dip with a Splash of Beer

This very good dip (one of the best reasons I know of for having some home-simmered pot beans in the freezer) gets much of its unique flavor from dried guajillo chile pods. Their sweet, berrylike heat makes the dip very hard to stop eating. The final simmering of the dip can be accomplished on a hot grill, if desired, for ultimate showmanship and rustic convenience. (Because of the tomatoes in the dip, you'll need a nonreactive pan or skillet.) The timings remain the same.

1. Using kitchen scissors, stem and seed the chiles and cut the pods into small pieces. In a medium heatproof bowl, combine the chile pieces and the water. Cover and let stand, stirring occasionally, until cool.

2. With a slotted spoon, transfer the soaked chile pieces to a food processor. Add ¼ cup of the chile soaking water and process, stopping several times to scrape down the sides of the work bowl, until the chiles are fairly smooth. Transfer to a sieve set over a bowl, and with a rubber scraper, force the chiles through the sieve. Discard any tough chile pieces that can't be sieved. There should be about 1 cup chile puree. (The puree can be prepared up to 3 days ahead and refrigerated, or frozen for up to 1 month.)

SERVES 6 TO 8

2 ounces dried guajillo
   chiles (about 12)
3 cups boiling water
3 cups Pot Beans with
   their broth (page 198)
2 tablespoons olive oil
2 strips thick-cut bacon,
   chopped
3 garlic cloves, chopped
¾ cup amber beer, such as
   Dos Equis
¼ cup canned crushed
   tomatoes with added
   puree
Salt
8 ounces Monterey Jack
   cheese, 6 ounces diced
   and 2 ounces shredded
½ cup thinly sliced green
   onions, tender tops
   included
Tostaditas (page 20) or
   purchased corn tortilla
   chips

3. In a food processor, puree the beans and their broth until fairly smooth (leave some texture).

4. In a heavy medium saucepan over low heat, warm the oil. Add the bacon and cook, stirring occasionally, until almost crisp, about 7 minutes. Stir in the garlic and cook until the garlic is tender and golden and the bacon is fairly crisp, another 3 minutes. Add the beans, the guajillo puree, beer, tomatoes, and ½ teaspoon salt. Bring to a simmer and cook uncovered, stirring often. As the dip begins to thicken, it will start to spatter and you will need to partially cover the pan.

5. When the dip is thick, after about 10 minutes, stir in the diced cheese and ⅓ cup of the green onions. Continue to cook, stirring often, until the cheese has melted and is stringy, another 3 to 4 minutes. Adjust the seasoning.

6. Transfer the dip to a serving dish and scatter the shredded cheese and the remaining green onions over the top. Serve immediately, accompanied by the tostaditas.

Queso Fundido with Mushrooms, Chiles, and Olives

Queso fundido is "baked cheese," an elementally simple and satisfying Mexican dish akin to fondue. Prepared on the grill in a cast-iron skillet over a smoky fire, it's about as rustic and pleasing as food can get. Set the skillet in the center of the table, supply guests with a basket (or several) of warmed corn tortillas and a salsa or two, and let them scrape, scoop, and eat to their heart's content.

1. In a well-seasoned 9- or 10-inch flameproof cast-iron skillet over low heat, warm the olive oil. Add the poblano strips, cover and cook, stirring once or twice, until almost tender, about 8 minutes. Increase the heat to medium and add the mushrooms, garlic, and salt. Cover and cook, stirring once or twice, until the mushrooms are tender and lightly browned, about 5 minutes. (The recipe can be prepared to this point several hours in advance. Cool, cover, and hold at room temperature.)

2. Light a direct-heat charcoal fire and let it burn down to medium-hot (5 seconds to "ouch") or preheat a gas grill to medium-high. Position the rack about 6 inches above the heat source. Preheat the oven to 400°F.

3. Wrap the tortillas in foil in 4 packets of 4 tortillas per package. Place in the preheated oven and heat for 10 minutes, until supple and warm.

4. Meanwhile, when the grill is ready, set the skillet on the rack. If the vegetable mixture has been prepared in advance, reheat it until sizzling. Scatter the cheese over the vegetables, cover the grill, and bake until the cheese is almost melted, about 4 minutes. Stir briefly, scatter the olives,

SERVES 4

1½ tablespoons olive oil
1 large poblano chile, stemmed, seeded, and cut into matchstick-thin strips
5 large cremini (brown) or cultivated white mushrooms (about ⅓ pound), trimmed and coarsely chopped
1 garlic clove, minced
¼ teaspoon salt
10 ounces Monterey Jack cheese, diced
⅓ cup sliced pimiento-stuffed green olives
2 green onions, tender tops included, trimmed and thinly sliced
1 fresh red jalapeño, stemmed and minced (optional)
16 (5-inch) corn tortillas
1 cup Avocado-Tomatillo Salsa (page 284) and/or Mango Pico de Gallo (page 281)

SMOKING CHIP OPTION: HICKORY

green onions, and jalapeño over the cheese, cover, and continue to bake, until bubbling and lightly browned, another 1 to 2 minutes (Do not overbake.)

5. Serve immediately, accompanied by the tortillas and one or both the salsas.

Skillets on the Grill

Cooking in a skillet over an open fire seems natural if you're camping out, odd in the backyard. But why? The same joy of cooking and eating something-or-other outdoors applies, as does the extra boost of flavor the smoke and flame supply. And, without a skillet, certain dishes just can't be cooked on a grill—gooey, drippy queso fundido being an ideal example. Cast-iron cooking is undergoing a renaissance these days, so finding a medium-priced, medium-sized (9- or 10-inch), skillet won't take a trip to the survivalist store. If it costs you more than twenty dollars, you've probably paid too much. Or, look for a used skillet at a yard sale for even less. The fire won't be as hard on the skillet as you may think (though it makes sense to avoid pricey enamel-painted pans or anything with a wooden handle, which might be damaged by the flame), so you won't need to dedicate the skillet to grill use only. In fact, using it as often as possible both indoors and out will help keep it seasoned. Brand new or used, first scrub your skillet well with hot water and detergent. Dry it, fill it with about 1 inch of cooking oil, and set it in a 300°F oven for an hour. Discard the oil, wash and dry the skillet, and it's ready to use. When it is well seasoned and depending on what you have cooked, you may be able to just wipe it clean. Otherwise, wash it by hand with hot water and detergent, dry it, set it on a medium-high burner, and, when it is hot, use a paper towel to lightly coat it with cooking oil, preferably peanut oil. Remove it from the burner, let it cool, and store it away until its next use.

Queso Fundido with Crab and Toasted Pumpkin Seeds

I confess to an uncontrollable liking for crabmeat in any form, if possible with cheese. That has led to this, one of the gooiest and most satisfying appetizers of my recipe-developing career and one of a handful of sure-fire starters that I rely on when I have guests I really, really need to impress. Corn chips are good for scooping here, but warmed corn tortillas are even better. Pass the pickled jalapeño slices at the table, for those who want to spice up this rich stuff a little.

1. Position a rack in the middle of the oven and preheat to 400°F. In a shallow metal pan, like a cake tin, toast the pumpkin seeds, stirring occasionally, until they are crisp, brown, and have begun to pop, 10 to 12 minutes. Cool and coarsely chop.

2. Light a direct-heat charcoal fire and let it burn down to medium-hot (5 seconds to "ouch") or preheat a gas grill to medium-high. Position the grill rack about 6 inches above the heat source.

3. Meanwhile, in a well-seasoned 9- or 10-inch flameproof cast-iron skillet over low heat, warm the olive oil. Add the garlic and cook without browning, stirring occasionally, for 2 minutes. Add the tomatoes, green chiles, and salt and cook uncovered, stirring occasionally, until thick, about 7 minutes.

4. Wrap the tortillas in foil in 4 packets of 4 tortillas each. Place in the oven for 10 minutes, until supple and warm.

5. Meanwhile, when the grill is ready, scatter the cheese over the tomato mixture. Scatter the crab over the cheese and sprinkle the green onions over the crab. Set the skillet on the rack, cover the

SERVES 4

¼ cup raw pumpkin seeds
1 tablespoon olive oil
3 garlic cloves, finely chopped
¾ cup diced tomato (from 2 plum tomatoes)
½ cup chopped roasted hot green chiles
¼ teaspoon salt
16 (5-inch) corn tortillas
10 ounces jalapeño Jack cheese, cubed
½ pound fresh blue or Dungeness crabmeat, preferably jumbo lump, picked over
3 green onions, tender tops included, trimmed and thinly sliced
Sliced pickled jalapeños, drained (optional)

SMOKING CHIP OPTION: HICKORY

grill, and bake until the cheese has almost all melted and is beginning to bubble, about 4 minutes. Stir briefly, replace the cover, and bake until all the cheese has melted and is just beginning to brown around the edges, another 2 to 3 minutes.

6. Remove the skillet from the grill. Scatter the pumpkin seeds over the queso fundido and serve immediately, accompanied by the tortillas and pickled chiles.

Queso Fundido with Ancho Chiles and Ham

SERVES 4

3 large ancho chiles
1 tablespoon olive oil
6 ounces smoky good-
   quality ham, in ¼-inch
   cubes
16 (5-inch) corn tortillas
5 ounces sharp cheddar
   cheese, diced
5 ounces jalapeño Jack
   cheese, diced
2 green onions, tender
   tops included, trimmed
   and thinly sliced
1 cup Chile de Arbol Salsa
   with Rosemary and
   Orange (page 288),
   Mango Pico de Gallo
   (page 281), and/or
   Avocado-Tomatillo
   Salsa (page 284)

SMOKING CHIP OPTION: HICKORY

Not a traditional queso fundido, but a tasty one. The strands of sweet, slightly chocolaty ancho chiles mingle with the smoky ham and molten cheese in a very satisfying way. You could use flour tortillas (or even pita bread) for the scooping and dipping, if desired, but as usual, corn tortillas have a way of making the dish, however unconventional, utterly southwestern.

1. Stem the anchos, slit them along one side, and open them out flat. Scrape off as many seeds as possible, then cut the anchos the short way into very thin strips. In a medium bowl, cover the ancho strips with hot tap water and let stand, stirring once or twice, for 10 minutes. Drain and pat dry.

2. In a well-seasoned 9- or 10-inch flameproof cast-iron skillet over medium heat, warm the olive oil. Add the ham and cook, stirring once or twice, until lightly browned, about 4 minutes. Stir in the ancho strips and cook another minute. (The recipe can be prepared up to this point several hours in advance. Cool, cover, and hold at room temperature.)

3. Light a direct-heat charcoal fire and let it burn down to medium-hot (5 seconds to "ouch") or preheat a gas grill to medium-high. Position the rack about 6 inches above the heat source. Preheat the oven to 400°F.

4. Wrap the tortillas in foil in 4 packages of 4 tortillas each. Place in the oven for 10 minutes, until supple and warm.

5. Meanwhile, when the grill is ready, set the skillet on the rack. If the ham mixture has been prepared in advance, reheat it until sizzling. Scatter the cheeses over the ham, cover the grill, and bake until the cheeses are almost melted, about 4 minutes. Stir briefly, scatter the green onions over the cheese, cover, and continue to bake, until bubbling and lightly browned, another 1 to 2 minutes. (Do not overbake.)

6. Serve immediately, accompanied by the tortillas and one or more of the salsas.

Grill-Baked Goat Cheese with Mango Pico de Gallo

H ere is a variation on the queso fundido theme, one I first served at my chili restaurant in New York years ago. The goat cheese doesn't so much melt as get hot and fluffy. Scooped onto warm flour tortillas or corn chips, its tangy taste spectacularly complemented by chiles, spices, and smoke, it's a vivid and lively way to kick off a southwestern grill supper. I like the sweet shock the mango salsa supplies, but several other salsa choices make good eating, too.

1. Light a direct-heat charcoal fire and let it burn down to medium-hot (5 seconds to "ouch") or preheat a gas grill to medium-high. Position the rack about 6 inches above the heat source. Preheat the oven to 400°F, if using corn tortillas.

2. Coat the bottom of a well-seasoned 9- or 10-inch flameproof cast-iron skillet with the olive oil. Slice the goat cheese into 5 pieces. Set the pieces, cut sides-up, in the oil in the skillet. Season generously with pepper.

SERVES 6

2 tablespoons olive oil
1 (11-ounce) log mild fresh goat cheese, chilled
Freshly ground black pepper
18 corn tortillas or Tostaditas (page 20)
2½ cups Mango Pico de Gallo (page 281), Chile de Arbol Salsa with Rosemary and Orange (page 288), and/or Golden Tomato Salsa Borracha (page 287)

SMOKING CHIP OPTION: HICKORY

3. Wrap the tortillas, if using, in foil in 3 packages of 6 tortillas each. Place in the oven for 10 minutes, until supple and warm.

4. Meanwhile, when the grill is ready, set the skillet on the rack. Cover the grill and bake until the oil in the skillet is sizzling and the goat cheese is hot and fluffy, about 8 minutes.

5. Serve immediately, accompanied by one or more salsas and tortillas or tostaditas.

Great Goat

Tangy goat cheese is reminiscent of several Mexican cheeses and more than holds its own with the region's assertive seasonings. There is, in fact, a tradition of goat cheesemaking in the Southwest, especially in New Mexico, where sheep- and goat-husbandry go back to the Spanish. (Because goats seem to be mentally grouped with sheep, they are less evident in cattle country—Texas and Arizona). Nowadays, the cattle wars are pretty much settled and imported French goat cheese is—like arugula, sun-dried tomatoes, and balsamic vinegar—a supermarket staple. Even better news, there are a number of artisanal makers of goat cheese throughout the Southwest. Working in the farmstead tradition, producing cheeses made from milk that comes only from their own herds, dairies with names like Sweetwood and Coon Ridge carry on the southwestern goat cheese tradition.

Grilled Quesadilla with Squash Blossoms and Goat Cheese

Throughout Mexico it seems, but especially in Oaxaca, squash blossoms find their way, along with cheese, into quesadillas. Their mild vegetable taste (not like flowers at all) and brilliant golden color make this quesadilla a very appealing starter. In Oaxaca, the base would be corn masa patted into a tortilla-like round or half-round and cooked on the comal, a type of griddle. I use purchased flour tortillas and turn the quesadillas on the grill, and the results are very good indeed. Salsa Verde (the variation without the pineapple) seems the tastiest and most authentic condiment for this delicate appetizer, but feel free to try another salsa you find appealing.

1. Light a direct-heat charcoal fire and let it burn down to medium-hot (5 seconds to "ouch") or preheat a gas grill to medium-high. Position the rack about 6 inches above the heat source.

2. Meanwhile, lay 1 tortilla on a cookie sheet without an edge. Spread the tortilla evenly with the goat cheese.

3. In a large skillet over low heat, warm the olive oil. Add the garlic and cook, stirring often, until fragrant but not browned, about 4 minutes. Add the squash blossoms and warm them in the oil, turning them once, until they are barely wilted, about 1 minute; do not overcook.

4. With tongs or a slotted spoon, transfer the blossoms to the prepared tortilla, arrange them spoke-fashion in a single layer. Sprinkle with the sage and season lightly with salt and generously with pepper. Scatter the Jack cheese over the squash blossoms, set the remaining tortilla atop them, and press gently with your palm to flatten slightly.

SERVES 2 TO 4

2 (10-inch) flour tortillas
2½ ounces mild fresh
  goat cheese, at room
  temperature
2 tablespoons olive oil
1 garlic clove, minced
12 large squash blossoms,
  prepared for cooking
  (see Scoping Out
  Squash Blossoms,
  page 36)
2 teaspoons finely
  chopped fresh sage
  (optional)
Salt and freshly ground
  black pepper
2 ounces shredded
  jalapeño Jack cheese
About 2 cups Salsa Verde
  (page 283), made
  without the pineapple

SMOKING CHIP OPTION: HICKORY

5. When the grill is ready, oil the rack. Slide the tortilla from the sheet pan onto the grill. Place a small plate on top of the quesadilla to ensure even cooking. Cover and grill for 1 minute. Rotate the quesadilla 45 degrees on the rack, cover, and continue grilling, until the grill lightly marks the bottom and the cheeses are beginning to melt, ½ to 1 minute. Remove the plate. With a wide spatula, flip the quesadilla, weight with the plate, cover, and grill for 30 seconds. Rotate again and continue grilling, until the grill lightly marks the bottom, the cheeses are melted, and everything is hot, another 30 to 45 seconds.

6. Transfer to a cutting board. With a pizza wheel or a long, sharp knife, cut the quesadilla into 4 wedges. Serve immediately, accompanied by the salsa.

Scoping Out Squash Blossoms

Squash blossoms are not rare, as most vegetable gardeners will tell you, but finding them for sale has been iffy until recently. Harvesting the female flowers (the ones with the infant squash attached) means one less adult vegetable for the farmer to harvest later, so they are not cheap; even then some growers are not anxious to make the sacrifice, uncertain if the demand will support it. Even the squash-less male flowers are highly perishable. Blossoms are beginning to show up more often now, however, due to their popularity in Italian cuisine, and, in the Southwest, thanks to the efforts of produce specialists, like my friend Elizabeth Berry, who grow them for farmers' markets and creative restaurant chefs.

The blossoms may be zucchini blossoms, or they may be the long-stemmed flowers of a pumpkinlike squash (likelier in Mexico and the Southwest). The ones I buy are the former. They come tied with string in bundles of twelve and are best used the same day harvested. Remove the stems, leaving enough of the flowers' bases to hold the petals in place. Use a soft-bristled brush inside and out to remove any clinging grit. (It's best not to rinse them unless they are very dirty.) If you are not cooking them immediately—the ideal plan—wrap them in lightly dampened paper towels and refrigerate for no more than a few hours, until use. Raw squash blossoms, prepared as described here, also make a dazzling addition to green salads.

Hot 'n' Cold Ceviche Nachos

Like several of the appetizers in this book, these nachos, topped with a tangy marinated raw fish salad, are grilled because they can be, not because they must be. If you like the backyard theatre that comes with pulling several courses in a row off the grill and passing them out to the eagerly waiting hungry hordes, then you'll understand. With enough smoking chips, the nachos do pick up an extra nuance of flavor, and it's always more convenient to cook the full meal in one place, rather than running indoors and out. But if need be, the nachos can be baked in the oven. Do it on the upper rack of a preheated 450°F oven; the timing is a little briefer, about 5 minutes.

1. Trim the fish and cut it into ½-inch pieces. In a medium bowl, combine the fish pieces and the ½ cup lime juice. Cover and refrigerate, stirring occasionally; the acid in the lime juice will change the texture of the fish, as if cooking it. The fish is "done" when it is completely opaque and will flake, about 12 hours.

2. Light a direct-heat charcoal fire and let it burn down to medium-hot (5 seconds to "ouch") or preheat a gas grill to medium-high. Position the rack about 6 inches above the heat source.

3. Meanwhile, drain the fish. In a medium bowl, combine the fish with the tomato, onion, cilantro, jalapeño, olive oil, remaining 2 teaspoons lime juice, and the salt. Adjust the seasoning.

4. Spread each chip with a thin layer of beans, arranging the chips as you go on a serving piece (even a baking sheet) that can go on the grill. Sprinkle the cheese over the bean-covered chips.

5. When the grill is ready, set the baking sheet on the grill. Cover the grill and bake, turning the sheet once to promote even heating, until the cheese has melted and the beans are sizzling, about 9 minutes.

6. Remove from the heat. Working quickly, top each nacho with some of the fish mixture, dividing it evenly and using it all. Serve immediately.

SERVES 4 TO 6

1¼ pounds boneless, skinless fillet of very fresh mild white fish, such as snapper or flounder
½ cup plus 2 teaspoons fresh lime juice
¼ cup finely diced tomato
3 tablespoons finely diced red onion
3 tablespoons finely chopped cilantro
1 fresh jalapeño, stemmed and finely chopped
1 tablespoon olive oil
¼ teaspoon salt
24 large Tostaditas (page 20) or commercial corn tortilla chips
About 3/4 cup refried black or pinto beans
6 ounces jalapeño Jack cheese, shredded

SMOKING CHIP OPTION: HICKORY

Tequila-Cured Salmon with Lime Cream

SERVES 12, WITH LEFTOVERS

⅓ cup sugar
1 tablespoon kosher salt
1 tablespoon freshly
  ground black pepper
1 whole side of salmon
  (2½ to 3½ pounds—
  choose the larger size if
  you want leftovers to
  grill), with the skin on
3 tablespoons tequila
Half a bunch of cilantro
12 very thin lime slices
1½ cups Lime Cream
  (page 296)
Sprigs of cilantro
  (optional)

In this recipe, the salmon undergoes the same curing process that produces the Scandinavian fish preparation known as gravlax. The salt and sugar change the texture of the raw fish into something silky and wonderful, while the tequila, lime, and cilantro infuse it with unique southwestern flavor. It makes an elegant first course or even a light main dish, especially during hot weather, and will feed a crowd with ease (although you will need a long, sharp knife to slice the salmon into properly thin slices). Since the slicing starts at the thin, tapered end of the salmon, the thicker end is frequently leftover. The lucky cook to whom this happens has a second wonderful meal in store: see the recipe for Grilled Tequila-Cured Salmon on the next page.

1. In a small bowl, stir together the sugar, salt, and pepper. Set aside.

2. With sterile tweezers or needle-nose pliers, pull out any bones remaining in the salmon. They are easy to locate by running your fingers along the side of fish. (There can be as many as 30.) Cut the side of salmon in half crosswise.

3. Lay one piece of salmon skin side-down in a shallow, nonreactive dish. Drizzle with half the tequila. Sprinkle with half the sugar mixture, patting it firmly into the fish. Layer the cilantro over the salmon; arrange the lime slices over the cilantro. Drizzle the second piece of salmon with the remaining tequila and sprinkle it with the remaining sugar mixture, patting it firmly into the fish. Lay the second piece of salmon on top, skin-side up. Cover with plastic wrap. Set a small, flat-bottomed dish atop the stack of salmon and weight it with 2 heavy cans or a small saucepan. Refrigerate for 24 hours.

4. Remove the weights, the dish, and the plastic wrap. With a spatula, flip the two pieces of salmon as one, so that the top piece is now on the bottom. With the spatula, lift the salmon piece now on top and baste the cilantro layer with the accumulated juices from the dish. Replace the salmon. Cover with plastic, top again with the dish and the weights, and refrigerate another 24 hours.

5. Remove the dish, weights, and plastic. Scrape off the cilantro, limes, and the salt mixture and pat the salmon dry with paper towels. Transfer to a cutting board. Beginning with the tapered tail-end piece of the salmon, using a long, thin, sharp knife, cut the salmon, across the grain and at an angle almost parallel to the work surface, into thin slices, releasing the slices from the skin as you go. Cut out and discard the darker v-shaped portion of each slice if desired.

6. Arrange the salmon on plates as you slice, overlapping slightly. About 2 ounces of salmon is a suitable portion (like all raw fish, it is rich). Drizzle decoratively with the lime cream, garnish with cilantro sprigs, and serve immediately.

Grilled Tequila-Cured Salmon
with
Mango Pico de Gallo

There's nothing wrong with the thick end of the tequila-cured salmon, it's just that since the slicing starts at the thin end, the thick end sometimes survives the party. When that happens, consider grilling your gravlax. Prepare a medium-hot (5 seconds to "ouch) charcoal fire or preheat a gas grill to medium high. Lightly oil the rack and place the salmon pieces skin-side up on the rack. Cover and grill for 4 minutes. Then turn, cover, and continue to grill until the salmon is done to your liking, another 4 minutes for medium-rare fish (because of the cure, the fish will flake even when undercooked). Serve with Mango Pico de Gallo (page 281).

Hickory-Smoked Salmon and Green Chile Spread

SERVES 10 TO 12
(MAKES ABOUT 3 CUPS)

6 ounces cream cheese, at
    room temperature
⅔ cup mayonnaise
⅓ cup finely chopped
    roasted hot green chiles
2 tablespoons fresh lime
    juice
2 teaspoons Dijon
    mustard
¼ teaspoon salt
1 pound Hickory-Smoked
    Salmon (page 117), skin
    removed, fish roughly
    flaked
Crisp ovals of toasted
    bread (see Crisp Toast
    Rounds, below)

By now I've smoked enough salmon on my kettle grill to be able to accomplish it in my sleep, so whipping up this party-sized batch of one of my favorite casual appetizers is no chore at all. It's also a good destination for the leftovers of a salmon that's been smoked for another meal and stashed in the freezer, perhaps; in that case, the recipe adjusts quite nicely to whatever amount of salmon dividend you are left with. Be sure your chiles are plenty picante, or the spread will seem too rich.

1. In a medium bowl, mix together the cream cheese and mayonnaise until smooth. Mix in the green chiles, lime juice, mustard, and salt. Add the salmon and fold until just combined; leave as much rough texture as possible. (The spread can be used immediately or it can be covered tightly and refrigerated for up to 2 days. Return the spread to room temperature if chilled.)

2. Transfer to a rustic dish, like a crock, and serve accompanied by the toasted bread.

Crisp Toast Rounds

To make the toasted bread, slice a baguette crosswise into 36 thin ovals. Brush lightly and evenly on both sides with about ⅓ cup olive oil. On a preheated gas grill set to medium-high (I wouldn't light a charcoal fire for this), or under a preheated broiler, toast the bread ovals, turning them once, until crisp and lightly browned, 3 to 4 minutes total. The breads can be toasted several hours in advance. Cool and store airtight until using.

Chipotle-Barbecued Shrimp with Goat Cheese Cream

There's a good grilling lesson to be learned from this shrimp appetizer's fiery sauce: Nothing ever tastes as spicy after it's spread onto something and grilled as it does on a spoon or a finger while being prepared. So, don't hesitate to proceed with the full amount of smoky chipotles. The final dish (especially when drizzled with mellow goat cheese cream), is merely habit-forming, not painful.

1. In a food processor or blender, combine the chipotles and their adobo, the lime juice, orange juice, tequila, ketchup, sugar, molasses, salt, and pepper.

2. In a shallow nonreactive dish, combine the chipotle mixture and the shrimp. Cover and let stand at room temperature, stirring once or twice, for 30 minutes. Transfer the goat cheese cream to a squeeze bottle, if desired.

3. Meanwhile, light a direct-heat charcoal fire and let it burn down to medium-hot (5 seconds to "ouch"), or preheat a gas grill to medium-high. Position the rack about 6 inches above the heat source.

4. Lift the shrimp from the marinade (reserve it), and divide them among 4 or 5 flat metal skewers. When the grill is ready, oil the rack. Lay the skewers on the rack. Baste with some of the marinade, cover and grill, turning 3 times and basting at each turn with some of the sauce, until the sauce is used up and the shrimp are curled, pink, and cooked through while remaining moist, about 6 minutes total.

5. Slide the shrimp from their skewers onto a platter or individual appetizer plates. Drizzle generously and decoratively with the goat cheese cream (you may not use all of it) and serve immediately.

SERVES 6 TO 8

8 chipotles en adobo, coarsely chopped, plus ¼ cup adobo from the can
6 tablespoons fresh lime juice
⅓ cup fresh orange juice
¼ cup tequila
¼ cup ketchup
2 tablespoons packed dark brown sugar
2 tablespoons unsulphured molasses
1 teaspoon salt
1 teaspoon freshly ground black pepper
1½ pounds large shrimp (about 36), shelled and deveined
Goat Cheese Cream (page 296), at room temperature

SMOKING CHIP OPTION: APPLE

Peel-and-Eat Shrimp with Grill-Roasted Green Chile Tartar Sauce

SERVES 4

1 pound medium-large
  shrimp (about 24)
1½ cups amber beer, such
  as Dos Equis
Grill-Roasted Green Chile
  Tartar Sauce (page 295)
Lime wedges

SMOKING CHIP OPTION: MESQUITE

Shrimp cooked in the shell always have more flavor, an axiom never truer than when those shrimp are first marinated in beer (which also plumps and firms them), grilled over a smoky fire, and then dunked into an absolutely habit-forming tartar sauce. Another plus is that, except for his or her own portion, the cook gets to skip the shrimp-shelling step—for my money, at least, the most annoying of all kitchen jobs. It's a messy business (though well rewarded) and really should only be attempted outside, with plenty of beer, napkins, maybe even wet towels at hand.

1. Rinse the shrimp under cold running water. In a large bowl, combine the shrimp and beer and let stand at room temperature, stirring once or twice, for 1 hour.

2. Light a direct-heat charcoal fire and let it burn down to medium-hot (5 seconds to "ouch") or preheat a gas grill to medium-high. Position the grill rack about 6 inches above the heat source.

3. Divide the tartar sauce among 4 ramekins. Drain the shrimp (discard the beer) and divide them among 4 flat metal skewers.

4. When the grill is ready, lay the skewers on the rack. Cover and grill, turning once, until the shrimp are pink, curled, and cooked through while remaining moist (test one to be certain), about 9 minutes total.

5. Transfer each skewer to a plate. Set a ramekin of sauce and some lime wedges on each plate and serve immediately, providing a bowl for discarded shells and napkins at the table.

Mango–Grilled Shrimp Cocktails

The popular seafood "coctels" served on Mexican beaches are very different from the typical horseradish-spiked American shrimp cocktail. Typically featuring an array of shellfish in a sweetish tomato-and-orange soft drink broth, and served in tall, soda fountain-type glasses, they can, with the addition of plenty of hot sauce and the drinking of much beer, be plenty satisfying. With a little tinkering (or maybe a lot), however, the general idea becomes something far more interesting, as this mango-touched grilled shrimp starter will prove. In Mexico, the "premium" coctels are made, like mine, with all shrimp, but if you would prefer more variety, add a few shucked clams or oysters to each serving.

1. In a blender, combine the tomato, mango nectar, tomato juice, lime juice, half of the jalapeño, and ¾ teaspoon salt. Process until smooth. Let the tomato broth stand at room temperature for 1 hour. (The broth can be prepared several hours in advance and refrigerated, if desired; let it come to room temperature before proceeding.)

2. Light a direct-heat charcoal fire and let it burn down to medium-hot (5 seconds to "ouch") or preheat a gas grill to medium-high. Position the rack about 6 inches above the heat source.

3. Meanwhile, thread the shrimp onto 4 or 5 flat metal skewers.

4. When the grill is ready, oil the rack. Lay the skewers on the rack. Cover and grill, turning once, until the shrimp are curled, pink, and just cooked through while remaining moist, about 5 minutes total.

5. Season the shrimp with salt and pepper and slide them off the skewers.

SERVES 6

1 large ripe tomato (about 10 ounces), seeded and chopped
⅓ cup canned mango nectar
⅓ cup best-quality canned tomato juice
2 tablespoons fresh lime juice
1 to 2 tablespoons minced fresh jalapeño
Salt
Freshly ground black pepper
1½ pounds large shrimp (about 36), shelled and deveined
1 large ripe but firm mango, peeled and diced
1 small avocado, diced
½ cup diced red radish
½ cup diced peeled jicama
⅓ cup diced red onion
⅓ cup finely chopped cilantro
Sprigs of cilantro (optional)

SMOKING CHIP OPTION: MESQUITE

6. In a medium bowl, gently combine the tomato broth, mango, avocado, radish, jicama, onion, chopped cilantro, and the remaining jalapeño. Taste and adjust the seasoning.

7. Divide the broth mixture evenly among 6 bowls. Divide the shrimp among the bowls, arranging them attractively. Garnish each bowl with the cilantro sprigs and serve immediately.

Managing Mangoes

Golden and fragrant, mangoes are among the most versatile and popular tropical fruits now used increasingly in southwestern cooking. Many come from Florida, but imports, primarily from Mexico and Haiti, are also showing up, and the fears of a few years ago that mangoes would disappear from the market now seem unfounded. They are only sporadically available still, however, so grab them and use them when you find them. There are various varieties (rarely labeled), but given that as much as half of the fruit is pit, it makes sense to buy the largest mangoes you can find. The stem end should give off a pleasant aroma. Ripen hard, green mangoes at room temperature (in the company of a ripening banana if desired) and enjoy them, if possible, without refrigeration.

Getting the flesh away from the large pit and off the peel (which can be bitter) is a challenge never better described than by Elizabeth Schneider in her book, *Uncommon Fruits & Vegetables*: "Set the mango stem end up with a narrow side facing you. Make a vertical slice about ½ inch to the right of the stem so it barely clears the long, flat, narrow stone that runs almost the length of the fruit. Do the same on the other side. Pare the skin from the seed section, then cut off the flesh from the seed. With a butter knife, score the flesh half in squares of desired size, cutting to but not through the skin. Press the skin so the cut side pops outward, hand grenade-like (also called hedgehog fashion). Slice the cubes from the skin." To eat, as is, as friends in El Paso like to do, impale a ripe mango on large fork (specially designed antique Mexican silver mango forks are coveted by collectors), score the peel into quarters, and peel each quarter back to expose the flesh. Eat from the fork, like eating a taffy apple on a stick.

Grill-Opened Clams on the Half Shell with Quick Rosemary-Bacon Salsa

The heat of the grill easily opens shellfish, adding a smoky edge to their briny flavor and creating a steamy, appetizing sizzle that will draw people from all around the yard, deck, beach, whatever. This easy clam preparation will remind you of clams casino, if you have ever had that warhorse appetizer, but with a bold, southwestern accent. The clams are served on a bed of rock salt on a platter, to hold them level.

1. Light a direct-heat charcoal fire and let it burn down to medium-hot (5 seconds to "ouch") or preheat a gas grill to medium-high. Position the rack about 6 inches above the heat source.

2. Spread 6 cups rock salt in a ½-inch-deep layer on 2 large platters.

3. In a bowl, stir together the salsa and rosemary.

4. When the grill is ready, arrange the clams directly on the rack. Cover and grill, turning occasionally, until the clams begin to open, about 8 minutes.

5. As they open, using potholders to protect your hands, twist off and discard the top shells. Arrange the opened clams, shells-down, on the platters of salt. Discard any clams that have not opened after 10 minutes or so. Working quickly, spoon salsa atop clams. Sprinkle the clams with the bacon and serve immediately.

SERVES 8

2 cups medium-hot, good quality homemade or store-bought salsa (see Note)
2 tablespoons finely chopped fresh rosemary
48 littleneck clams, scrubbed
10 strips thick bacon, cooked almost crisp, chopped

SMOKING CHIP OPTION: MESQUITE

Note: Given the quantity of salsa called for, this recipe is probably most conveniently made with purchased bottled salsa. Choose one with a relatively thick texture. On the other hand, I have had it made with Chile de Arbol Salsa with Rosemary and Orange (page 288), omitting the additional 2 tablespoons chopped rosemary, and it was superb.

Appetizers, Starters, and Snacks

Grilled Mini Crab Cakes with Mango Pico de Gallo

SERVES 6 TO 8

½ cup mayonnaise
1 large egg
2 tablespoons finely diced red bell pepper
1 tablespoon finely diced fresh jalapeño
1 tablespoon Dijon mustard
1 pound lump blue or Dungeness crabmeat, picked over
1 cup fine, fresh bread crumbs
¾ cup Lime Cream (page 296)
2¼ cups Mango Pico de Gallo (page 281)

SMOKING CHIP OPTION: APPLE

Foodwise, you never really know what will work until you try. No one was more surprised than I at how easily and deliciously crab cakes grill, picking up a hint of smoky flavor that complements the sweet meat wonderfully. Topped with chunky, mango-studded salsa, the cakes can be passed as somewhat messy finger food or plated for a more formal (and less drippy) presentation. Of course, if there's gridlock on the grill or snow in the forecast, these can be sautéed indoors in butter in a skillet, the old-fashioned way.

1. In a medium bowl, whisk together the mayonnaise, egg, bell pepper, jalapeño, and mustard. Fold in the crabmeat. Add the bread crumbs and mix well. Let stand for 15 minutes. Using 2 tablespoons per cake, form the crab mixture into about eighteen 3-inch cakes, transferring them as you go to a sheet pan.

2. Meanwhile, light a direct-heat charcoal fire and let it burn down to medium (7 to 8 seconds to "ouch") or preheat a gas grill to medium. Position the rack about 6 inches above the heat source.

3. When the grill is ready, lightly oil the rack. Working quickly, arrange the crab cakes on the rack. Cover and grill, carefully turning the crab cakes once, until they are firm and lightly marked by the rack, about 12 minutes total.

4. Transfer the crab cakes to a platter or small plates. Drizzle decoratively with the lime cream, spoon a small dollop of salsa atop each, and serve immediately.

Note: Depending on the crab and on the bread you use, the recipe may not need added salt. (Dungeness is more prone to being salty than is blue crabmeat; some breads are saltier than others.) To check, form and sauté one crab cake in butter in a small skillet until lightly browned. Taste the cake and adjust the seasoning in the remaining crab mixture accordingly.

Santa Fe Chicken Satays with Red Chile–Peanut Sauce

The concept of satay itself is from Indonesia, not New Mexico, but the love of eating smoky bites of just-grilled meat off a skewer is ancient and universal. The skewers really ought to be of bamboo, for both aesthetics and safety, but if metal is all you have, slide the finished chicken onto a platter, drizzle with the sauce and serve, accompanied by long cocktail toothpicks, for spearing the chicken morsels. Drizzling with sauce as opposed to setting it out in a communal bowl, is a good idea in general, actually: It prevents "double-dipping" and looks colorful and festive at the same time.

1. Soak 30 long bamboo skewers in water to cover for at least 2 hours.

2. Separate and trim the chicken breasts and remove all fat. Cut the chicken breasts on an angle into ½-inch strips. Cut the longer strips in half crosswise. Drain the skewers and pat dry. Thread a strip of chicken onto each skewer, positioning the chicken on the skewer so that the pointed tip end of the wood is protected by chicken and not visible. In a small bowl, mix together the cumin, cayenne, and salt. Sprinkle the cumin mixture lightly but evenly over the chicken.

3. Meanwhile, light an indirect charcoal fire, banking the coals on one side of the kettle, and let it burn down to hot (3 seconds to "ouch"), or preheat the front burner of a gas grill to high. Position the rack about 6 inches above the heat source.

4. When the grill is ready, oil the rack. Lay the skewers on the rack. If you are grilling over charcoal, position the skewers so that the chicken strips are over the coals and the exposed skewers are over the unheated side of the grill or overhanging the

SERVES 8

2¼ pounds (1½ large whole) boneless, skinless chicken breasts
4 teaspoons freshly ground cumin (preferably from toasted seeds)
½ teaspoon cayenne pepper
Pinch salt
1½ cups Red Chile–Peanut Sauce (page 291)
¼ cup finely chopped cilantro (optional)

SMOKING CHIP OPTION: MESQUITE

grill altogether. If you are grilling over gas, position the skewers so that the chicken strips are on the heated section of the grill rack while the skewers extend over the cool section or overhang the grill.

5. Grill, turning the skewers occasionally (with tongs if necessary) and always working to prevent the skewers from burning up (a few inevitably will), until the meat is lightly browned and cooked through while remaining juicy, about 6 minutes.

6. Remove from the fire and arrange the skewers on a large platter. Drizzle decoratively with the peanut sauce, sprinkle the cilantro over all, and serve immediately. Pass the remaining peanut sauce at the table.

Cumin-Oregano Chicken Wings

SERVES 6 TO 8

2½ pounds chicken wing drumettes
¼ cup Cumin-Oregano Rub (page 267)
Salt
1½ cups Cool Green Dipping Sauce (page 291), Red Chile–Peanut Sauce (page 291), or Roasted Garlic Aioli (page 294)

SMOKING CHIP OPTION: MESQUITE

Chicken wings, designed for gnawing, are one of the great backyard nibbles, particularly good for occupying the hungry hordes while you concentrate on grilling the main course. These wings, coated with a pungent rub, are actually "drumettes," the meatiest third wing segment, now fairly widely available in supermarkets. The trick with chicken drumettes is to cook them low and slow, rendering them smoky and tender.

1. Light a direct-heat charcoal fire and let it burn down to medium (7 to 8 seconds to "ouch") or preheat a gas grill to medium. Position the rack about 6 inches above the heat source.

2. Pat the drumettes dry. On a sheet pan, sprinkle the drumettes with the rub, turning to coat evenly.

3. When the grill is ready, oil the rack. Working quickly, lay the drumettes on the rack. Cover and grill, turning every 4 or 5 minutes, until the drumettes are lightly browned, crisp, and cooked through while remaining moist, about 25 minutes total.

4. Transfer to a platter, season lightly with salt, and serve hot, accompanied by one or more of the dipping sauces.

Steak and Grilled Green Onion Quesadilla

SERVES 2 TO 4

6 large green onions, tops
  trimmed to no more
  than 3 inches long
About ¼ pound grilled
  steak, trimmed and
  finely diced
Salt and freshly ground
  black pepper
2 (10-inch) flour tortillas
2 ounces sharp cheddar
  cheese, shredded
2 ounces jalapeño Jack
  cheese, shredded
¼ cup Lime Cream (page
  296) or Goat Cheese
  Cream (page 296)
¾ cup Grilled Three-Chile
  Salsa with Black Beans
  and Corn (page 280),
  Cantina Red Table Sauce
  (page 290), or any good-
  quality bottled salsa

SMOKING CHIP OPTION: HICKORY

I'm always squirreling away bits of leftover grilled steak in the freezer, so I can enjoy this meaty treat spontaneously (leftovers from Beef Tacos "al Carbon," page 79, are particularly good), but die-hard types can always start from scratch. With a green salad, this quesadilla is substantial enough to serve as a supper for one.

1. Light a direct-heat charcoal fire and let it burn down to medium-hot (5 seconds to "ouch"), or preheat a gas grill to medium-high. Position the rack about 6 inches above the heat source.

2. When the grill is ready, lightly oil the rack. Lay the onions on the rack, cover, and grill, turning them once, until they are lightly marked and almost tender, about 5 minutes total. Transfer the onions to a cutting board, cool slightly, and coarsely chop. Season the steak and onions with salt and pepper to taste.

3. Lay 1 tortilla on a cookie sheet without an edge. Scatter the cheddar over the tortilla. Scatter the steak and onions over the cheddar. Scatter the Jack cheese over the steak. Top with the second tortilla. Press lightly with the palm of your hand.

4. Re-oil the grill rack if necessary. Slide the quesadilla from the sheet pan onto the grill. Place a small plate on top to ensure even cooking. Cover and grill for about 1 minute. Rotate the quesadilla on the rack 45 degrees, cover, and continue to grill, until the grill lightly marks the bottom and the cheeses are beginning to melt, ½ to 1 minute. Remove the plate. With a wide spatula, flip the quesadilla, replace the plate, cover, and grill for 30 seconds. Rotate again and continue grilling, until the grill lightly marks the bottom, the cheeses are melted, and everything is hot, another 30 to 45 seconds.

5. Transfer to a cutting board. With a pizza wheel or a long, sharp knife, cut the quesadilla into 4 wedges. Transfer to plates, drizzle decoratively with lime or goat cheese cream and serve immediately, accompanied by one of the salsas.

Small Grilled Pizzas with Chorizo, Goat Cheese, and Green Chile "Jam"

SERVES 4

4 ounces chorizo
1 tablespoon olive oil
2 garlic cloves, finely chopped
Pinch crushed red pepper flakes
1 cup chopped roasted hot green chiles
½ teaspoon packed light brown sugar
¼ teaspoon salt
2 (6-inch) prebaked pizza shells, such as Boboli
2 ounces fresh mild goat cheese, at room temperature

SMOKING CHIP OPTION: MESQUITE

Quesadillas are referred to as "Mexican pizzas" so often, it was inevitable that the idea of an actual pizza topped with something southwestern would occur. Even more so with appetizer pizzas than with meal-type ones, the toppings must be intensely flavorful. A touch of smoke is a welcome plus, recalling pizzas baked in real wood-burning ovens. On the other hand, purchased pizza shells are a great convenience and are improved by being baked on the grill. The green chile topping is not really a jam, though a touch of brown sugar helps caramelize the chiles and brings out their natural sweetness.

1. Remove the chorizo from its casings and crumble it into a small skillet. Set over medium-low heat and cook, breaking up the chorizo, until it has rendered its fat and is lightly browned, 5 to 7 minutes. With a slotted spoon, transfer to paper towels to drain. (The chorizo can be prepared up to 1 day ahead. Wrap well and refrigerate, returning it to room temperature before using.)

2. In a small skillet over low heat, warm the olive oil. Add the garlic and red pepper and cook without browning, stirring often, for 4 minutes. Add the green chiles, sugar, and salt and continue to cook, stirring occasionally, until the chile mixture is thick and lightly browned, about 10 minutes. Cool to room temperature. (The chile jam can be prepared up to 1 day ahead. Cover tightly and refrigerate, returning it to room temperature before using.)

3. Light a direct-heat charcoal fire and let it burn down to medium (7 to 8 seconds to "ouch") or preheat a gas grill to medium. Position the grill rack about 6 inches above the heat source.

4. Meanwhile, divide the chile jam over the pizza shells, spreading it almost to the edges. Crumble the cheese over the jam. Scatter the chorizo over the cheese.

5. When the grill is ready, invert a baking sheet with sides (like a jelly roll pan; it can be disposable) onto the grill rack. Set the pizzas on the inverted pan, cover, and grill, rotating the pizzas occasionally to promote even baking and checking that the bottoms are not getting too dark, until the chorizo is sizzling and the cheese is lightly browned, about 10 minutes.

6. Transfer to a cutting board, cut into wedges, and serve immediately.

Chili Meatballs with Hot Pepper Jelly Dipping Sauce

SERVES 6 TO 8

2 large eggs
¼ cup minced green
    onions, tender tops
    included
3 garlic cloves, crushed
    through a press
1 tablespoon
    Worcestershire sauce
1 tablespoon chili powder
    seasoning blend
2 teaspoons soy sauce
½ teaspoon freshly ground
    cumin (preferably from
    toasted seeds)
¼ teaspoon dried oregano,
    crumbled
1½ pounds butcher's meat-
    loaf blend (typically
    50 percent ground
    chuck, 25 percent
    ground veal and 25
    percent ground pork),
    at room temperature
1 cup fine dry bread
    crumbs
Hot Pepper Jelly Dipping
    Sauce (page 289),
    warmed

SMOKING CHIP OPTION: MESQUITE

Meatballs have a universal appeal, grilled meat-balls even more so. Add a tangy, sweet-hot dipping sauce, and you'll be a backyard hero. Designed to skewer, these meatballs don't require a light touch. In fact, if you don't shape them firm-ly, they'll fall apart on the grill. But don't worry, even with all that brusque handling, the finished product will be tender and tasty.

1. In a large bowl, whisk together the eggs, onions, garlic, Worcestershire, chili powder, soy sauce, cumin, and oregano. Add the meat and bread crumbs and knead until thoroughly com-bined. Firmly shape the meat mixture into about forty 1-inch balls.

2. Meanwhile, light a direct-heat charcoal fire and let it burn down to medium-hot (5 seconds to "ouch") or preheat a gas grill to medium-high. Position the rack about 6 inches above the heat source.

3. Divide the meatballs among 6 or 8 flat metal skewers. When the grill is ready, lightly oil the rack. Lay the skewers on the rack, cover, and grill, turn-ing occasionally, until the meatballs are crisp, nice-ly browned, and done through while remaining moist, about 12 minutes total.

4. Slide the meatballs off the skewers onto a platter and serve, accompanied with long sandwich picks for spearing and the sauce for dipping.

Grilled Beef Heart Skewers with Cascabel–Roasted Garlic Salsa

Marinated and grilled hot and fast, beef heart is meaty, tender, and delicious—one of the great carnivorous nibbles. This skewered appetizer, called *anticuchos*, is pretty much a traditional Peruvian recipe—but in spirit, especially with the post-grill application of a deliciously garlicky salsa, it is very southwestern. To really turn this into party fare, offer small corn tortillas, the salsa, and even some guacamole (page 21), and let guests compose their own small tacos.

1. In a food processor, combine the vinegar, oil, garlic, ancho powder, achiote paste, sugar, cumin, salt, pepper, oregano, and chile de árbol powder. Process until fairly smooth.

2. In a nonreactive dish, combine the vinegar mixture with the cubed beef heart and marinate, stirring once or twice, for 4 hours at room temperature or overnight in the refrigerator.

3. Light a direct-heat charcoal fire and let it burn down to hot (3 seconds to "ouch), or preheat a gas grill to high. Position the rack about 6 inches above the heat source.

4. Remove the cubed meat from the marinade and divide the meat among 4 to 6 flat metal skewers. When the grill is ready, lay the skewers on the rack. Cover and grill, basting with the reserved marinade and turning every 2 minutes, until the marinade is used up. Continue grilling until the meat is nicely browned but not dry, 6 to 8 minutes total.

5. Slide the grilled meat from the skewers onto plates and serve immediately, accompanied by the salsa.

SERVES 4 TO 6

½ cup sherry wine vinegar
⅓ cup olive oil
4 garlic cloves, chopped
1 tablespoon ancho chile powder
1 tablespoon achiote paste
1 tablespoon packed dark brown sugar
2 teaspoons freshly ground cumin (preferably from toasted seeds)
2 teaspoons salt
1 teaspoon freshly ground black pepper
1 teaspoon dried oregano, crumbled
1 teaspoon chile de árbol or chipotle chile powder
1 trimmed beef heart (about 2¼ pounds), cut into approximately ¾-inch cubes
1½ cups Cascabel–Roasted Garlic Salsa (page 285)

SMOKING CHIP OPTION: MESQUITE

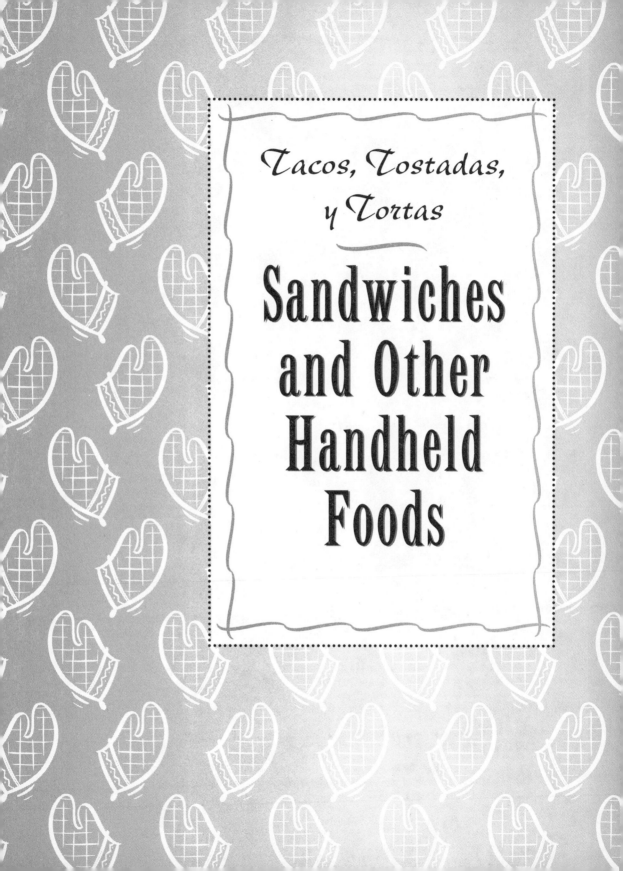

Tacos, Tostadas,
y Tortas

Sandwiches and Other Handheld Foods

Tacos, Tostadas, y Tortas
SANDWICHES AND
OTHER HANDHELD FOODS

Spice-Rubbed Buffalo Burgers with
Coffee Barbecue Sauce 80

Valle Grande Lamb Burgers with
Green Chiles and Goat Cheese 81

Portobello Mushroom Burgers with Cheese and Salsa Mayonnaise

Oversized portobello mushrooms are super-market darlings these days, in the Southwest and across the country. Sometimes compared to that most delicious of all wild mushrooms, the porcini (a.k.a. cèpes or boletes, which are, in fact, often found in wild abundance in forests through-out the Southwest), portobellos, being cultivated, are necessarily milder in flavor. Still, they make a satisfying meatless "burger," especially when topped with melted cheese and a zippy salsa-infused mayonnaise.

1. Light a direct-heat charcoal fire and let it burn down to medium-hot (5 seconds to "ouch") or preheat a gas grill to medium-high. Position the rack about 6 inches above the heat source.

2. Meanwhile, brush the mushroom caps and onion slices on both sides with the garlic oil.

3. When the grill is ready, lay the onion slices on the rack. Cover and grill for 2 minutes. Add the mushroom caps, cover, and grill for 4 minutes. Season the mushrooms with salt, turn the mush-rooms and onions, and salt the mushrooms again. Arrange the cheese slices over the mushrooms, cover, and grill until the cheese has melted, another 4 to 5 minutes.

4. Meanwhile, toast the cut sides of the ham-burger buns (use the grill, if desired).

5. Spread the cut sides of the buns generously with the mayonnaise. Set the mushroom caps on the bun bottoms. Separate the onions into rings and divide them over the mushrooms. Set the bun tops in place and serve immediately.

SERVES 4

4 very large portobello
  mushrooms (about
  1½ pounds total),
  stems removed
2 thick slices from a very
  large red onion
¼ cup roasted garlic oil
  (available in gourmet
  shops and some
  supermarkets) or
  plain olive oil
Salt
6 ounces provolone, sharp
  cheddar, or jalapeño
  Jack cheese, thinly
  sliced
4 large hamburger buns or
  sandwich rolls
1 cup Salsa Mayonnaise
  (page 292)

SMOKING WOOD OPTION: MESQUITE

Sandwiches and Other Handheld Foods

Grill-Baked Eggplant, Poblano, and Two-Cheese Sandwiches

MAKES 4 SANDWICHES

2 eggplants (about 1½ pounds total)

3 tablespoons roasted garlic-flavored olive oil (available in gourmet shops and some supermarkets) or plain olive oil

4 poblano chiles

4 large hamburger buns or sandwich rolls

Salt and freshly ground black pepper

4 tablespoons mild fresh goat cheese, at room temperature

¼ pound jalapeño Jack cheese, thinly sliced

About ½ cup Chipotle Mayonnaise (page 293), Roasted Garlic Aioli (page 294), or plain mayonnaise

SMOKING CHIP OPTION: MESQUITE

Always a more than acceptable stand-in for meat, rich and satisfying eggplant stars in these meatless sandwiches, a creation of the modern, rather than the historical, Southwest. Taste your poblanos after roasting: If they are on the mild side, add a few slices of pickled jalapeño to each sandwich, in order to keep things lively.

1. Light a direct-heat charcoal fire and let it burn down to medium-hot (5 seconds to "ouch") or preheat a gas grill to medium-high. Position the rack about 6 inches above the heat source.

2. Meanwhile, cut eight ¾-inch-thick round or slightly oval slices of eggplant about the same size as the buns you are using. Brush the slices on both sides with the garlic oil.

3. When the grill is ready, lay the eggplant slices and poblanos on the rack. Cover and grill, turning once, until the eggplant slices are well marked and tender and the poblano peels are lightly but evenly charred, about 10 minutes total. Remove the vegetables from the grill. Transfer the chiles to a paper bag, close the bag, and steam the chiles until cool. Rub away the burnt peel and stem and core the chiles.

4. Toast the cut sides of the buns (use the grill, if desired).

5. Season the eggplant slices and poblanos with salt and pepper. Spread one side of 4 eggplant slices with a tablespoon of goat cheese. Lay the eggplant slices in a disposable foil pan. Top each with a poblano, cutting to fit if necessary. Top the poblanos with the Jack cheese, dividing it evenly. Set the remaining 4 eggplant slices atop the Jack cheese.

6. Set the disposable foil pan on the grill rack, cover, and bake, turning each eggplant stack once, until the cheeses are hot and bubbly, about 8 minutes total.

7. Spread the cut sides of each bun with about 1 tablespoon mayonnaise. Set an eggplant stack on each bun bottom. Set the bun tops in place and serve immediately.

Note: If it is more convenient, the baking of the assembled eggplant stacks can be done in a preheated 400°F oven, rather than on the grill. The baking time is the same.

Grilled Salmon Burgers with Rosemary-Achiote Mop

When people see me ready to toss patties of nothing more than ground raw salmon on the grill, they always ask, "Will it work?" Yes, it works (and why not, burgers of ground raw beef work), and if you love salmon as much as I do, it works spectacularly well.

1. With sterile tweezers or needle-nosed pliers, remove the thin pin bones that run in a line down the side of salmon. Cut the salmon into 1-inch chunks. In a food processor, with short bursts of power, chop the salmon medium-fine (this is easier to do if the fish is cold); leave some texture. Shape the salmon into 4 thick 5-inch burgers, transferring them to a plate as you go. Cover with plastic and refrigerate. (The burgers can be prepared several hours in advance.)

2. Light a direct-heat charcoal fire and let it burn down to hot (3 seconds to "ouch"), or preheat a gas grill to high.

3. When the grill is ready, lightly oil the rack. Carefully lay the burgers on the rack. Baste with some of the Rosemary-Achiote Mop, cover, and

SERVES 4

2 pounds skinless salmon fillet, well chilled
1¼ cups Rosemary-Achiote Mop (page 269)
4 large hamburger buns or sandwich rolls
¾ cup Lime Cream (page 296) or 1 cup Avocado-Tomatillo Salsa (page 284)
Salt
4 thin slices from a large tomato
4 thin onion slices (optional)

SMOKING CHIP OPTION: MESQUITE

grill, turning the burgers once and basting with the mop until it is used up and the burgers are done to your liking, about 8 minutes total for fish that is fully cooked through but very moist.

4. Meanwhile, lightly toast the cut sides of the buns (use the grill, if desired).

5. Spread the cut sides of the buns with the lime cream or the salsa. Season the burgers with salt to taste and set one on each bun bottom. Top with the tomato and onion slices. Set the bun tops in place and serve immediately.

Café Pasqual's Grilled Salmon Burritos with Cucumber Salsa

SERVES 4

4 (6-ounce) skinless salmon fillets (see Note)

1 tablespoon medium-hot unblended powdered red chile, preferably from Chimayo

Salt and freshly ground black pepper

4 (10-inch) flour tortillas

¾ cup mild fresh goat cheese, at room temperature

1⅓ cups Black Pot Beans (page 199), heated to simmering

Café Pasqual's Cucumber Salsa (page 282)

SMOKING CHIP OPTION: MESQUITE

Chef Katherine Kagel, of Café Pasqual's in Santa Fe, has a unique way of combining authentic southwestern flavors with atypical ingredients and inventive, sometimes even startling, presentations. Among those items that never seem to leave the popular café's ever-changing menu are these burritos. There are not a lot of traditional dishes combining tortillas and seafood in the Southwest (since until modern times there was not much seafood), but that doesn't mean the pairing can't be wildly successful, as this simplified version of Kagel's recipe proves.

1. Light a direct-heat charcoal fire and let it burn down to medium-high (5 seconds to "ouch") or preheat a gas grill to medium-high. Position the rack about 6 inches above the heat source. Preheat the oven to 400°F.

2. Meanwhile, with sterile tweezers or needle-nosed pliers, remove any bones remaining in the salmon. Dust the fillets on all sides with the chile powder, patting it firmly to adhere.

3. When the grill is ready, lightly oil the rack. Lay the fillets on the rack, cover, and grill, turning once, until well-marked by the grill and done to your liking, about 8 minutes total for medium-rare fish. Remove from the grill and season with salt and pepper.

4. Meanwhile, wrap the tortillas in foil. Place in the oven until warm and supple, about 10 minutes.

5. Spread 3 tablespoons of the goat cheese down the center third of each warm tortilla. Divide the beans over the cheese. Set the salmon atop the beans. Fold the sides of the tortilla over the short ends of the fillets, then roll up the opposite sides of the tortillas, enclosing the salmon completely. Transfer to plates. Spoon the salsa over and around the burritos, dividing it evenly and using it all. Serve immediately.

Note: The fillets should be cut from the thicker (or head) end of the salmon, so that each is rectangular (burrito-shaped, in effect), rather than triangular.

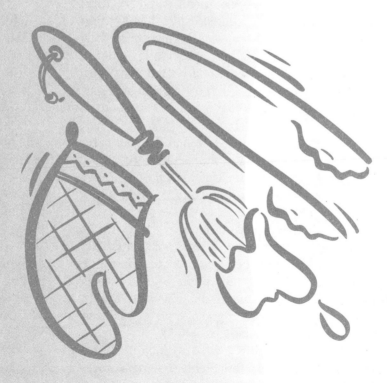

Garlicky Fish Tostadas with Guacamole

SERVES 4

7 tablespoons olive oil
6 tablespoons fresh lime
  juice
4 garlic cloves, crushed
  through a press
1 teaspoon granulated
  brown sugar
Salt
Freshly ground black
  pepper
1½ pounds firm, flaky
  white-fleshed fish,
  such as striped bass,
  in a single, thick fillet
About ¼ cup corn oil
8 (5-inch) corn tortillas
Guacamole (page 21)
2½ cups finely shredded
  inner romaine lettuce
  leaves
Pickled jalapeño slices

SMOKING CHIP OPTION: MESQUITE

The main difference between fish tostadas and fish tacos is that the tostadas are even messier to eat. Choose your company carefully, therefore (some people are just not suited for tostada-eating, which requires the fingers) and provide them with plenty of napkins.

1. In a shallow nonreactive dish, whisk together 3 tablespoons of the oil, 3 tablespoons of the lime juice, the garlic, sugar, ½ teaspoon salt, and ½ teaspoon pepper. Add the fish, skin side-down, and let stand at room temperature for 1 hour.

2. In a medium skillet over moderate heat, warm the corn oil. One or two at a time, add the corn tortillas and fry, turning once or twice, until almost crisp, 1 to 2 minutes. Transfer to paper towels to drain. Season lightly with salt.

3. Meanwhile, light a direct-heat charcoal grill and let it burn down to medium-hot (5 seconds to "ouch") or preheat a gas grill to medium-high. Position the rack about 6 inches above the heat source.

4. When the grill is ready, lightly oil the rack. Lift the fish from the marinade (reserve it) and lay it skin side-up on the rack. Cover and grill for 9 minutes, turn, baste with the marinade, and continue to grill, covered, until the fish is just cooked through and flaking while remaining moist, another 5 minutes or so.

5. Remove the fish from the grill and cool slightly. Remove the skin and flake the fish. Transfer to a medium bowl. Add the remaining 4 tablespoons olive oil and 3 tablespoons lime juice. Add ¼ teaspoon salt and a generous grinding of pepper and toss gently to avoid breaking up the fish pieces any more than necessary.

6. Spread about ¼ cup of the guacamole on each tostada. Set 2 tostadas on each of 4 plates. Top each tostada with some of the lettuce. Top the lettuce with the fish and its dressing, using it all. Top each tostada with a dollop of the remaining guacamole. Scatter a few pickled jalapeño slices over each tostada and serve immediately.

Grilled Fish Tacos with Citrus Slaw

Along the coast of the Sea of Cortez, fish tacos are a popular street snack, one that has now established a beachhead in San Diego, becoming a fast-food phenomenon. Typically made with battered, deep-fried fish (junky, but fun), the tacos become something vividly light and flavorful when the fish is instead grilled over a smoky fire. The touches of orange juice and zest are my own embellishments. Each taco is made with two tortillas stacked, to prevent them from bursting at their overstuffed seams. Try to serve the tacos while the fish mixture is still warm.

SERVES 4 TO 6

2¼ cups homemade or storebought hot red or green salsa
1 tablespoon olive oil
4 thick (1½-inch) mahi mahi fillets or swordfish or shark steaks (about 2 pounds total)
1½ cups corn oil
25 (5-inch) corn tortillas
¾ cup Lime Cream (page 296)
1 garlic clove, crushed through a press
1 medium-large ripe avocado, cut into ½-inch chunks
⅓ cup diced red onion
⅓ cup finely chopped cilantro
¼ teaspoon salt
Citrus Slaw (page 212)

SMOKING CHIP OPTION: MESQUITE

1. In a shallow nonreactive dish, stir together 1 cup of the salsa and 1 tablespoon olive oil. Add the fish, cover, and marinate at room temperature, turning once or twice, for 1 hour.

2. In a large skillet over medium heat, warm the oil. With tongs, dip the tortillas one at a time in the hot oil, turn them, and then transfer to paper towels to drain. The tortillas should not be in the oil more than a few seconds, and they should not blister or become crisp. Set aside at room temperature.

3. Combine the lime cream and the garlic and transfer, if desired, to a squeezed bottle.

4. Meanwhile, light a direct-heat charcoal fire and let it burn down to medium-hot (5 seconds to "ouch") or preheat a gas grill to medium-high. Position the grill rack about 6 inches above the heat source.

5. When the grill is ready, lift the fish from the marinade (reserve it) and lay the fish on the rack. Cover and grill, turning the fish once and basting with the reserved marinade, until the marinade is used up and the fish is just cooked through while remaining moist, about 9 minutes total. Transfer to a cutting board.

6. Roughly chop the fish and transfer to a bowl. Add the avocado, onion, cilantro, ¼ cup salsa, and salt. Toss gently. Adjust the seasoning.

7. For each taco, stack 2 tortillas on a plate. Top each with about ⅓ cup of the fish mixture and about ¼ cup of the slaw. Squirt with lime cream and serve immediately, passing the remaining 1 cup salsa at the table.

Yucatan Shark "Bread"

SERVES 4

⅔ cup fresh orange juice
3 tablespoons fresh lime
   juice
2 tablespoons achiote
   paste
1¼ pounds shark, cut in
   1 or 2 thick (1½-inch)
   steaks
16 (5-inch) corn tortillas
Salt and freshly ground
   black pepper
About 1½ cups refried
   black beans (preferably
   homemade), heated
2½ cups Yucatan
   Habanero Salsa
   (Xnipec) (page 286)

SMOKING CHIP OPTION: MESQUITE

Shark bread *(pan de cazon)* is a common snack in the Yucatan, although my experience with these taco-like grilled fish roll-ups is that they are so good, they deserve to be a full-fledged, albeit light, meal, hence their inclusion in this chapter. (If you do serve them as snacks, plan on two roll-ups per person.) Shark is not a requirement here—swordfish works wonderfully well—but the Xnipec is essential: Its fruity, fiery heat brings the dish to life.

1. In a shallow nonreactive dish, whisk together the orange juice, lime juice, and achiote until smooth. Add the steaks, cover, and marinate at room temperature, turning once or twice, for 2 hours. (If you use swordfish or something else less resilient than shark, shorten the marinating time to 1 hour, to avoid making the fish mushy.)

2. Light a direct-heat charcoal fire and let it burn down to medium-hot (5 seconds to "ouch") or preheat a gas grill to medium-high. Position the rack about 6 inches above the heat source. Preheat the oven to 400°F.

3. When the grill is hot, lightly oil the rack. Lift the steaks from the marinade (reserve it) and lay them on the rack. Cover and grill, basting the steaks with the reserved marinade and turning them once, until the marinade is used up and the steaks are done to your liking, about 8 minutes total for shark that is just cooked through while remaining moist (other fish may take less time).

4. Meanwhile, wrap the tortillas in foil in 4 packets of 4 tortillas each. Place the tortillas in the preheated oven, until warm and supple, about 10 minutes.

5. When the steaks are cooked through, transfer to a cutting board and let them rest for a few minutes.

6. Coarsely chop the fish, season it with salt and pepper, and transfer it to a communal bowl or to 4 individual plates. Serve immediately, accompanied by the tortillas, beans, and salsa. To eat, spread a thin layer of beans on a tortilla. Top the beans with a few spoonfuls of fish, add salsa to taste, then roll up and eat, taco-fashion.

Soft Tacos of Grilled Orange-Garlic Shrimp

Like most of the world's great pick-up meals, these messy tacos are compelling food: Start and you won't want to stop. Those really getting into the back-to-basics mode may wish to omit the salsa, feeling that the combined flavors of smoky, orange-scented shrimp and corn tortillas are sufficient (as, indeed, they are), but since I never met a ripe avocado I didn't like, I find the cool green stuff essential. Lots of napkins are also a good idea, as is plenty of beer. To turn the tacos into a meal instead of just a divine snack, add Orzo, Black Bean, and Cherry Tomato Salad (page 210) and Sweet and Smoky Corn Relish (page 195).

1. Position a rack in the middle of the oven and preheat to 375°F.

2. Remove the loose, papery outside peels of the garlic bulbs. With a sharp knife, cut off the top one-quarter of the garlic heads, exposing the cloves inside the peels. Partially enclose each garlic bulb in a packet of heavy-duty foil. Drizzle the garlic evenly with the sherry and olive oil. Seal the packets tightly, set them on the oven rack, and bake until the garlic is fragrant and tender enough to pierce easily with a paring knife, about 1 hour. Cool, then squeeze or scoop the softened garlic out of the peels.

3. In a food processor, combine the garlic puree, wine, orange juice, zest, sugar, achiote paste, 1 teaspoon salt, 1 teaspoon black pepper, and the red pepper. Process, stopping once or twice to scrape down the sides of the work bowl, until the mixture is fairly smooth.

SERVES 4 TO 6

2 large bulbs regular (not elephant) garlic
2 tablespoons dry sherry
2 tablespoons olive oil
½ cup dry white wine
½ cup fresh orange juice
2 tablespoons minced orange zest
2 tablespoons packed dark brown sugar
1 tablespoon achiote paste
Salt
Freshly ground black pepper
½ teaspoon crushed red pepper flakes
2 pounds large shrimp (about 48), peeled and deveined
16 to 18 (5-inch) flour tortillas
2 cups Avocado-Tomatillo Salsa (page 284) (optional)

SMOKING CHIP OPTION: MESQUITE

Sandwiches and Other Handheld Foods

4. In a shallow nonreactive bowl, combine the garlic mixture and the shrimp. Cover and let stand at room temperature, stirring once or twice, for 1 hour.

5. Meanwhile, light a direct-heat charcoal fire and let it burn down to medium-hot (5 seconds to "ouch") or preheat a gas grill to medium-high. Position the grill rack about 6 inches above the heat source.

6. Lift the shrimp from the marinade (reserve it) and divide them among 4 or 5 flat metal skewers. Preheat the oven to 400°F.

7. When the grill is ready, lightly oil the rack. Lay the skewers on the rack, cover, and grill, basting once or twice with the marinade and turning once, until the shrimp are lightly marked by the grill and just cooked through while remaining moist, 6 to 8 minutes total.

8. Meanwhile, wrap the tortillas in 2 or 3 foil packets. Place in the oven until warm and supple, about 10 minutes.

9. Remove the shrimp from the grill and transfer to a cutting board. Coarsely chop the shrimp, then season them with salt and pepper. Transfer the shrimp to a communal dish or divide among individual plates. Serve immediately, accompanied by the tortillas and the salsa. Encourage guests to tear off pieces of tortillas and wrap portions of shrimp and salsa into them, to make informal soft tacos.

Grilled Chicken Breast Sandwiches with Bacon and Avocado Mayonnaise

These sandwiches are not better than a BLT (because what could be?), but certainly they are a close cousin and a very tasty, slightly southwestern one at that. Add Potato Salad with Roasted Garlic Aioli (page 206) and Jicama and Grilled Red Pepper Slaw (page 211) and you have the kind of brilliantly casual meal that defines what grilling, southwestern or otherwise, is all about.

1. In a shallow nonreactive dish just large enough to hold the chicken breasts in a single layer, whisk together the olive oil, lime juice, sugar, and garlic. Add the chicken breasts, cover, and marinate at room temperature, turning once or twice, for 1 hour.

2. Meanwhile, light a direct-heat charcoal fire and let it burn down to medium-hot (5 seconds to "ouch") or preheat a gas grill to medium-high. Position the grill rack about 6 inches above the heat source.

3. When the grill is almost ready, lift the chicken breasts from the marinade (reserve it). Lay the breasts on the grill rack. Cover and grill for 5 minutes. Baste with half the reserved marinade, turn the breasts, baste with the remaining marinade, cover, and continue to grill at least two minutes after the marinade is used up, until the chicken breasts are just cooked through while remaining moist, another 4 to 5 minutes total.

4. Transfer the chicken breasts to a cutting board and let them rest for a few minutes.

5. Meanwhile, lightly toast the bread slices on one side only (use the grill, if desired).

SERVES 4

¼ cup olive oil
¼ cup fresh lime juice
4 teaspoons packed light
  brown sugar
2 garlic cloves, crushed
  through a press
1½ large whole boneless,
  skinless chicken breasts
  (2¼ pounds total),
  halves separated and
  trimmed of visible fat
8 slices from an oval loaf
  of good-quality sour-
  dough bread
Salt and freshly ground
  black pepper
Avocado Mayonnaise
  (page 293)
2 tomatoes, thinly sliced
8 thick-cut bacon strips,
  cooked
4 romaine lettuce leaves

SMOKING CHIP OPTION: MESQUITE

6. With a sharp knife, cut the chicken breasts across the grain and at an angle into thin slices. Season with salt and pepper. Generously spread the untoasted sides of each bread slice with the mayonnaise. Divide the chicken over the mayonnaise on 4 of the bread slices. Top the chicken with the tomato slices. Top the tomatoes with the bacon strips, 2 per sandwich, and top the bacon with lettuce. Set the remaining 4 bread slices mayonnaise side-down atop the lettuce. Press gently with a palm to flatten the sandwiches slightly, cut them in half and serve immediately.

Chicken!

I know cooks who believe boneless chicken breasts on the grill are inevitably dry and dull. To them and to you I say, don't be chicken! There are two simple tricks that can make the grilled boneless breast—already one of the quickest things you'll ever pull off the coals—also one of the moistest and tastiest. First, choose larger, thicker chicken breasts. I go out of my way to shop at a store that stocks breasts that run almost 1½ pounds, nearly ¾ pound per half. An inch thick at their thickest, these breasts stay on the grill longer (9 to 10 minutes total grilling time), browning nicely and picking up more flavor while still remaining moist. Second, marinate or use a rub on the breasts. Both add color and surface flavor, and even when the chicken is being used with other assertive dressings or seasonings, I never skip this step. Marinades with a touch of sugar are particularly successful. The finished chicken doesn't taste sweet, but the sugar caramelizes, and when the chicken breasts are rotated about 45 degrees halfway through each side's cooking time, the breasts are attractively crosshatched by the hot grill rack—tasty enough and eye-appealing enough to serve whole. One word of caution: when basting with a marinade that has been in contact with raw chicken, be certain to use up all the marinade and to stop basting several minutes before the end of the cooking time in order to avoid any bacterial contamination.

Chipotle-Orange Turkey Burgers with Lime Cream

Neither dull nor dry, these burgers are so good they've been known to convert red meat lovers to the leaner ways of the turkey. Don't overcook them—the burgers are perfect when the last trace of pink at their centers has just disappeared—and do baste them often while they grill with the zesty chipotle mop. It not only lightly glazes them with sweet and smoky flavor, it contributes moisture as well.

1. Light a direct-heat charcoal fire and let it burn down to medium-hot (5 seconds to "ouch") or preheat a gas grill to medium-high. Position the grill rack about 6 inches above the heat source. Transfer the mop to a measuring cup or pitcher with a pouring lip.

2. When the grill is ready, lightly oil the rack. Lay the burgers on the rack. Cover and grill, basting often with the mop (pour directly from the measuring cup onto the burgers to avoid cross-contamination) and carefully turning once, until the mop is used up and the burgers are just cooked through while remaining juicy, about 10 minutes. Remove from the heat and season with salt and pepper to taste.

3. Meanwhile, toast the cut sides of the hamburger buns (use the grill, if desired).

4. Set a burger on each bun bottom and serve immediately, letting guests add mayonnaise, tomato, onion, and lettuce as desired.

Note: There is a good bit of shrinkage when grilling turkey, which is why the amount of meat called for is a bit larger than my usual. Ground turkey is more flavorful and less likely to dry out than ground turkey breast (not coincidentally, it's also higher in fat and calories). Both seem to include a lot of water and the burgers will remain very soft and hard to turn on the grill until almost done. Don't futz: Use a wide spatula and limit yourself to one careful turn, or you'll break up the burgers.

SERVES 6

1⅓ cups Chipotle-Orange Mop (page 268)
3 pounds ground turkey, formed into 6 thick 5-inch burgers
Salt and freshly ground black pepper
6 large hamburger buns or sandwich rolls
¾ cup Lime Cream (page 296)
2 medium tomatoes, thinly sliced
1 large red onion, peeled, thinly sliced and separated into rings
4 romaine lettuce leaves

SMOKING CHIP OPTION: MESQUITE

Grilled Pork Tenderloin Tortas with Smoky Black Beans and Pickled Onions

SERVES 4

3 (¼-inch) onion slices
2 tablespoons sherry wine
   vinegar
¼ cup water
Salt
2 pork tenderloins (about
   1¾ pounds total),
   trimmed
3½ tablespoons Quick Red
   Rub (page 266)
2 chipotle chiles en
   adobo, minced
1 tablespoon adobo sauce
   from chipotles
¾ cup canned or home-
   made refried black or
   pinto beans
1 avocado
1 teaspoon fresh lime
   juice
4 (6-inch) soft hero rolls
   or similar-sized
   segments cut from
   2 baguettes
¼ cup mayonnaise
Whole or sliced pickled
   jalapeños

SMOKING CHIP OPTION: MESQUITE

Tortas are Mexican hero- or hoagie-type sand-wiches, featuring, at the very least, meats, maybe cheeses, something crunchy, and some-thing spicy. My tortas are somewhat more complex and meant to be enjoyed on purpose, not as part of a clean-out-the-fridge expedition. Casual enough for a weekday supper, they're also special enough to be served to company, at least the kind of company that enjoys gutsy, slightly messy food and cold beer. There are three types of chiles involved here, cre-ating layers of flavor and a slow build of heat that are eventually very pleasurable indeed. A great backyard meal might consist of these, ac-companied by Grilled Calabacitas Salad (page 202) and followed by Frozen Raspberry Margarita Pie (page 242).

1. Separate the onion slices into rings. Combine the onions with the vinegar, water, and a pinch of salt in a bowl. Let stand, stirring once or twice, while making the sandwiches.

2. Meanwhile, light a direct-heat charcoal fire and let it burn down to medium-hot (5 seconds to "ouch") or preheat a gas grill to medium-high. Position the rack 6 inches above the heat source.

3. Evenly coat the tenderloins with the rub, using it all and patting it firmly into the meat.

4. When the grill is ready, lightly oil the rack. Lay the tenderloins on the rack, cover, and grill, turning every 4 minutes, until the meat is just done through while remaining juicy, about 16 minutes total. The spice coating will be fairly dark and an instant-read thermometer inserted into the meat should read 140° to 150°F.

5. Transfer the meat to a cutting board and let it rest for 5 minutes.

6. Meanwhile, drain the onion rings. In a medium bowl, combine the chipotles, their sauce, and the beans. Peel and pit the avocado and scoop the flesh into a medium bowl. Coarsely mash the avocado and stir in the lime juice and a big pinch of salt. Split the rolls horizontally lengthwise and with your fingers pull the excess crumb, leaving a shell of bread.

7. Carve the tenderloins by slicing across the grain and at an angle to the cutting board, into thin slices. Season with salt.

8. Spread the bottom cut surfaces of the rolls with the beans, dividing them evenly and using them all. Spread the top cut surfaces of the rolls with the mayonnaise. Arrange the pork slices over the beans (for properly robust tortas, use all the pork). Spread the avocado mixture over the pork, dividing it evenly and using it all. Top the avocado layer with the onions. Close up the sandwiches, cut them in half crosswise if desired, and serve, accompanied with whole pickled chiles for eating alongside or sliced jalapeños for tucking into the tortas.

Terrific Tenderloin

I can't say enough about how convenient and delicious the pork tenderloin is. Especially when it comes to grilling with southwestern flavors, this lean, tender cut shines. Not inexpensive (each pig comes with two only), tenderloins are nearly waste-free and so quick to prepare and so pleasing to eat, the steep tab is a small price to pay. They do go on sale occasionally, so stock up. Typically packed two to a plastic package, they're good for a couple of weeks in the refrigerator or a couple of months in the freezer.

Tenderloins can be used all sorts of ways (diced or sliced for stir-fries, for example, or skewered as they are on page 157), but grilled whole is when they really come into their own. Remove any visible surface fat and slice away the silverskin, a tough, fibrous tissue that resembles strapping tape. Rub them if desired, marinate them if you must (I rarely do), or merely mop them with one sort of glazing sauce or other. The latter, if sweet, should not be applied until the pork has had about 5 minutes grilling per side. A typical tenderloin weighs about ¾ pound, for which the cooking time, on a medium-hot grill, is 16 to 18 minutes. Ideally, the meat will still be ever so slightly pink at the center and juicy, while being crusty and well browned on the outside (the tapering tip will be somewhat more well done, for those who don't want pink pork). An instant-read thermometer inserted in the thick center of the meat will read 140° to 150°F.

Assume two diners per loin, though when guests serve themselves, this formula can change drastically. I often cook an extra tenderloin, in case of extreme appetites, and, anyway, there's nothing quite so cheering as leftover pork for lunch the next day.

Unconventional Pork Tortas with Citrus Slaw

SERVES 4

1½ cups Chipotle-Peanut
  Barbecue Sauce (page
  276)
2 pork tenderloins (about
  1½ pounds total),
  trimmed
4 large hamburger buns or
  sandwich rolls, split
Salt
Citrus Slaw (page 212)

SMOKING CHIP OPTION: HICKORY

Among my favorite sandwiches are those southern specialties combining well-sauced barbecue-smoked pork and coleslaw, piled high on a bun. Using them as my guideline, and with some of my favorite Mexican sandwiches as inspiration, I concocted these terrific tortas. Neither southern nor authentically southwestern, they're nevertheless just about as satisfying to eat as any sandwich on the planet. Serve Potato Salad with Roasted Garlic Aioli (page 206) and pour a big glass of iced tea (page 258).

1. Light a direct-heat charcoal fire and let it burn down to medium-hot (5 seconds to "ouch") or preheat a gas grill to medium-high. Position the grill rack about 6 inches above the heat source. Reserve ½ cup of the barbecue sauce for the sandwiches.

2. When the grill is ready, lay the tenderloins on the rack, cover, and grill for 8 minutes, turning them once. Brush generously with sauce, turn, cover, and grill for 4 minutes. Continue to brush with sauce, turn, and grill, until the sauce is used up and the pork is just cooked through while remaining juicy, 16 to 18 minutes total grilling time. An instant-read thermometer inserted in the thick center of the meat should read 140° to 150°F.

3. Transfer the meat to a cutting board and let it rest for 5 minutes.

4. Meanwhile, lightly toast the cut sides of the buns (use the grill, if desired).

5. Carve the tenderloins by slicing thinly across the grain and at a slight angle to the cutting board. Season with salt.

6. Arrange the pork over the bun bottoms, dividing it evenly and using it all. Top the pork slices with the reserved ½ cup barbecue sauce, then with the coleslaw, using all of it. (These sandwiches should be big and a little messy.) Cut the sandwiches in half, if desired, and serve immediately.

West Texas Drive-In Chilidogs with the Works

Maybe a drive-in still exists, in Texas or somewhere, where the chilidogs are as good as these. Or maybe it's just my fantasy, more Larry McMurtry than Rand-McNally. Sometimes you've just got to do these things for yourself. Though you can get by with passable (read: canned) chili if the dogs are top-quality, homemade chili makes these a superb eating experience. For chiliburgers, simply substitute thin 5-inch patties of ground chuck, grilled about 4 minutes per side, for the knockwurst.

1. Light a direct-heat charcoal fire and let it burn down to medium-hot (5 seconds to "ouch") or preheat a gas grill to medium-high. Position the rack about 6 inches above the heat source.

2. When the grill is ready, brush the knockwurst on both sides with the oil. Lay them on the rack, cover, and grill, turning once, until lightly browned and crisp, about 6 minutes total.

3. Meanwhile, lightly toast the cut sides of the buns (use the grill, if desired).

4. Spread the cut side of each bun bottom with 1 tablespoon mustard or ketchup, as desired. Set the knockwurst on the bun bottoms. Top with chili, dividing it evenly and using it all. Top the chili with cheese, dividing it evenly and using it all. Sprinkle on the onions, if you are using them (you'd be crazy not to), add as many pickled jalapeño slices as each diner likes, set the bun tops in place, and serve immediately.

SERVES 4

*4 premium knockwurst
(about 1 pound total),
split lengthwise*
*About 2 tablespoons
vegetable oil*
*4 large hamburger buns or
sandwich rolls*
Mustard
Ketchup
*1½ cups West Texas Chili
for Dogs and Tacos
(page 76), heated to
simmering*
*1½ cups shredded sharp
cheddar cheese*
*½ cup diced onion
(optional)*
*Thinly sliced pickled
jalapeños*

West Texas Chili for Dogs and Tacos

3 tablespoons bacon
   drippings or olive oil
3 cups chopped onions
5 garlic cloves, minced
2 pounds butcher's meat-
   loaf blend (typically 50
   percent ground chuck,
   25 percent ground pork,
   and 25 percent ground
   veal)
2 tablespoons medium-
   hot unblended red chile
   powder
1 tablespoon dried
   oregano, crumbled
1 tablespoon freshly
   ground cumin (prefer-
   ably from toasted seeds)
2 teaspoons salt
1 teaspoon freshly ground
   black pepper
1 teaspoon chipotle chile
   powder
2 cups tomato juice
2 cups canned beef broth
½ cup chopped roasted hot
   green chiles
2 tablespoons masa
   harina

Thick and smooth, this hot and smoky chili is primarily designed to stay put as much as possible on a sandwich. The recipe makes more than you'll need for four chilidogs, but it freezes well and besides, there's really no such thing as excess chili. Use it as a taco filling, for example, adding shredded cheese, shredded lettuce and salsa. Or, stir in a well-drained can or two of red kidney or black beans and enjoy as you would any good bowl of red, garnished as you desire, accompanied with crackers, and washed down with cold beer.

1. In a large, heavy nonreactive pan over low heat, warm the bacon drippings or olive oil. Add the onion and garlic, cover and cook, stirring once or twice, until the vegetables have softened, about 10 minutes. Add the meatloaf blend, increase the heat, and cook, breaking up the meat with the edge of a spoon, until it is evenly crumbled and gray, about 8 minutes. Add the powdered chile, oregano, cumin, salt, pepper, and chipotle powder. Cook, stirring often, for 3 minutes. Add the tomato juice, beef broth, and green chiles and bring to a simmer.

2. Partially cover, decrease the heat, and cook, stirring occasionally, until the chili has reduced to about 6 cups, about 1½ hours.

3. Sprinkle the masa over the surface of the chili, then whisk it in. Simmer for another minute or two, until thick. The chili can be served now, refrigerated for up to 3 days, or frozen for up to 1 month.

Hatch Surprise Burgers with Green Chile–Cheese Stuffing

The tiny farming village of Hatch is the self-proclaimed chile capital of the world (big chile festival doings are held every Labor Day weekend), but the entire state of New Mexico embraces the green chile cheeseburger as its own. The best GCCB's are indeed made with chiles from Hatch, but their peak season is brief, and milder Anaheims, untraditional poblanos or (confession time) widely available frozen chopped hot green chiles are employed the rest of the year. Stuffing the chiles and cheese inside the burgers, instead of piling them on top, is one of those things you do because you can, not because you have to, and besides, they're fun to eat. A practical note: provide a lot of napkins.

1. Divide the ground beef into 8 equal portions. Form each into a 4-inch patty. Trim the cheese slices into 3-inch rounds (use a cookie cutter for best results). Center a round of cheese on each of 4 beef patties. Top the cheese rounds with the green chiles, dividing them equally. Top the chiles with the remaining cheese rounds. Top the cheese rounds with the remaining beef patties. Thoroughly pinch the edges of each pair of beef patties together to seal tightly. (The stuffed burgers can be prepared several hours in advance. Cover and refrigerate.)

2. Light a direct-heat charcoal fire and let it burn down to medium-hot (5 seconds to "ouch") or preheat a gas grill to medium-high. Position the rack about 6 inches above the heat source.

3. When the grill is ready, lay the onion slices on the rack. Cover and grill for 2 minutes. Turn the onions, add the stuffed burgers, cover, and grill, turning the onions every 2 minutes and the burgers

SERVES 4

2 pounds ground beef (not too lean)
8 slices sharp cheddar cheese, preferably Kraft "Old English"
½ cup finely chopped roasted hot green chiles
4 thick slices from a large red or white sweet onion
4 large hamburger buns or sandwich rolls, split
¼ cup ketchup
¼ cup mayonnaise
About 20 dill pickle slices, patted dry
Salt and freshly ground black pepper

SMOKING CHIP OPTION: HICKORY

once, until the onions are nicely browned, about 10 minutes total, and the cheese inside the burgers has melted and the meat is done to your liking, about 8 minutes total for medium-rare.

4. Meanwhile, lightly toast the cut sides of the buns (use the grill, if desired).

5. Spread the cut side of each bun top with 1 tablespoon ketchup. Spread the cut side of each bun bottom with mayonnaise. Arrange the pickle slices over the mayonnaise.

6. When the onions and burgers are done, season them to taste with salt and pepper. Set a burger on each bun bottom. Top each with an onion slice. Set the bun tops in place, and serve immediately.

Soft Tacos of "Next Day" Brisket with Barbecue Sauce

SERVES 2 TO 4

1 pound thinly sliced, well-trimmed Slow and Smoky Beef Brisket (page 174)
4 (10-inch) flour tortillas
Salt
¾ cup Chipotle-Peanut Barbecue Sauce (page 276) or Coffee Barbecue Sauce (page 275)
1 cup shredded sharp cheddar cheese
1 cup shredded romaine lettuce
1 cup diced tomato

Leftover grill-smoked brisket is a great treat in any form, though as the filling for these very unconventional tacos, it really is spectacular. Perhaps it's the ease with which the sandwich-like tacos go together or maybe it's just the pick-up-and-eat informality of them. Since the brisket is home-smoked, only homemade barbecue sauce makes sense as a condiment.

1. Position a rack in the middle of the oven and preheat to 350°F. Wrap the brisket tightly in foil. Set the wrapped brisket in the oven and heat until steaming, about 25 minutes.

2. Wrap the tortillas in foil in 2 packages of 4 tortillas each. Place in the oven until warm and supple, 10 to 15 minutes.

3. Working quickly, open the foil. Season the brisket to taste with salt. Divide the brisket slices among the 4 tortillas. Spread the barbecue sauce over the meat. Top the meat with cheese, lettuce, and tomato. Roll up the tortillas, enclosing everything. Serve immediately.

Beef Tacos "al Carbon"

This charcoal-grilled specialty of Northern Mexico has the same roll-your-own informality as fajitas, though the meat is diced rather than cut into strips and the tortillas are more likely to be of corn rather than flour (though this is up to you). Grilled whole green onions, one per taco, are tucked into the tacos or just enjoyed alongside. Offer freshly made guacamole and a good basic salsa or two and keep stacks of warmed tortillas coming. In my rendition, the meat is not marinated (there's really not much point to that), but a lime-and-garlic seasoning paste and a dry rub add welcome complexity. For maximum tenderness, buy best-quality flank steak, grill it hot and fast, and serve it rare.

1. Light a direct-heat charcoal fire and let it burn down to hot (3 seconds to "ouch") or preheat a gas grill to high. Position the rack about 6 inches above the heat source. Preheat the oven to 400°F.

2. Meanwhile, in a small bowl, stir together 1 tablespoon of the oil, the lime juice, soy sauce, and garlic. Spread the oil mixture evenly over both sides of the flank steak. Brush the green onions with the remaining 2 tablespoons oil.

3. When the grill is ready, sprinkle the top side of the steak evenly with half the rub. Lay the steak on the rack rub side-down, cover, and grill for 5 minutes. Sprinkle the remaining rub evenly over the steak and turn it. Lay the onions on the rack, cover, and grill, turning the onions once, until the onions are marked by the grill and tender, 4 minutes, and the steak is done to your liking (rare is best, another 5 minutes).

SERVES 6

3 tablespoons olive oil
1 tablespoon fresh lime juice
2 teaspoons soy sauce
3 garlic cloves, crushed through a press
1 flank steak (about 1½ pounds)
3½ tablespoons Quick Red Rub (page 266)
18 large green onions, tops trimmed to no more than 3 inches long
18 (5-inch) corn tortillas
Salt
Guacamole (page 21)
About 2 cups Salsa Verde (page 283), made without the pineapple
2 cups Cascabel–Roasted Garlic Salsa (page 285)
About 12 ounces feta cheese, grated (optional)

SMOKING CHIP OPTION: MESQUITE

4. Transfer the steak to a cutting board and let it rest for 10 minutes. Transfer the onions to a platter.

5. Meanwhile, wrap the tortillas in foil in 3 packets of 6 tortillas each. Place in the preheated oven for 10 minutes, until warm and supple.

6. Carve the steak across the grain and at a slight angle into slices; then cut the slices into cubes. Transfer the cubes to the platter with the onions. Season the meat and onions lightly with salt.

7. Serve the meat and onions immediately, accompanied by tortillas, guacamole, salsa, and feta.

Note: I love a soft tangy cheese as one element of the many hot-and-cool layers in these tacos. Feta works well and recalls Mexican cheeses that are not widely available here, but the inclusion of cheese is not traditional and it can be omitted.

Spice-Rubbed Buffalo Burgers with Coffee Barbecue Sauce

SERVES 4

1½ pounds ground buffalo
3½ tablespoons Quick Red
  Rub (page 266)
4 slices from 1 or 2 very
  large red onions, cut
  ½-inch thick
About 1¼ cups Coffee
  Barbecue Sauce (page
  275), plus additional
  sauce for serving, if
  desired
Salt and freshly ground
  black pepper
4 large hamburger buns or
  sandwich rolls

SMOKING CHIP OPTION: HICKORY

While it harks nicely back to the Old West, my choice of buffalo—actually bison—meat for these burgers has practical, modern aspects as well. Namely, buffalo (now farm-raised, of course) tastes great and is quite low in fat. Got no buffalo? You can find it in some supermarkets and health food stores or you can order it by mail (see Mail-Order Sources, page 321). Ground beef, lean or otherwise, is terrific here, too.

1. Light a direct-heat charcoal fire and let it burn down to medium-hot (5 seconds to "ouch") or preheat a gas grill (medium-high). Position the rack about 6 inches above the heat source.

2. Divide the meat into 4 equal portions. Form each portion into a 5-inch burger. Dust the burgers on both sides with the rub, dividing it evenly and using it all.

3. When the grill is ready, lightly oil the rack. Lay the onion slices on the rack and grill for 2 minutes. Brush the onions with some of the barbecue sauce and turn. Lay the buffalo burgers on the rack. Cover and continue to grill, brushing the onion slices with sauce and turning them every 2 minutes, and turning the burgers once, until the sauce is used up, the onions are tender and brown (about 10 minutes total), and the meat is done to your liking, about 8 minutes total for medium-rare. After the final turn, season the onion slices and burgers with salt and pepper to taste.

4. Meanwhile, toast the cut sides of the buns (use the grill, if desired).

5. Set a burger on each bun. Top each burger with an onion slice. Set the bun tops in place and serve immediately, offering additional barbecue sauce at the table if desired.

Valle Grande Lamb Burgers with Green Chiles and Goat Cheese

These burgers celebrate the terrific churro lamb produced by Ganados del Valle, although you can make them with any freshly ground lamb you find. (Many supermarkets offer ground lamb. This meat can be quite fatty and may not make the best possible burger, but it is worth a try.) Teamed with tangy goat cheese, for which it has a natural affinity, lamb makes rich burgers, which are enlivened by chiles (use the spiciest you can find) and by sweet, juicy tomatoes.

1. On a preheated grill, under a preheated broiler, or directly on the ring of a gas burner set on high, roast the chiles, turning them occasionally, until the peels are charred. Transfer to a paper bag, close the bag, and let the chiles steam until cool. Rub away the burnt peel, stem and core the chiles, and cut them lengthwise into ½-inch strips; cut the strips in half crosswise.

SERVES 4

*4 long green chiles, prefer-
    ably New Mexican, or
    3 large poblanos*
1½ pounds ground lamb
Salt
*5-inch log mild fresh goat
    cheese, cut into 8 slices,
    at room temperature*
*Freshly ground black
    pepper*
*4 large hamburger buns or
    sandwich rolls*
*4 slices from a large
    tomato*

SMOKING CHIP OPTION: MESQUITE

2. Light a direct-heat charcoal fire and let it burn down to medium-hot (5 seconds to "ouch") or preheat a gas grill to medium-high. Position the rack about 6 inches above the heat source.

3. Divide the meat into 4 equal portions. Form each portion into a 5-inch burger.

4. When the grill is ready, lay the lamb burgers on the rack. Cover and grill for 4 minutes. Turn the burgers, season them with salt, and divide the chile strips over them. Top the chile strips with the cheese slices, cover, and continue to grill until the cheese is hot and fluffy and the burgers are done to your liking, another 4 minutes for medium rare.

5. Meanwhile, toast the cut sides of the buns (use the grill, if desired).

6. Set a burger on each bun bottom. Top each with a tomato slice and serve immediately.

Lamb of the Valley

The Valle Grande ("big valley"), in mountainous northern New Mexico, is a caldera—the crater of an extinct volcano. It's spectacular country, parts of it slated for federal parks protection, other parts of it used for ranching, especially sheep ranching. Some of these ranchers have been organized into a cooperative, Ganados del Valle, to raise churro sheep. Originally brought to the area by the Spanish, the churro has distinctively silky wool, which was coveted by local settlers and Navajo weavers. The delicious meat is prized as well, and now, with the establishment of the cooperative, and the return of the nearly defunct churro to New Mexico, both wool and meat are once again available. The lamb is sold at the Santa Fe Farmer's Market and at Pastores Feed and General Store in Los Ojos, New Mexico. It can be ordered by mail, preferably in the fall or early winter when supplies are greatest; call 505-588-7896.

Ensaladas Grandes

Main-Dish Salads

Ensaladas Grandes
MAIN-DISH SALADS

*Garlic Shrimp and Pasta Salad with
Charred Tomato Dressing 87*

Grilled Spiny Lobster Salad with Avocado and Papaya 88

*Grilled Squid and Noodle Salad with
Avocado, Pineapple, and Pine Nuts 90*

Grilled Chicken "Totopo" Salad 92

*Warm Chicken Caesar Salad with
Cornbread Croutons 94*

*Hickory-Smoked Chicken and Potato Salad with
Apples and Pecans 96*

*Sage-and-Coffee-Rubbed Quail and
Marinated Mushroom Salad 97*

*Grilled Tamarind Pork and Noodle Salad
with Smoky Vegetables 99*

Barbecued Hill Country Sausage and Lima Bean Salad 101

Salpicon of Grill-Smoked Brisket 102

Warm Grilled Chile-Lime Beef Salad 103

Grilled Cumin Lamb, Orange, and Onion Salad 105

Garlic Shrimp and Pasta Salad
with
Charred Tomato Dressing

This salad fairly explodes with garlicky grill and seafood flavor. If summer weather has appetites down, this will wake them up, guaranteed. It's an all-in-one meal, and it's done ahead, so the cook stays cool. Just bake some Cornbread with Red Chile–Pecan Streusel (page 214), or, if it's too hot to light the oven, grill some Texas Toast (page 217).

1. In a bowl, whisk together 2 tablespoons of the olive oil and the sherry. Force 4 of the garlic cloves through a press into the bowl. Stir in the red pepper and add the shrimp. Cover and marinate at room temperature for 1 hour, stirring once or twice.

2. In a metal pan under a preheated broiler (or directly on a hot grill rack if desired), roast the tomatoes, turning them once, until the peels are well-charred, about 15 minutes total. Remove and cool. Core the tomatoes but do not peel; reserve all juices.

3. Bring a large pot of salted water to a boil. Add the pasta and cook, partially covered, stirring occasionally, until almost tender, according to the package directions. Add the corn and cook until the pasta is tender, another minute or so. Drain and cool.

4. Meanwhile, light a direct-heat charcoal fire and let it burn down to medium-hot (5 seconds to "ouch") or preheat a gas grill to medium-high. Position the rack about 6 inches above the heat source.

SERVES 4

7 tablespoons olive oil
¼ cup medium-dry sherry
6 garlic cloves
¼ teaspoon crushed red pepper flakes
1½ pounds large shrimp (about 36), shelled and deveined
4 plum tomatoes (about ¾ pound total)
Salt
½ pound imported semolina short pasta, such as tortiglioni or fusilli
1 cup tender fresh or frozen corn kernels
2 (½-inch-thick) slices from a large red onion
3 tablespoons sherry wine vinegar
⅔ cup thickly sliced pimiento-stuffed green olives

SMOKING CHIP OPTION: MESQUITE

5. Lift the shrimp from the marinade (reserve it) and thread them onto flat metal skewers. Brush the onion slices with 1 tablespoon of the oil.

6. When the grill is ready, lay the skewers and onion slices on the rack. Cover and grill, basting the shrimp often with the marinade and turning the skewers and onion slices once, until the shrimp are pink, curled, and just cooked through while remaining moist, about 6 minutes total, and the onions are well browned, about 10 minutes total.

7. Transfer the skewers to a plate and the onion slices to a cutting board.

8. In a food processor, combine the charred tomatoes with their peels and all juices, the remaining 4 tablespoons oil, the vinegar, the remaining 2 cloves garlic and ¼ teaspoon salt. Process until fairly smooth. Adjust the seasoning.

9. Chop the onions. In a large bowl, toss together the pasta and corn, the tomato dressing, onions, and olives. Slide the shrimp from their skewers into the bowl. Toss again, adjust the seasoning, and serve more or less at once.

Grilled Spiny Lobster Salad
with
Avocado and Papaya

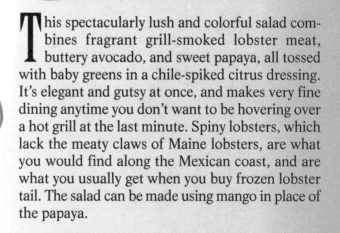

T his spectacularly lush and colorful salad combines fragrant grill-smoked lobster meat, buttery avocado, and sweet papaya, all tossed with baby greens in a chile-spiked citrus dressing. It's elegant and gutsy at once, and makes very fine dining anytime you don't want to be hovering over a hot grill at the last minute. Spiny lobsters, which lack the meaty claws of Maine lobsters, are what you would find along the Mexican coast, and are what you usually get when you buy frozen lobster tail. The salad can be made using mango in place of the papaya.

1. Light a direct-heat charcoal fire and let it burn down to medium-hot (5 seconds to "ouch") or preheat a gas grill to medium-high. Position the grill rack about 6 inches above the heat source.

2. Meanwhile, using a long, heavy knife (or kitchen scissors), cut the lobster tails in half lengthwise. Remove the intestinal tract.

3. When the grill is ready, lay the lobster tails on the rack, cut sides-up. Cover and grill for 6 minutes. Turn, cover, and continue to grill until the lobster meat is white, opaque, and just cooked through, another 5 to 7 minutes. Cool slightly, then remove the meat from the shells and cut into ½-inch pieces.

4. In a medium bowl, whisk together the orange juice, lime juice, jalapeño, lime zest, orange zest, and ½ teaspoon salt. Gradually whisk in the oil; the dressing will thicken. Adjust the seasoning.

5. In a medium bowl, toss together the lobster, avocados, tomatoes, papaya, and ¾ cup of the dressing. Season generously with pepper and add salt, if necessary.

6. In a large bowl, toss the greens with the remaining dressing. Season generously with pepper.

7. Divide the greens among 4 plates. Top the greens with the lobster mixture and serve immediately.

Note: To use Maine lobsters in this recipe, substitute 3 live lobsters, about 1½ pounds each. Follow the pre-grill preparation steps given in the recipe for Grilled Split Lobsters with Lime Aioli on page 128. Then proceed with the grilling and salad making as above.

Main-Dish Salads

4 large lobster tails (about 2½ pounds total), thawed if frozen
½ cup fresh orange juice
3 tablespoons fresh lime juice
1 tablespoon minced fresh jalapeño
1 tablespoon minced lime zest
1½ teaspoons minced orange zest
Salt
9 tablespoons olive oil
2 ripe avocados, cut into ½-inch pieces
4 tomatoes, seeded and cut into ½-inch pieces
1 large papaya, peeled, seeded, and cut into ½-inch pieces
8 ounces mixed baby salad greens (mesclun)
Freshly ground black pepper

SMOKING CHIP OPTION: MESQUITE

Grilled Squid and Noodle Salad with Avocado, Pineapple, and Pine Nuts

SERVES 6

6 tablespoons pine nuts
½ pound imported thin
  semolina pasta, such as
  spaghettini
Salt
1 cup chopped cilantro,
  plus ¼ cup minced
¾ cup thinly sliced green
  onions, tender tops
  included
1 large fresh jalapeño,
  stemmed and chopped
5 garlic cloves, chopped
5 tablespoons olive oil
2 tablespoons dry white
  wine
2 teaspoons granulated
  brown sugar
Freshly ground black
  pepper
6 squid, bodies only,
  dressed (about 1 pound
  total)
¼ cup fresh orange juice
½ cup diced (¼ inch)
  pineapple
1 small, buttery-ripe
  black-skinned (Hass)
  avocado, halved and
  pitted

SMOKING CHIP OPTION: MESQUITE

This wonderfully spicy seafood and noodle salad is descended from one I had several years ago at Ovens, an Arizona restaurant. The garnishes of avocado, pineapple, and pine nuts marked the dish as falling somewhere along the Thailand/Tucson axis. I've removed the definite Asian touches of sesame oil and ginger, and replaced crabmeat with grilled squid, but the salad has survived the adaptation with all its eating excitement intact. A hunk of garlic toast and a big glass of Triple-Citrus-Ade (page 259) complete the menu for a great hot-weather lunch or supper.

1. Position a rack in the middle of the oven and preheat to 375°F. In a shallow metal pan, like a cake tin, toast the pine nuts, stirring once or twice, until crisp and golden, 8 to 10 minutes. Remove from the pan and cool.

2. Bring a large pot of salted water to a boil. Add the pasta and cook, partially covered, according to the package directions, until the pasta is just cooked through while remaining firm. Drain, rinse under cold water, and drain again.

3. In a food processor, combine the 1 cup chopped cilantro, ½ cup of the green onions, half the jalapeño, the garlic, 2 tablespoons of the olive oil, the wine, sugar, ½ teaspoon salt, and ½ teaspoon pepper. Process, stopping several times to scrape down the sides of the work bowl. Reserve ⅓ cup of the resulting puree.

4. Slice the squid open along one side and open them out. Rinse well. With a sharp knife, score a shallow crosshatch pattern into the outer side of each squid. In a shallow, nonreactive dish, combine the squid and the remaining ⅔ cup cilantro puree. Marinate for 1 hour at room temperature, turning once or twice.

5. Light a direct-heat charcoal fire and let it burn down to high (3 seconds to "ouch") or preheat a gas grill to high. Position the rack about 6 inches above the heat source.

6. Meanwhile, make the dressing. In a blender or small food processor, combine the reserved ⅓ cilantro puree, orange juice, the remaining 3 tablespoons olive oil, the remaining jalapeño, ½ teaspoon salt, and ½ teaspoon pepper. Process until smooth.

7. In a large bowl, combine the pasta, dressing, remaining ¼ cup cilantro, remaining ¼ cup green onions, the pineapple, and 4 tablespoons of the pine nuts. Toss.

8. Divide the noodle mixture among 6 plates. Halve and pit the avocados and, with a table knife, score the flesh down to the peel into ½-inch cubes. With a spoon, scoop the cubes of avocado out of the peels. Scatter evenly over the noodles.

9. When the grill is ready, lightly oil the rack. Lay the squid on the rack, cover, and grill until the squid are lightly marked, about 2 minutes. Drizzle the squid with any marinade remaining in the dish, turn, cover, and grill until the squid are just cooked through and tender, 1½ to 2 minutes.

10. Remove the squid from the grill. Season the squid with salt and pepper and set 1 atop each portion of salad. Scatter the remaining pine nuts over the squid and serve immediately.

The Secrets of Squid

In better fish stores and supermarkets, squid are available defrosted, with bodies (or "tubes") and tentacles sold mixed. For this recipe, only bodies are required. Some markets stock only frozen blocks of squid and will saw off a portion for you to take home and defrost. Since this naturally results in some pieces too odd-shaped to use (as well as tentacles not desired here), order more than you need in order to be able to get 6 whole bodies. The secret to achieving tender squid is to either cook it very fast (a few minutes at most) or very slow (and hour or more), hence the brief time on the grill. Leave the squid on the grill too long, and it will be inedibly tough.

Grilled Chicken "Totopo" Salad

SERVES 6

About ¾ cup corn oil
6 (5-inch) corn tortillas
Salt
2 cups frozen mixed peas
  and carrots
1½ large boneless, skinless
  chicken breasts (2¼
  pounds total), halves
  separated and trimmed
  of fat
1 cup Chipotle Vinaigrette
  (page 298)
1½ cups homemade or
  canned refried pinto or
  black beans
8 cups chopped romaine
  lettuce
Freshly ground black
  pepper
2 avocados, cut into thin
  strips
½ pound jalapeño Jack
  cheese, in thin 4-inch
  strips, at room
  temperature
24 small cherry tomatoes,
  stemmed
12 pitted black Greek
  olives (Kalamatas)
4 ounces drained feta
  cheese, finely grated
6 large whole pickled
  jalapeños

SMOKING CHIP OPTION: MESQUITE

This slightly loopy dish—in essence a south-western-styled chef's salad presented in the conical form of a volcano or an Aztec temple, depending on who you listen to—is a Tucson, Arizona, specialty. Best purveyed (and possibly created) at the legendary El Charro restaurant, it is more than a novelty, however: It tastes good, too. My recipe is loosely based on El Charro's version, although I like the kick chipotle gives to the salad dressing, and I naturally think grilled chicken is preferable to the more traditional poached. Festive-looking as it is, urge your guests to dig right in: Like most vertical food, the totopo needs to be knocked over before it can be eaten.

1. In a medium skillet over moderate heat, warm the oil. One or two at a time, add the corn tortillas and fry, turning once, until almost crisp, 1 to 2 minutes. Transfer to paper towels to drain. Season lightly with salt.

2. Bring a saucepan of salted water to a boil. Add the peas and carrots and cook until tender, about 5 minutes. Drain, rinse with cold water, and drain again.

3. Light a direct-heat charcoal fire and let it burn down to medium-hot (5 seconds to "ouch") or preheat a gas grill to medium-high. Position the rack about 6 inches above the heat source.

4. Brush ⅓ cup of the vinaigrette over the chicken breasts. When the grill is ready, lay the breasts on the rack. Cover and grill, turning once, until the chicken is well marked by the grill and just cooked through while remaining juicy, about 9 minutes total. Transfer to a cutting board and let rest for a few minutes. Cut the breasts into thin strips and season lightly with salt.

5. Meanwhile, warm the beans (for a quantity this small, the microwave may be the best method). In a large bowl, combine the lettuce, peas and carrots, and ⅓ cup of the remaining vinaigrette. Add ¼ teaspoon salt and a generous grinding of pepper and toss. Adjust the seasoning and toss again.

6. Spread each tortilla with about ¼ cup of the beans. Working quickly, pack about ⅛ of the romaine mixture firmly into a 4-inch, 2-cup conical mold (such as a kitchen funnel or an oversized martini glass). Invert a tortilla, bean side-down, over the mold. Invert the 2 together onto a salad plate. Lift off the mold; repeat with the remaining romaine mixture and tortillas. Arrange the chicken breasts strips, cutting them to fit, the avocado strips and the cheese strips, alternating, around the sides of the salad cones. Arrange the tomatoes and olives on the plates around the bases of the cones, dividing them evenly. Drizzle the chicken, avocado, and cheese with the remaining vinaigrette. Sprinkle the feta over the salads, dividing it evenly and using it all. Garnish with the pickled jalapeños. Serve immediately.

Warm Chicken Caesar Salad
with
Cornbread Croutons

SERVES 4

2½ cups cubed (¾ inch)
    Plain Cornbread (page
    215)
2 tablespoons roasted
    garlic oil (available in
    gourmet shops and
    some supermarkets) or
    plain olive oil
1 tablespoon medium-hot
    unblended red chile
    powder
¼ cup Dijon mustard
1 tablespoon fresh lime
    juice
1 tablespoon olive oil
2 garlic cloves, crushed
    through a press
1 teaspoon Worcestershire
    sauce
1½ large boneless, skinless
    chicken breasts (2¼
    pounds), halves
    separated and trimmed
    of visible fat
2 large heads romaine
    lettuce, trimmed and
    torn into bite-sized
    pieces (about 16 cups)

By now almost everyone must know that the Italian-seeming Caesar salad was actually created in Tijuana, Mexico, albeit by an Italian, sometime during the 1920s. Even if that weren't so, this reworking of it into a chicken-topped main dish with various southwestern touches would still earn it a logical place in this book. Few summertime meals are as satisfying, particularly if you have timed things so that you can serve the salads while the chicken is still warm from the grill.

1. Position a rack in the middle of the oven and preheat to 400°F.

2. In a medium bowl, toss the cornbread cubes with the garlic oil until evenly coated. Continue tossing the cubes while sprinkling them evenly with the chile powder. Spread the cubes in a single layer on a sheet pan and bake, stirring occasionally, until lightly browned, about 15 minutes.

3. Meanwhile, in a shallow nonreactive bowl, whisk together the mustard, lime juice, olive oil, garlic, and Worcestershire sauce. Add the chicken breasts, turn to coat, and marinate at room temperature for 30 minutes.

4. Light a direct-heat charcoal fire and let it burn down to medium-hot (5 seconds to "ouch") or preheat a gas grill to medium-high. Position the rack about 6 inches above the heat source.

5. When the grill is ready, lift the chicken breasts from the marinade (reserve it) and lay them on the rack. Cover and grill for 5 minutes. Baste with half the marinade, turn, baste with the remaining marinade, using it all, cover, and continue to grill until the chicken breasts are just cooked through while remaining juicy, another 4 to 5 minutes.

6. Transfer the chicken to a cutting board and keep warm.

7. In a large bowl, toss together the lettuce, dressing, croutons, and cheese. Season generously with pepper and toss again. Divide among 4 plates.

7. Cut the chicken across the grain and at a slight angle into thin strips, season with salt and pepper, and arrange atop the salads. Serve immediately.

Note: Manchego is a Spanish sheep's milk grating cheese that is particularly good in the salad. Parmigiano-Reggiano or a young, not-too-salty Romano can be substituted.

1 cup Lime Caesar Dressing (page 297)
½ cup grated Manchego cheese (see Note)
Freshly ground black pepper

SMOKING CHIP OPTION: MESQUITE

Main-Dish Salads

Hickory-Smoked Chicken and Potato Salad with Apples and Pecans

SERVES 6 TO 8

1 pound red-skinned new
   potatoes, scrubbed,
   trimmed, and quartered
Salt
1 cup pecan halves (about
   5 ounces)
1 Sweet Hickory Whole
   Smoked Chicken (page
   145)
¾ cup Lime Cream (page
   296)
¼ cup mayonnaise
¼ cup fresh lime juice
1 tablespoon minced lime
   zest
½ teaspoon hot pepper
   sauce, such as Tabasco
2 large, tart, red-skinned
   apples
3 celery ribs, trimmed and
   sliced
Freshly ground black
   pepper
Lettuce leaves

This terrific salad is the usual destination for the smoked chicken I make from the recipe on page 145. Full of contrasting flavors and textures, with just a subtle touch of hickory smoke and plenty of tangy lime zest and juice, it's just right for a summer supper when I want to impress people but don't want to go to a lot of last-minute fuss. Start the menu with something like the Grilled Eggplant Dip with Sweet and Smoky Flavors (page 26), serve some Cornbread with Red Chile–Pecan Streusel (page 214) alongside the salad, and end with Frozen Raspberry Margarita Pie (page 242).

1. In a medium saucepan, cover the potatoes with salted cold water. Bring to a brisk simmer over medium heat. Cook, partially covered, stirring occasionally, until the potatoes are just tender, about 12 minutes. Drain and cool.

2. Position a rack in the middle of the oven and preheat to 375°F. In a shallow metal pan, like a cake tin, toast the pecans, stirring them occasionally, until they are crisp and fragrant, about 8 minutes. Cool to room temperature and coarsely chop.

3. Remove and discard the skin from the chicken. Pull all the meat from the bones and cut it into 1-inch chunks.

4. In a large bowl, whisk together the Lime Cream, mayonnaise, lime juice, zest, and pepper sauce. Add the chicken, potatoes, apples, half the pecans, and the celery. Season generously with pepper and toss well. Adjust the seasoning and toss again.

5. To serve, line a platter with the lettuce. Spoon the salad onto the lettuce, scatter the remaining pecans over all, and pass the salad at the table.

Sage-and-Coffee-Rubbed Quail and Marinated Mushroom Salad

At The Double A, an ambitious Santa Fe nouvelle cowboy restaurant that debuted and then flamed out all too quickly several years ago, one signature item was a brace of quail, rubbed with a mixture of ground coffee beans and sage and roasted in cast-iron skillets. The crisp little birds, with their boldly flavored crust, were attention-getting and unexpectedly but undeniably delicious, although not enough, apparently, to keep the place going. At the restaurant, the quail were accompanied by cheese grits. My version serves them atop a tangy salad of mixed baby greens, with smoky grilled and marinated mushrooms as accent. Add a chunk of Cornbread with Red Chile–Pecan Streusel (page 214) for a completely wonderful plate of food.

1. In a small bowl, combine the garlic, sage, and ¾ teaspoon salt. With the back of a spoon, thoroughly mash the mixture. Add the coffee, sugar, and 1 teaspoon of the pepper and mix well. On a baking sheet pan, sprinkle the skin sides of the quail with the coffee mixture, dividing it evenly and patting it firmly into the birds to encourage it to adhere.

2. Divide the mushrooms among 3 or 4 skewers, preferably of flat metal.

3. Meanwhile, light a direct-heat charcoal fire and let it burn down to medium-hot (5 seconds to "ouch" or preheat a gas grill to medium-high. Position the rack about 6 inches above the heat source.

4. When the grill is ready, brush the mushrooms with 2 tablespoons of the olive oil. Lightly

SERVES 4

5 garlic cloves, crushed through a press
4 teaspoons minced fresh sage
Salt
¼ cup finely ground medium-dark roast coffee beans
1 teaspoon granulated brown sugar
Freshly ground black pepper
8 (5-ounce) farm-raised quail, butterflied and at room temperature
24 cremini mushrooms, stems trimmed flat with caps
7 tablespoons olive oil
4 teaspoons sherry wine vinegar
8 ounces mixed baby salad lettuces (mesclun)

SMOKING CHIP OPTION: MESQUITE

oil the grill rack. Lay the quail on the rack, rub side-up, and lay the mushroom skewers beside them. Cover and grill, turning once, until the quail are crisp, brown, and done to your liking, about 8 minutes total for slightly pink meat, and the mushrooms are well-marked by the grill and tender, about 10 minutes total. Transfer the quail to a plate. Slide the mushrooms from the skewers onto a cutting board.

5. Halve the mushrooms, and, while still warm, combine them with 1 tablespoon of the olive oil, 1 teaspoon of the vinegar, and a generous pinch of salt and pepper. Toss.

6. In a large bowl, toss the salad greens with the remaining 4 tablespoons olive oil. Add ¼ teaspoon salt and toss again. Add the remaining 3 teaspoons vinegar and a generous grinding of pepper and toss once more.

7. Divide the salad greens among 4 plates. Set 2 quail atop each portion of greens. Spoon the mushrooms and their marinade over the quail, dividing them evenly and using them all. Serve immediately.

Note: Only farmed quail are suitable for this recipe. Look for them at specialty supermarkets or see the Mail-Order Sources (page 321). The quail may be available butterflied (or "spatchcocked") or a butcher will do it for you. Or, one at a time, set the quail upright on their tail ends. With a thin, sharp knife, cut down through the quail along both sides of the backbone and through the thigh joints. Discard the backbone. Flatten the quail gently with the palm of your hand until the breastbones crack, letting the birds lie flat.

Grilled Tamarind Pork and Noodle Salad with Smoky Vegetables

A grilled pork, noodle, and vegetable salad can sound more than a little Southeast Asian—unless, or course, the cook who's in charge is in a southwestern frame of mind. Far from anything even remotely authentic, this rousing and colorful combination is nevertheless just as at home in Santa Fe as in Saigon. The noodles and dressing for this zesty and colorful all-in-one dish can be prepared in advance, but the salad tastes best if the pork and vegetables are still warm. If ever a dish was designed to be enjoyed with a cold beer, this is it.

1. Bring a large pot of salted water to a boil. Add the noodles and cook, partially covered, until just tender, according to the package directions. Drain, rinse thoroughly under cold water, and drain again.

2. In a food processor, combine the cilantro, green onions, vinegar, chiles, lime juice, honey, garlic, and 1 teaspoon salt. Process until fairly smooth. With the motor running, gradually add the ½ cup olive oil through the feed tube. The dressing will thicken. Adjust the seasoning.

3. Light a direct-heat charcoal fire and let it burn down to medium-hot (5 seconds to "ouch") or preheat a gas grill to medium-high. Position the grill rack about 6 inches above the heat source.

4. When the grill is ready, lightly oil the rack. Lay the pork tenderloins on the rack. Cover and grill for 10 minutes, turning the tenderloin once. Begin basting with the tamarind glaze and continue to grill, turning and basting every 4 minutes, until the glaze is used up. Continue to grill until the pork is just cooked through while remaining slightly pink and juicy, about 25 minutes total.

SERVES 6 TO 8

Salt
12 ounces fresh Chinese egg noodles
¾ cup chopped cilantro leaves and stems
½ cup chopped green onions, tender tops included
3 tablespoons unseasoned rice wine vinegar
2 serrano chiles, stemmed and chopped
1 tablespoon fresh lime juice
1½ teaspoons honey
2 garlic cloves, chopped
½ cup plus 1½ tablespoons olive oil
2 large pork tenderloins (about 2 pounds total), trimmed
1½ cups Tamarind-Honey Glaze (page 270)
2 medium-large zucchini, trimmed and quartered lengthwise
2 yellow squash, trimmed and quartered lengthwise
2 medium-large red bell peppers

SMOKING CHIP OPTION: MESQUITE

5. Meanwhile, brush the zucchini and squash with the remaining 1½ tablespoons oil. Place them on the grill, cover, and grill, turning them occasionally, until well marked on all sides, about 10 minutes total. Grill the peppers until the peels are lightly but evenly charred, about 12 minutes.

6. Transfer the pork, zucchini, and squash to a cutting board. Transfer the peppers to a paper bag, close the bag, and steam the peppers until cool.

7. Rub away the burnt peel and cut the peppers into long, thin strips. Cut the zucchini and squash quarters crosswise into 1-inch pieces. Slice the pork across the grain and at a slight angle into thin slices. Season the pork and vegetables to taste with salt.

8. In a large bowl, toss together the noodles, dressing, and vegetables. Adjust the seasoning.

9. Transfer the salad to a large platter. Arrange the pork slices over the noodle salad and serve immediately.

Note: The best noodles for this dish are thick rather than thin and cut about ¼-inch wide. If Asian noodles are not available, fresh linguine (the kind that comes in refrigerated plastic trays), can be substituted, as can such dried semolina pasta noodles as fettuccine.

Barbecued Hill Country
Sausage and Lima Bean Salad

Many Germans settled in the beautiful Texas Hill Country, establishing a smokehouse tradition—the original Lone Star barbecue—that still endures. Inspired by that tradition, but in no way a part of it, this tangy, smoky creation makes a great, easy one-dish meal (though some Sweet Texas Slaw [page 212] wouldn't be out of place on the side). I can eat grilled sausages any day of the year, but the robust flavors in this dish may be most appropriate when the first signs of fall are in the air.

1. In a large bowl, cover the beans with cold water and let soak overnight. Drain, transfer to a large pan, and cover with fresh cold water. Lightly salt the water, set over medium heat, and bring to a simmer. Partially cover and cook, stirring occasionally, until just tender, about 50 minutes, but bean cooking times vary widely. Drain and cool.

2. Light a direct-heat charcoal fire and let it burn down to medium-hot (5 seconds to "ouch") or preheat a gas grill to medium-high. Position the grill rack about 6 inches above the heat source.

3. Stir together the barbecue sauce and the adobo. Measure out ¼ cup of the barbecue sauce mixture and reserve. Thread the sausage slices onto 3 flat metal skewers.

4. When the grill is ready, brush the sausage skewers generously with some of the remaining barbecue sauce mixture. Lay the sausage skewers on the rack, cover, and grill for 4 minutes. Continue grilling, turning, brushing with the sauce, grilling and moving the skewers around on the grill to avoid flare-ups, until the sauce is used up and the slices are crisp and well-browned, 12 to 15 minutes total.

5. Meanwhile, in a small bowl, whisk together the reserved barbecue sauce mixture, vinegar, and ½ teaspoon salt. Gradually whisk in the oil; the mixture will thicken.

SERVES 6

2 cups dried baby lima beans (about 1 pound), picked over
Salt
1 cup prepared traditional-style homemade or store-bought barbecue sauce
2 tablespoons adobo from canned chipotles
1 pound kielbasa sausage, diagonally-cut into ¾-inch slices
2 tablespoons cider vinegar
¼ cup corn oil
3 carrots, diced
3 sweet gherkin pickles, coarsely chopped (⅓ cup)
⅓ cup finely chopped pickled jalapeños
Freshly ground black pepper

6. In a large bowl, toss together the beans, carrots, pickles, and jalapeños. Add the barbecue dressing from the small bowl, season generously with pepper, and toss.

7. Transfer the beans to a serving bowl or platter. Slide the sausage slices from the skewers onto the bean salad and serve immediately. The salad tastes best when the sausages are still warm.

Salpicon of Grill-Smoked Brisket

SERVES 4

4½ cups diced, well-
  trimmed Slow and
  Smoky Beef Brisket from
  the Grill (page 174)
  (about 1¾ pounds
  brisket before trimming),
  at room temperature
6 ounces jalapeño Jack
  cheese, at room
  temperature, diced
½ cup diced red onion
½ cup pitted black Greek
  olives (Kalamatas),
  drained and halved
1 cup Chipotle Vinaigrette
  (page 298)
½ cup coarsely chopped
  cilantro
Salt and freshly ground
  black pepper
Tender inner leaves from 2
  heads of romaine lettuce
2 ripe tomatoes, cored and
  cut into quarters
1 large avocado, cut into
  eighths
½ cup diced radish

Salpicon is a meaty main-course salad and one of the great original dishes of the El Paso, Texas–Juarez, Mexico, area. Consisting of shredded, poached beef brisket and a welter of other colorful and crunchy ingredients, all in a smoky chipotle vinaigrette, it is hearty, sturdy, and yet somehow appetite-arousing—perfect hot weather fare. Made with smoked rather than poached brisket, salpicon rises to another level of deliciousness, really a remarkable plate of food. The lazy and/or the wealthy may prefer to buy a brisket from a neighborhood smokehouse, while the rest of us will have to smoke our own. I have made this with leftover (even defrosted) meat, but it's at its most succulent with brisket that has never been chilled.

1. In a large bowl, combine the beef, cheese, onion, olives, about half the dressing, and the cilantro. Toss, season to taste with salt and pepper, and toss again.

2. Line a serving platter with the romaine leaves. Spoon the beef mixture into the center of the platter. Surround the beef mixture with the tomato and avocado wedges. Drizzle the tomatoes, avocado, and lettuce leaves with the remaining vinaigrette. Scatter the radishes over all and serve immediately.

Warm Grilled Chile-Lime Beef Salad

When hot weather inspires mealtime lethargy, few dishes will do more to wake up lazy appetites than salads combining hot and cold elements. Based on a favorite Thai dish, this warm and tangy beef salad is one of my favorite summertime alarm clocks. No one—not even the family salad-hater—can resist the combination of tart, smoky meat, crisp vegetables, and chipotle-spiked dressing. For a heart-of-summer backyard party, precede the salad with Grilled Mini Crab Cakes with Mango Pico de Gallo (page 46) and serve Frozen Raspberry Margarita Pie (page 242) by way of a cool-down.

1. In a small food processor or blender, combine the lime juice, sugar, olive oil, jalapeño, garlic, and ½ teaspoon pepper. Process until fairly smooth. In a nonreactive dish, pour the lime mixture over the flank steak. Cover and let stand at room temperature, turning once or twice, for 2 hours.

2. Bring a medium pot of salted water to a boil. Add the green beans and cook, uncovered, stirring once or twice, until the beans are just tender, about 6 minutes. Drain and transfer to a bowl of iced water. When cool, drain immediately and pat dry.

3. Meanwhile, light a direct-heat charcoal fire and let it burn down to hot (3 seconds to "ouch") or preheat a gas grill to high. Position the rack about 6 inches above the heat source.

4. Brush the green onions with the vegetable oil. When the grill is ready, lift the steak from the marinade (reserve it) and lay it on the rack. Lay the onions on the rack, cover, and grill, turning once and basting the steak occasionally with the reserved marinade, until the onions are tender and marked by the grill, about 5 minutes total, and the

SERVES 6

½ cup fresh lime juice
3 tablespoons packed dark brown sugar
3 tablespoons olive oil
1 fresh jalapeño, stemmed and chopped
4 garlic cloves, chopped
Freshly ground black pepper
1¾-pound flank steak (preferably prime grade)
¾ pound green beans, trimmed and halved
6 large green onions, trimmed
2 teaspoons vegetable oil
8 ounces mixed baby salad greens (mesclun)
2 ripe tomatoes, cored and cut into sixteenths
1 medium-large cucumber, peeled if necessary, seeded, and cut into ¾-inch chunks
1 small red onion, halved and thinly sliced
1 cup Chipotle Vinaigrette (page 298)
Salt

SMOKING CHIP OPTION: MESQUITE

Main-Dish Salads

marinade is used up and the steak is done to your liking. For rare steak (my preference), grill for about 9 minutes total.

5. Transfer the steak to a cutting board and let it rest for 5 minutes.

6. Meanwhile, divide the salad greens among 6 plates. In a bowl, combine the green beans, tomatoes, cucumber, and red onion with ½ cup of the vinaigrette. Season to taste with salt and pepper and toss again. Divide the vegetable mixture into 6 portions and spoon atop the salad greens.

7. Carve the steak across the grain and at a slight angle to the cutting board into very thin slices. Season to taste with salt and pepper. Arrange the slices over the vegetable mixture on the plates, dividing them evenly and using them all. Drizzle the remaining ½ cup vinaigrette evenly over the meat and greens. Garnish each salad with a grilled green onion and serve immediately.

Grilled Cumin Lamb, Orange, and Onion Salad

In the unlikely event you have leftover Cumin-Grilled Leg of Lamb, this is the thing to make with it. Meaty, colorful, even—yes—refreshing, it makes a fine lunch or a casual and rustic light supper. Or, to make it for a party, multiply the recipe accordingly, grill the lamb on purpose, earlier in the day, and offer the salad on a big platter. In that case, try to time things so that the lamb is never refrigerated—it will be much more moist and tender, and the salad really will be fit for a celebration.

1. Trim the lamb and slice it across the grain and at a slight angle to the cutting board into thin slices.

2. Zest the oranges. Mince the zest and reserve. Cut a slice from the top and bottom of each orange. Set the oranges on a cutting board. With a serrated knife, cut away the orange peels by slicing downward, following the curve of the oranges, to the board. Thinly slice the oranges (but not so thinly the slices fall apart).

3. On 4 plates, arrange the lamb, orange, and onion slices in overlapping layers. Season with salt and pepper. Stir the reserved orange zest into the dressing. Drizzle each salad with 2 tablespoons of dressing. Scatter the olives over the salads. Sprinkle the salads with the cilantro and serve immediately, passing the remaining dressing at the table.

SERVES 4

About 1½ pounds Cumin-Grilled Butterflied Leg of Lamb (page 184)
2 oranges
1 sweet red onion, thinly sliced
Salt and freshly ground black pepper
1 cup Chipotle Vinaigrette (page 298)
3 cups coarsely chopped pitted black Greek olives (Kalamatas)
⅓ cup finely chopped cilantro

Pescados y Mariscos

Fish
and
Shellfish

Pescados y Mariscos
FISH AND SHELLFISH

Grilled New Mexico Mountain Trout with Cider, Bacon, and Piñon Sauce

Although all sorts of seafood now can be found in the Southwest's better supermarkets, only freshwater trout can be considered native to its heartland. Especially in New Mexico's icy northern mountain streams, trout (typically cutthroat, though rainbows and German browns are stocked) can be found and they make fine fishing. Since northern New Mexico is also home to numerous apple orchards as well as wild piñon trees that provide a free annual harvest of pine nuts, this dish is actually a lot more indigenous than, say, fajitas or guacamole. Not indigenous, however, is wild rice, which makes an ideal accompaniment to this very flavorful dish.

1. Position a rack in the middle of the oven and preheat to 375°F. In a shallow metal pan, like a cake tin, toast the pine nuts, stirring them often, until they are lightly browned and fragrant, 8 to 10 minutes. Remove from the pan and cool.

2. In a medium nonreactive saucepan over low heat, cook the bacon, stirring occasionally, until almost crisp, about 8 minutes. With a slotted spoon, transfer the bacon to paper towels to drain. Discard the bacon drippings, but do not clean the saucepan.

3. Return the saucepan to low heat. Add 4 tablespoons of the butter and when it foams, stir in the onion and garlic. Cover and cook, stirring once or twice, for 5 minutes. Uncover, add the cider and ½ teaspoon salt, and increase the heat. Bring to a brisk simmer and cook uncovered, skimming any foam from the surface, until the sauce is reduced by about half, 15 to 20 minutes. (The sauce can be prepared to this point several hours in advance.)

SERVES 4

¼ cup pine nuts (see Note)
8 thick-cut bacon strips, cut into ½-inch pieces
6 tablespoons unsalted butter
1 onion, thinly sliced
2 garlic cloves, finely chopped
3⅓ cups fresh apple cider
Salt
4 (1-pound) trout, cleaned and scaled
2 tablespoons vegetable oil
Freshly ground black pepper
3 tablespoons finely chopped flat-leaf parsley

SMOKING CHIP OPTION: APPLE

4. Light a direct-heat charcoal fire and let it burn down to medium (7 to 8 seconds to "ouch") or preheat a gas grill to medium. Position the rack about 6 inches above the heat source.

5. Meanwhile, with a sharp knife, make 3 diagonal slashes through the skin and flesh on each side of each trout, cutting down to the bone. Brush the trout with the oil. When the grill is ready, lay the fish on the rack. Cover and grill, turning once (use a long spatula), until the trout is fully cooked through and flaking while remaining moist, about 12 minutes total. Transfer the trout to plates.

6. While the trout grills, finish the sauce. Stir in the bacon and rewarm the mixture, if necessary, over low heat. Divide the remaining 2 tablespoons butter into 8 pieces and whisk the pieces into the cider mixture one at a time, adding a new piece just before the previous piece is fully incorporated; the sauce will thicken slightly. Season generously with pepper. Taste and add more salt, if necessary. Stir in the parsley.

7. Spoon the sauce over and around the trout, dividing it evenly and using it all. Scatter the pine nuts over the trout and serve immediately.

Note: So small an amount of pine nuts can burn easily. If desired, toast a larger amount, measure out the ¼ cup needed for the recipe, and store the rest in an airtight jar in a cool place. They will be good for at least a month.

Is It Done?

The doneness of fish didn't used to be a matter of opinion, but that was before the days of tuna seared on the outside and sashimi raw on the inside and restaurant critics who like their finfish lukewarm and barely gelled. If you do much grilling (and I hope you will), you may find yourself asking "Who wants their sea bass rare, who wants it well-done?" The instant-read thermometer is not much help here, and so visual cues will need to be your guide.

For most fish fillets, press gently on one at its thickest point; if it just moistly flakes, it is fully cooked. Learning how to estimate when a minute or two before that condition is will enable you to satisfy various tastes. It comes with practice. With fish like tuna, which do not readily flake, cutting into a piece is the most reliable way of assessing its doneness. Shrimp and scallops should be cut into also.

Grilled Dorado Fillets with Red Pipian

Pipian is one of Mexico's oldest sauces, consisting chiefly of seasonings thickened with ground squash or pumpkin seeds. Typically, the pipian would be stirred into the braising liquid in which the duck (or whatever) had been simmered. At La Serenata de Garibaldi, a wonderful Mexican restaurant in Los Angeles, however, the sauces are prepared separately from the food to be sauced (primarily seafood) and spooned elegantly over just before service. I had this terrific combination of lean dorado and rich, nutty pipian there one evening and finally duplicated it at home, successfully enough, at least, to tide me over until my next trip to L.A. Dorado, a delicious fish that swims Mexico's coastal waters, is also known as mahi mahi and dolphinfish.

SERVES 4

4 skinless dorado fillets
   (about 2 pounds total)
1 tablespoon Simple Rub
   for Fish (page 265)
1⅓ cups Red Pipian
   (page 272), heated just
   to simmering
Lime wedges

SMOKING WOOD OPTION: MESQUITE

1. Light a direct-heat charcoal fire and let it burn down to medium-hot (5 seconds to "ouch") or preheat a gas grill to medium-high. Position the rack about 6 inches above the heat source.

2. Lightly dust the fillets all over with the rub, using it all.

3. When the grill is ready, lightly oil the rack. Lay the fish on the rack, cover and grill, turning once, until the fish is lightly marked by the rack and just cooked through while remaining moist, 8 to 9 minutes.

4. Transfer the fish to plates. Spoon a generous dollop (about ⅓ cup) of pipian over the fish and serve immediately, accompanied by the limes for squeezing on the fish as desired.

Spice-Coated Catfish with Bumpy Avocado "Butter"

The Southwestern Grill

SERVES 4

1 perfectly ripe avocado
1 garlic clove, crushed
through a press
½ teaspoon fresh lime
juice
½ teaspoon freshly ground
black pepper
¼ teaspoon salt
4 (8-ounce) catfish fillets
3½ tablespoons Quick Red
Rub (page 266)

SMOKING CHIP OPTION: MESQUITE

You can actually combine avocado and sweet butter to make a truly luscious topper for grilled fish. Avocado is rich enough on its own, however, to render the butter superfluous. In this recipe, roughly mashed and minimally seasoned avocado functions on its own to add a layer of cool green color and buttery richness to the spicy, smoky fish. Complete the menu with Orzo, Black Bean, and Cherry Tomato Salad (page 210) and Sweet and Smoky Corn Relish (page 195).

1. Light a direct-heat charcoal fire and let it burn down to medium-hot (5 seconds to "ouch") or preheat a gas grill to medium-high. Position the grill rack about 6 inches above the heat source.

2. Meanwhile, halve and pit the avocado and scoop the flesh out of the peel into a small bowl. Add the garlic, lime juice, pepper, and salt. With a fork, roughly mash the avocado, leaving plenty of bumps.

3. Dust the fillets with the rub, using it all and patting it firmly into the fish to encourage it to adhere.

4. When the grill is ready, lightly oil the rack. Lay the fillets on the rack, cover, and grill, turning once, until the fish is just cooked through while remaining moist, 7 to 8 minutes total.

5. Transfer the fish to plates. Spread the avocado mixture in an even layer over the fillets, dividing it evenly and using it all. Serve immediately.

A favorite place of mine to eat when visiting the border town of Nogales is Elvira's, a restaurant that has evolved over the years from a small funky place into a rather large, glitzy one. The welcome has remained warm, however (including the roving refiller of tequila shot glasses, most of which somehow never end up on the bill), and the food delicious. Fish Elvira is one house specialty, consisting of cabrilla, a lean, flavorful fish of the grouper and bass clan, baked in foil packets with onions and a generous coating of what appears to be nothing more than mayo from a jar. For a grilled version, I've rearranged the elements slightly, but the results are every bit as good. Naturally you will need to provide your own tequila.

1. Light a direct-heat charcoal fire and let it burn down to medium-hot (5 seconds to "ouch") or preheat a gas grill to medium-high. Position the rack about 6 inches above the heat source.

2. Meanwhile, dust the fish on all sides with the rub. Brush the onion slices with the oil.

3. When the grill is ready, lightly oil the rack. Lay the fish and onions on the rack, cover, and grill, turning the fish once, until it is just cooked through and beginning to flake while remaining moist, about 8 minutes, and turning the onions several times, until tender and nicely browned, 8 to 10 minutes.

4. Transfer the fish to plates. Season with salt and pepper. Top each piece of fish with a slice of onion, separating the rings slightly. Season with salt and pepper. Generously drizzle the lime cream from a squeeze bottle and serve immediately, accompanied by the lime wedges.

SERVES 4

4 cabrilla, sea bass, or
  grouper fillets (about
  2 pounds total)
1 tablespoon Simple Rub
  for Fish (page 265)
4 (½-inch-thick) slices
  from a very large red
  onion
2 tablespoons olive oil
Salt and freshly ground
  black pepper
¾ cup Lime Cream (page
  296)
Lime wedges

SMOKING CHIP OPTION: MESQUITE

Halibut Escabeche

SERVES 4

⅓ cup plus 2 tablespoons
  olive oil
1 cup diced carrot
1 cup diced red bell pepper
1 cup sliced green beans
2 bay leaves
1 cup diced onion
1 cup diced yellow squash
4 garlic cloves, thinly
  sliced
1 to 2 serrano chiles,
  stemmed and thinly
  sliced into rounds
½ teaspoon dried oregano,
  crumbled
Salt
¼ cup sherry wine vinegar
¼ cup water
4 thick (1½-inch) halibut
  steaks (about 2 pounds
  total)

SMOKING CHIP OPTION: MESQUITE

South of the border, an escabeche is a light, fresh pickle (no canning is involved). Both cooked seafood and vegetables can get the tangy treatment, so for this recipe I combined the two, producing a nearly perfect hot-weather main course. Almost any fish steak or fillet you like on the grill can be used if halibut is not available. The dish is best at room temperature, easing pressure on the cook. For a more informal presentation, coarsely flake the marinated fish, mix it back into the pickled vegetables and serve with warmed corn tortillas, encouraging diners to assemble rustic tacos. These are good with Avocado-Tomatillo Salsa (page 284) or a fairly fiery salsa, like Chile de Arbol Salsa with Rosemary and Orange (page 288).

1. In a large skillet over medium heat, warm ⅓ cup of the olive oil. Add the carrots, bell pepper, green beans, and bay leaves. Cook, uncovered, stirring once or twice, for 5 minutes. Add the onion, squash, garlic, serranos, oregano, and ¼ teaspoon salt. Cook, stirring occasionally, until the vegetables are almost tender and are lightly colored, about 4 minutes. Remove from the heat and transfer to a bowl. Stir in the vinegar and water. Cool to room temperature and adjust the seasoning.

2. Meanwhile, light a direct-heat charcoal fire and let it burn down to medium-hot (5 seconds to "ouch") or preheat a gas grill to medium-high. Position the grill rack about 6 inches above the heat source.

3. Brush the halibut steaks with the remaining 2 tablespoons olive oil. When the grill is ready, lay the steaks on the rack. Cover and grill, turning once, until the fish is just cooked through while remaining juicy, 8 to 9 minutes.

4. Transfer to a deep serving platter and season lightly with salt. Discard the bay leaves and spoon the vegetable mixture and all its liquid over the fish. Let cool just to room temperature before serving.

Hickory-Smoked Salmon with Habanero-Pineapple Butter

This salmon, which bears no resemblance to the silky cold-smoked salmon of fine restaurant menus, could also be called "grill-baked." The salmon is brined first (soaked in a salt-and-sugar solution), which helps keep it moist and tender, then indirectly grilled at a very low temperature with plenty of wood chunks to supply smoky flavor. This method, one I developed many years ago while working on a book with Park Kerr of The El Paso Chile Company, produces two types of fish. After an hour or so, the salmon is fully cooked and flaking, very moist and tender and only slightly smoky. After another half-hour on the grill, the meat is firmer (though still moist) and significantly smokier. Either is good for eating hot, straight from the grill, with a salsa, sauce, or compound butter. The smokier variation works best if you're using the fish cold, in a salad, say, or in the Hickory-Smoked Salmon and Green Chile Spread (page 40).

SERVES 4, WITH LEFTOVERS

⅔ cup kosher salt
½ cup packed light brown sugar
1 side skin-on salmon fillet (about 3½ pounds)
½ cup Habanero-Pineapple Butter (page 301), softened at room temperature

SMOKING WOOD CHUNKS: HICKORY

1. Soak six 3-inch hickory wood chunks in water for at least 24 hours.

2. To make the brine, bring 8 cups water to a boil in a saucepan. Add the salt and sugar and stir until dissolved. Remove from the heat and cool to room temperature.

3. With sterile tweezers or needle-nose pliers, pull out any bones remaining in the salmon. They are easy to locate by running your fingers along the side of fish. (There can be as many as 30.)

4. Lay the salmon skin side-up in a nonreactive dish just large enough to hold it, and cover it with the cooled brine. Weight the salmon with a plate to keep it submerged and refrigerate for 24 hours. Discard the brine, cover the salmon with fresh cold water, and let soak for 1 hour. Drain the salmon and pat it dry. Lay it on a shallow disposable foil pan just large enough to hold it.

5. Meanwhile, ignite about 30 charcoal briquettes, preferably in a chimney starter. When the briquettes are covered with white ash and glowing orange, arrange them in a kettle grill following the directions for indirect grilling on page 8. Drain the hickory chunks and arrange them atop the briquettes, spacing them apart. Set the grill rack in place. Set the pan with the salmon on the portion of the grill rack not over the briquettes. Cover the grill. Regulate the lower and upper vents to maintain a temperature between 230° and 250°F. (Generally, the lower vent should be about 25 percent open; the upper vent barely open, but grills vary.) (For smoking on a gas grill, see the box below.)

6. Smoke, rotating the position of the pan on the rack once, for about 1 hour for fully cooked but very moist and only slightly smoky salmon, or about 1½ hours for moist but firmer and much smokier salmon.

7. With a wide spatula, transfer the salmon to a cutting board. To make 3-inch-wide serving pieces, cut down through the salmon to, but not through, the skin. With the spatula, lift the salmon off the skin and transfer it to plates. Top each portion with one-fourth of the butter and serve immediately. (Leftover salmon can be refrigerated for up to 2 days or frozen for up to 1 month.)

Smoking Salmon on a Gas Grill

Salmon can also be smoked on some gas grills. Those with lava stones work best, and a grill with three separate burners is preferable to one with only two. Soak the hickory chunks as directed. Preheat one burner (in some grills, only one of the burners can operate alone; be sure to select this burner) to 250°F. Arrange the wood chunks on the lava stones over the lit burner and set the rack in place. Set the pan with the salmon on that portion of the rack over the cold burners. Cover and lower the heat, adjusting it to maintain a steady temperature of about 250°F. Turn the pan on the rack once or twice to promote even smoking. If you have successfully maintained the desired temperature, the salmon will be done in the same time frame. If your grill can't maintain a temperature that low, monitor the salmon for signs of doneness and take it off when it is fully cooked but still juicy. It may be a little less smoky, simply because it has spent less time over the wood chunks. Certain grills, with v-shaped ceramic bars as part of their grilling system, are not as suitable for smoking unless they come with a separate side smoking chamber. If you use such a grill, follow the manufacturer's directions for using the side smoking chamber.

Cornhusk-Steamed Salmon Steaks with Corn, Mushrooms, and Chiles

The sauce takes its inspiration from the Mexican delicacy known as *huitlacoche*. Also called "the truffle of Mexico," huitlacoche is a kind of fungus (mushroom if you prefer) that infests ears of corn in the field. Harvested rather than discarded, it is cooked and served on its own or in elegant sauces, sometimes in combination with green chiles. Although easier to find than it once was, huitlacoche is still a rarity, which is why I developed this corn, mushroom, and poblano chile sauce, which brilliantly complements salmon that has been grill-steamed inside cornhusk packets. The husks char and supply a little additional corn flavor; the packets are then opened on the plates and the sauce spooned over, for a striking and rustic presentation.

1. Separate the cornhusks, place in a large bowl, and cover them with cold water. Let stand for at least 1 hour or as long as overnight.

2. In the open flame of a gas burner, under a preheated broiler, or on the grill, roast the poblanos, turning them occasionally, until they are lightly but evenly charred. Transfer to a paper bag, close the bag, and steam the chiles until cool. Rub away the burnt peel and stem and chop the chiles.

3. In a large skillet over low heat, melt the butter. Add the poblanos and garlic, cover, and cook, stirring once or twice, for 5 minutes. Add the mushrooms, oregano, and salt. Increase the heat slightly. Cover and cook, stirring once or twice, until the mushrooms begin to give up their juices and are becoming tender, 5 to 7 minutes. Add the corn kernels and juices and cook, covered, for 3 minutes. Stir in the cream and a generous grinding

SERVES 6

About 30 large dried corn-husks (hojas de maiz)
2 large fresh poblano chiles
2 tablespoons unsalted butter
2 garlic cloves, finely chopped
¾ pound brown (cremini) mushrooms, trimmed and chopped
2 tablespoons finely chopped fresh oregano
¾ teaspoon salt
Kernels and juices cut and scraped from 2 ears sweet corn
½ cup whipping cream
Freshly ground black pepper
6 (8-ounce) salmon steaks

of pepper. Bring to a simmer and cook, stirring occasionally, until the corn is tender and the sauce has thickened, about 4 minutes. (The sauce can be prepared several hours in advance. Shorten the cooking time slightly and hold it, covered, at room temperature.)

4. Drain the cornhusks. Tear several of the smaller husks lengthwise into ¼-inch strips, to use as ties. On a work surface, slightly overlap 2 husks, placing the narrow end of one at the wide end of the other. Set a salmon steak in the center. Season the fish with salt and pepper. Overlap two more husks on top of the salmon, orienting the second set of cornhusks in the same direction as the first set. Tuck the sides and ends under. Tie each end with a strip of cornhusk. Use a toothpick to secure the seam of the packet if necessary. Repeat with the remaining cornhusks and salmon. (The salmon packets can be prepared up to 1 hour ahead. Refrigerate until you are ready to grill.)

5. Light a direct-heat charcoal fire and let it burn down to medium-high (5 seconds to "ouch") or preheat a gas grill to medium-high. Position the rack about 6 inches above the heat source.

6. When the grill is ready, set the packets directly on the rack. Cover and grill, turning once, until the corn husks are lightly charred and the fish is done to your liking, about 8 minutes total for medium-rare fish, 12 minutes total for fully cooked but moist and flaky fish (open 1 packet to check).

7. While the salmon cooks, reheat the sauce to simmering, if necessary.

8. Transfer the packets to plates. Cut off the ties and open the packets to expose the fish. Spoon the sauce over and around the fish, dividing it evenly and using it all. Serve immediately.

Note: Salmon fillets can replace the steaks if desired, for those who don't like dealing with bones. Shorten the grilling time by about 2 minutes total.

Grilled Salmon Steaks
with
Chipotle Cream Sauce

Cream and honey mustard modify the smoky heat of chipotles without actually taming them, producing a sauce that manages to be both mellow and fiery at the same time. Salmon pairs nicely with the sauce as illustrated here (fillets work just as well as steaks if you prefer them), resulting in a dish sophisticated enough for company.

1. Light a direct-heat charcoal fire and let it burn down to medium-hot (5 seconds to "ouch") or preheat a gas grill to medium-high. Position the grill rack about 6 inches above the heat source.

2. Dust the salmon steaks with the rub, using it all and patting it into the fish to encourage it to adhere.

3. When the grill is ready, lightly oil the rack. Lay the fish on the rack, cover, and grill, turning once, until just cooked through to your liking, about 8 minutes total for medium-rare salmon.

4. Meanwhile, heat the cream sauce to simmering.

5. Transfer the salmon to plates. Spoon the sauce over and around the fish, dividing it evenly and using it all. Serve immediately.

SERVES 4

4 (8-ounce) salmon steaks
1 tablespoon Simple Rub
   for Fish (page 265)
1¼ cups Chipotle Cream
   Sauce (page 273)

SMOKING CHIP OPTION: APPLE

Grilled Swordfish Steaks
with
Avocado Mayonnaise

SERVES 4

1 cup thinly sliced green
   onions, tender tops
   included
¾ cup packed cilantro
   leaves and tender stems
3 tablespoons olive oil
3 tablespoons fresh lime
   juice
1½ tablespoons minced
   lime zest
1½ tablespoons packed
   light brown sugar
1 tablespoon minced
   jalapeño
½ teaspoon salt
½ teaspoon freshly ground
   black pepper
4 thick (1-inch) swordfish
   steaks (about 2 pounds
   total)
1½ cups Avocado
   Mayonnaise (page 293)

SMOKING CHIP OPTION: MESQUITE

This is an easy recipe, but a delicious one, grilling at its uncomplicated best. Swordfish, which can be dry, is here kept moist by a chile-spiked marinade and then served topped with a dollop of luscious avocado mayonnaise. Accompany it with Jicama and Grilled Red Pepper Slaw (page 211) and Grilled Polenta with Green Chiles and Corn (page 213).

1. In a food processor, combine the green onions, cilantro, olive oil, lime juice, lime zest, sugar, jalapeño, salt, and the pepper. Transfer the mixture to a shallow nonreactive dish. Add the fish steaks, cover, and marinate at room temperature, turning once or twice, for 1 hour.

2. Meanwhile, light a direct-heat charcoal fire and let it burn down to medium-hot (5 seconds to "ouch") or preheat a gas grill to medium-high. Position the grill rack about 6 inches above the heat source.

3. When the grill is ready, lift the fish steaks from the marinade (reserve it) and lay them on the rack. Cover and grill, basting with the marinade and turning once, until the fish is done to your liking, about 8 minutes total for fish slightly undercooked at the center.

4. Transfer the fish to plates, top with a dollop of the mayonnaise, and serve immediately.

Cumin Tuna Steaks
with
Lime Cream and Salsa

Robust fish like tuna stands up particularly well to assertive southwestern seasonings. Here, thick steaks are rubbed with little more than ground cumin, then briefly grilled to a succulent medium-rare. A drizzle of lime cream makes a fine flavor and color contrast with the cumin crust; any one of a number of salsas adds color and heat. This recipe is also good made with swordfish steaks.

1. Light a direct-heat charcoal fire and let it burn down to medium-hot (5 seconds to "ouch") or preheat a gas grill to medium-high. Position the grill rack about 6 inches above the heat source.

2. Meanwhile, season the tuna steaks on all sides with salt and pepper to taste. Evenly dust the steaks all over with the cumin, patting it firmly into the fish to encourage it to adhere.

3. When the grill is ready, lightly oil the rack. Lay the steaks on the rack. Cover and grill, turning once, until done to your liking, about 6 minutes total for medium-rare fish.

4. Transfer the steaks to plates. Generously drizzle the lime cream onto and around the steaks (you will not use all of it). Spoon a generous dollop of salsa alongside each steak, dividing it evenly and using it all. Serve immediately.

SERVES 4

4 thick (1½-inch) tuna steaks (about 2 pounds total)
Salt and freshly ground black pepper
4 teaspoons freshly ground cumin (preferably from toasted seeds)
½ cup Lime Cream (page 296)
1 cup Avocado-Tomatillo Salsa (page 284), Mango Pico de Gallo (page 281), or Golden Tomato Salsa Borracha (page 287)

SMOKING CHIP OPTION: MESQUITE

Fear of Fish

Afraid to grill fish and shellfish? It's not as tricky as you might imagine. Certainly a piece of halibut will overcook more quickly than a pork chop, and turning a fillet of red snapper without leaving much of it behind requires more experience than flipping a burger. Nevertheless, grilling—preferably with bold southwestern seasonings—is one of the best ways to cook seafood, and it's worth getting really good at. Here are some tips:

- Work with fish that is easy to handle, like the red meats you are comfortable grilling. This means start with steaks. Cut to an even thickness, swordfish, tuna, shark, halibut, and salmon steaks cook evenly and are easier to turn than fillets, which vary in thickness and have delicate edges.

- Grill shrimp. Nearly foolproof on the grill, all it takes to master this popular shellfish is a set of flat metal skewers. Turning a few skewers filled with shrimp instead of dozens of individuals makes the process speedy, and on a flat skewer the shrimp stay in perfect alignment for even cooking.

- Clean your grill rack. Fish won't stick as readily to a clean rack.

- Lightly oil your grill rack (use a paper towel dipped into oil; never aim a can of nonstick spray at an open flame). If you're not grilling a naturally oily fish (like salmon), or it hasn't been in a marinade containing oil or another fat, this will also reduce sticking.

- It may sound unlikely, but be sure the rack is very hot before laying the fish on. A hot rack sears and seals the fish, forming a crust that readily releases when you're ready to turn the fish.

- Give that crust plenty of time to form. Poking and turning fish shortly after it goes on the rack is a sure way of tearing delicate fillets or even hearty steaks. Allow at least 2 minutes of uninterrupted grilling.

- Buy the biggest spatula you can find, preferably one with a bent or offset handle; a restaurant supply house is a good source. The larger the spatula, the more reliably the fish can be turned.

- Create attractive marks on the fish by rotating it 45 degrees about halfway through grilling each side.

- Buy fresh fish, from a store dedicated to seafood, if possible. If it must be a supermarket, choose a busy one with a good turnover of product. Avoid fish on trays sealed in plastic wrap. In all but the busiest of stores, seafood comes in only a couple of days a week. Ask your fishmonger what his delivery days are, shop on those days, and cook the fish within a few hours.

Jalapeño-Cilantro Scallop Skewers
with Salsa Verde

The sweet heat of the thick green cilantro puree accents the natural sweetness of the scallops, making this one of the best ways of preparing them I know. Salsa Verde with Pineapple adds a lush touch to the lean bivalves (and the assorted colors are beautiful), but shellfish purists may want to skip it and just enjoy the scallops on their own.

1. In a food processor, combine the cilantro, onions, garlic, jalapeño, oil, wine, sugar, ½ teaspoon salt, and ½ teaspoon pepper. Process, stopping several times to scrape down the sides of the work bowl, until fairly smooth.

2. In a shallow nonreactive dish, combine the puree and the scallops. Marinate at room temperature, stirring once or twice, for 1 hour.

3. Meanwhile, light a direct-heat charcoal fire and let it burn down to medium-hot (5 seconds to "ouch") or preheat a gas grill to medium-high. Position the rack about 6 inches above the heat source.

4. Lift the scallops from the puree (reserve what little remains) and divide them among several flat metal skewers.

5. When the grill is ready, lightly oil the rack. Lay the skewered scallops on the rack, cover, and grill for 4 minutes. Baste with the remaining puree, turn, cover, and continue to grill until the scallops are lightly browned and just cooked through while remaining moist, another 4 to 5 minutes.

6. Slide the scallops from the skewers onto plates. Season with salt and pepper. Spoon the salsa over the scallops and serve immediately.

SERVES 4

1 cup coarsely chopped cilantro
½ cup thinly sliced green onions, tender tops included
4 garlic cloves, chopped
½ fresh jalapeño, stemmed and chopped
2 tablespoons olive oil
2 tablespoons white wine
2 teaspoons granulated brown sugar
Salt
Freshly ground black pepper
20 large sea scallops (about 2½ pounds total)
1⅓ cups Salsa Verde with Pineapple (page 283)

SMOKING CHIP OPTION: MESQUITE

Grilled Bacon Shrimp with Molasses Adobo

The Southwestern Grill

SERVES 4

⅓ cup tequila
¼ cup fresh lime juice
2 garlic cloves, crushed
through a press
Freshly ground black
pepper
1½ pounds large shrimp
(about 36), peeled and
deveined
1 cup Mexican Barbecue
Sauce (Adobo) (page
277)
¼ cup unsulphured
molasses
18 thin-cut strips bacon,
halved crosswise
Salt

SMOKING CHIP OPTION: APPLE

"Bacon and anything" pretty much sums up my food philosophy. Here that all-purpose kitchen mantra results in extra-succulent shrimp, extra-smoky from the bacon drippings that baste them as they grill. The deeply spicy-sweet adobo sauce with which they are glazed illustrates a new part of the philosophy, still evolving, tentatively: "Adobo on anything."

1. In a nonreactive bowl, stir together the tequila, lime juice, garlic, and ½ teaspoon pepper. Add the shrimp, cover, and marinate at room temperature, stirring once or twice, for 30 minutes.

2. In a small bowl, whisk together the barbecue sauce and molasses.

3. Meanwhile, light a direct-heat charcoal fire and let it burn down to medium-hot (5 seconds to "ouch") or preheat a gas grill to medium-high. Position the rack about 6 inches above the heat source.

4. Remove the shrimp from the marinade (discard it). Wrap each shrimp in a piece of bacon, threading the shrimp onto flat metal skewers as you go. Secure the bacon strips so that they will not unwrap.

5. When the grill is ready, lay the skewers on the rack. Brush lightly with some of the sauce, cover, and grill for 2 minutes. Turn, brush with more sauce, cover, and grill for 2 minutes. Continue grilling, turning the shrimp every 2 minutes, brushing them with sauce each time, until the sauce is used up and the shrimp are just cooked through while remaining moist, about 10 minutes total. (The bacon will be cooked through but will not be particularly crisp.)

6. Season the shrimp with salt and pepper. Slide them from the skewers onto plates and serve immediately.

Grilled Rocky Point "Scampi" Diablo

Rocky Point is a rough-and-ready beach town near the northernmost end of the Sea of Cortez. Promise of development has not yet led to an expected Acapulco-like transformation. Prices are still low, amenities simple, and crowds, except those during spring break, are manageable. Seafood prices, especially, remain gentle, which means jumbo shrimp, caught that very morning, are an affordable treat. They're not actually scampi (a Mediterranean spiny lobster), but they are delicious when butterflied, basted with a scampi-type garlic-and-white-wine marinade on the grill, and drizzled with chipotle mayonnaise at the table. Lime Cream (page 296) can be substituted for the mayo.

SERVES 4

24 very large shrimp
   (about 2 pounds)
1 cup dry white wine
⅔ cup fresh orange juice
8 garlic cloves, crushed
   through a press
½ teaspoon crushed red
   pepper flakes
Salt
Freshly ground black
   pepper
1 cup Chipotle
   Mayonnaise (page 293)
Lime wedges (optional)

SMOKING CHIP OPTION: MESQUITE

1. To butterfly the shrimp, remove the legs. With a small knife, cut the shrimp through just to the shells. Spread them open (like opening a book) and transfer them to a shallow, nonreactive dish.

2. In a small bowl, combine the wine, orange juice, garlic, pepper flakes, and ¼ teaspoon salt. Pour the wine mixture over the shrimp and let stand at room temperature, turning occasionally (be sure the shrimp stay open, for maximum exposure to the marinade) for no more than 1 hour.

3. Meanwhile, light a direct-heat charcoal fire and let it burn down to high (about 3 seconds to "ouch") or preheat a gas grill to high. Position the grill rack about 6 inches above the heat source.

4. Lift the shrimp from the marinade (reserve it) and thread them onto skewers, securing the shrimp open and flat, for maximum exposure to the fire.

5. When the grill is ready, oil the rack. Lay the skewers on the rack shell side-down, cover, and grill for 3 minutes, basting occasionally with the marinade. Turn and continue to grill, basting the shrimp with the last of the marinade, until they are lightly marked by the grill and just cooked through while remaining moist, about 7 minutes total.

6. Season the shrimp with salt and pepper and slide from the skewers onto plates. Drizzle the chipotle mayonnaise and serve immediately, with lime wedges for squeezing over the shrimp if desired. Pass the extra mayonnaise at the table.

Grilled Split Lobsters with Lime Aioli

SERVES 2 TO 4

Salt
2 (1¾-pound) live lobsters
¾ cup Lime Cream (page 296)
1 garlic clove, crushed through a press
8 to 12 (5-inch) corn tortillas

SMOKING CHIP OPTION: APPLE

This is more method than recipe, but when you've tried lobsters grilled this way, you'll want to prepare them often. (Just remember that at the height of grill season—summer—lobsters are molting and not at their sweet, meaty best; try to make this in late fall or early spring—or even winter—instead.) I like these as the main course of an informally messy meal for two, but you can also serve half a lobster per person as a starter, or pair half-lobsters with other grilled seafood, such as the Soft Tacos of Grilled Orange-Garlic Shrimp (page 67) or the Grill-Opened Clams (page 45), as part of a briny main course mixed grill.

1. Bring a large pot of water to a boil. Salt it lightly. Drop the lobsters headfirst into the boiling water. Cover, return to a boil, and cook for 2 minutes. Transfer the lobsters to a work surface. Using a clean kitchen towel to protect your hands, split the lobsters in half lengthwise with a long, sharp knife. Crack the claws.

2. Meanwhile, light a direct-heat charcoal fire and let it burn down to medium-hot (5 seconds to "ouch") or preheat a gas grill to medium-high. Position the rack about 6 inches above the heat source. Preheat the oven to 400°F.

3. When the grill is ready, lay the lobsters, cut sides-up, on the rack. Cover and grill for 5 minutes. Turn the lobsters cut sides-down, cover, and continue to grill until the lobster meat is just cooked through while remaining moist, another 5 to 6 minutes.

4. Meanwhile, wrap the corn tortillas in foil, dividing them into 2 packets. Heat them in the oven until supple and warm, about 10 minutes. Stir together the lime cream and the garlic in a small bowl.

5. Transfer the lobsters to plates. Serve, accompanied by the aioli and the tortillas. Encourage guests to use the tortillas to form small tacos of lobster meat topped with the aioli.

Aves

Chicken, Turkey, and Other Poultry

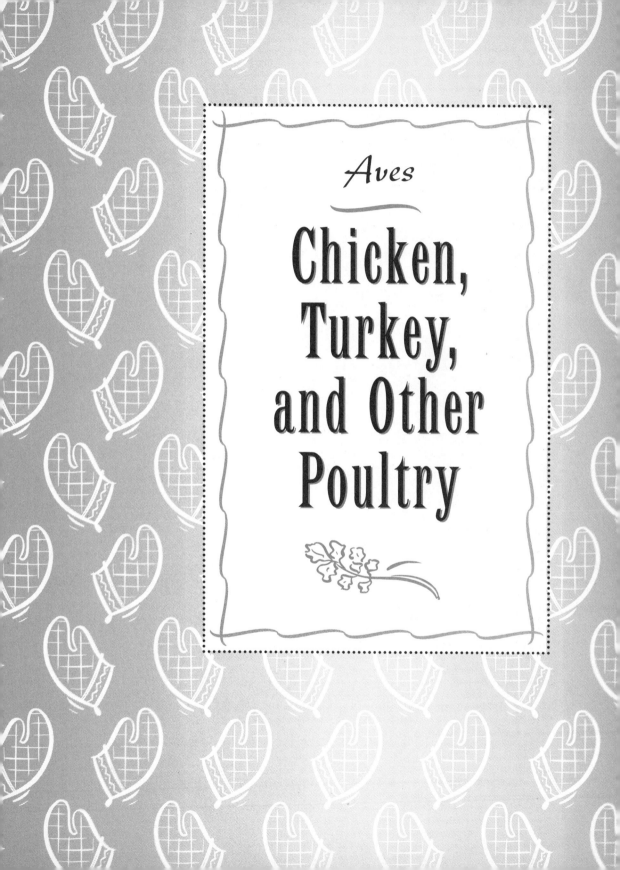

Aves

CHICKEN, TURKEY, AND OTHER POULTRY

Chicken Breasts in Pineapple-Tequila Marinade

This easy little fat-free marinade adds a flavor and color boost to grilled chicken breasts, transforming them from merely tasty into something very special indeed. Keep the marinating time to the minimum, or the pineapple juice will make the chicken breasts mushy. Good accompaniments would be Smoky Grill-Roasted Corn on the Cob (page 193) and Orzo, Black Bean, and Cherry Tomato Salad (page 210).

1. Light a direct-heat charcoal fire and let it burn down to medium-high (5 seconds to "ouch") or preheat a gas grill to medium-high. Position the rack about 6 inches above the grill rack.

2. Meanwhile, in a shallow nonreactive dish, stir together the pineapple juice, tequila, sugar, achiote paste, ketchup, lime juice, hot sauce, soy sauce, and garlic. Add the chicken breasts and marinate at room temperature for no more than 30 minutes, turning once or twice.

3. When the grill is ready, lightly oil the rack. Lay the chicken breasts on the rack. Cover and grill, basting often with the reserved marinade until it is used up, and turning the breasts every 2 minutes. Continue to grill for at least 2 minutes after the marinade is used up, turning the breasts once, until just done through while remaining juicy. Total grilling time should be about 8 minutes.

4. Transfer the chicken breasts to a cutting board and let them rest for 3 or 4 minutes.

5. Across the grain and at a slight angle, carve the chicken breasts into thin slices. Season to taste with salt and pepper and serve hot or warm.

SERVES 4

⅔ cup unsweetened pineapple juice
⅓ cup tequila
2 tablespoons packed dark brown sugar
2 tablespoons achiote paste
2 tablespoons ketchup
1 tablespoon fresh lime juice
1 tablespoon habanero hot sauce
1 tablespoon soy sauce
2 garlic cloves, crushed through a press
2 large whole boneless, skinless chicken breasts (3 pounds total), halves separated and trimmed of visible fat
Salt and freshly ground black pepper

SMOKING CHIP OPTION: MESQUITE

Marinades and Food Safety

When marinades do double-duty as a baste, there is a question of whether it is safe to baste with a marinade that has come in contact with raw poultry. Some people deal with the problem by making large quantities of the marinade and setting some aside to use as a baste. I hate to do that because it is a waste of ingredients; a lot of expensive extra-virgin olive oil ends up going down the drain. My preferred solution is to reuse the marinade as a baste, but to make sure that the baste is thoroughly cooked by the heat of the grill, I stop basting a few minutes before the poultry is done. The intense heat of the grill will destroy any bacteria. If the marinade is doing double-duty as a table sauce, however—no contact with the heat of the grill—then I always set some aside.

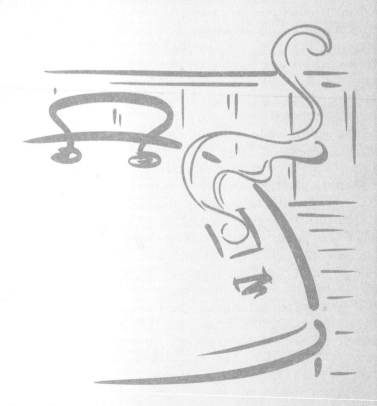

Easy BBQ Chicken Breasts on a Bed of Calabacitas Salad

Barbecued chicken and corn—two backyard grill supper classics—get slightly rearranged and significantly improved in this attractive southwestern rendition. Don't feel guilty about starting with a bottled barbecue sauce (I do it all the time), but do doctor it a bit, as suggested below, for extra zip. As a third element on the plate, serve Heirloom Bean Salad (page 203) or just grill up some Texas Toast (page 217).

SERVES 6

2 cups thick barbecue sauce, homemade or store-bought
⅓ cup maple syrup
1½ tablespoons Dijon mustard
1½ tablespoons adobo from canned chipotle chiles
3 large whole boneless, skinless chicken breasts (4½ pounds total), halves separated and trimmed of visible fat
Salt and freshly ground black pepper
Grilled Calabacitas Salad (page 202)

SMOKING CHIP OPTION: MESQUITE

1. In a small bowl, whisk together the barbecue sauce, maple syrup, mustard, and adobo. Set aside ½ cup of this mixture.

2. In a shallow dish, combine the chicken breasts with remaining barbecue sauce mixture and marinate for up to 1 hour at room temperature.

3. Meanwhile, light a direct-heat charcoal fire and let it burn down to medium-hot (5 seconds to "ouch") or preheat a gas grill to medium-high. Position the rack about 6 inches above the heat source.

4. When the grill is ready, lightly oil the rack. Lay the chicken breasts on the rack. Cover and grill, basting often with the reserved marinade until it is used up, and turning the breasts every 2 minutes. Continue to grill for at least 2 minutes after the marinade is used up, turning the breasts once, until just done through while remaining juicy. Total grilling time should be about 9 minutes.

5. Transfer the chicken breasts to a cutting board and let them rest for a few minutes.

6. Carve the chicken breasts across the grain and at a slight angle to the cutting board into thin slices. Season with salt and pepper.

7. Divide the salad among 6 plates. Arrange the chicken slices over the salad. Drizzle the chicken with the remaining ½ cup barbecue sauce mixture and serve immediately.

Chicken, Turkey, and Other Poultry

Sour Orange Chicken Breasts
with
Chile-Dusted Melon Skewers

SERVES 4

1 cup fresh orange juice
¼ cup fresh lime juice
¼ cup packed dark brown
  sugar
2 tablespoons olive oil
2 tablespoons Mexican
  hot sauce (Bufalo brand
  jalapeño Mexican hot
  sauce is recommended)
2 garlic cloves, crushed
  through a press
2 large boneless, skinless
  chicken breasts (3
  pounds total), halves
  separated and trimmed
  of visible fat
4 teaspoons medium-hot
  pure unblended red chile
  powder (preferably from
  Chimayo)
Salt
24 (1-inch) cubes juicy,
  red-ripe or golden
  watermelon
Freshly ground black
  pepper

SMOKING CHIP OPTION: MESQUITE

A sweet and tangy sour orange mop adds an edge of flavor to these simple chicken breasts and keeps them moist as well, while the garnish recalls a popular Mexican street snack of sweet, juicy watermelon chunks sprinkled with hot red chile powder. Here cubes of the fruit are skewered (though not grilled), and served as a cool and colorful garnish to the chicken. Complete this easy meal with Grilled Calabacitas Salad (page 202) and Double-Smoky Baked Black Beans (page 197).

1. In a shallow nonreactive dish, whisk together the orange juice, lime juice, sugar, olive oil, hot sauce, and garlic. Add the chicken breasts to the orange juice mixture and marinate at room temperature, turning once or twice, for no more than 1 hour.

2. Meanwhile, light a direct-heat charcoal fire and let it burn down to medium-hot (5 seconds to "ouch") or preheat a gas grill to medium-high. Position the rack about 6 inches above the heat source.

Chile-Dusted Melon

Something I learned the first time I sampled chile-spiked watermelon (also the first—and only—time I ever attended a bullfight): The combination just doesn't taste right if the melon isn't as sweet, ripe, juicy, and flavorful as it's possible to get.

Is It Done?

Chicken and turkey should be fully cooked through, showing no trace of pink, while retaining their natural moisture. With boneless breasts, this is a little hard to determine, unless you cut into one at its thickest (if you do, save this less than lovely portion for yourself). Chicken pieces or split birds on the bone are done when the meat of the thighs, pricked at its thickest spot, yields juices that are clear and yellow, not pink. Again, cut to be certain. An instant-read thermometer can be used to help determine doneness, but may not be entirely reliable on very thin cuts, like boneless breasts. Insert the thermometer into the poultry at its thickest, avoiding bone, fat, or any stuffing. In general, a reading of 160° to 170°F should yield fully cooked but juicy meat.

3. When the grill is ready, lightly oil the rack. Lay the chicken breasts on the rack. Cover and grill, basting often with the reserved marinade until it is used up, and turning the breasts every 2 minutes. Continue to grill for at least 2 minutes after the marinade is used up, turning the breasts once, until just done through while remaining juicy. Total grilling time should be about 9 minutes.

4. Meanwhile, in a small bowl, stir together the chile powder and ¼ teaspoon salt. Divide the watermelon cubes among 4 thin bamboo skewers. Evenly sprinkle the melon cubes with the chile mixture, using it all.

5. When the chicken is done, transfer the breasts to a cutting board and let them rest for a few minutes.

6. Carve the breasts across the grain and at a slight angle to the cutting board into thin slices. Season with salt and pepper.

7. Divide the chicken among 4 plates. Set a melon skewer atop each portion of chicken and serve immediately.

Spice-Rubbed Chicken with Branding Iron Barbecue Sauce

SERVES 4 TO 6

2 (3¼-pound) small
  chickens or 6½ pounds
  chicken parts
7 tablespoons Quick Red
  Rub (page 266)
2 cups Branding Iron
  Barbecue Sauce (page
  279)
Salt and freshly ground
  black pepper

SMOKING CHIP OPTION: MESQUITE

This recipe illustrates an interesting technique that can be applied to almost any meat, poultry, or seafood you want to grill. The chicken is first rubbed, then grilled to set and char the rub slightly, then sauced and grilled further. The layers the two flavoring agents create provide wonderful contrast and an overall sensory boost that makes for great eating. When people say they are craving really good barbecued chicken, this is the recipe I make for them. For a really great backyard grill meal, accompany the chicken with Sweet Texas Slaw (page 212), Potato Salad with Roasted Garlic Aioli (page 206), and Smoky Grill-Roasted Corn on the Cob (page 193) with Green Chile–Cheese Butter (page 300).

1. If you are starting with whole chickens, cut out the chicken backbones and reserve for another purpose. Separate the chicken thighs and legs. Separate the wings from the breasts. Cut the breasts in half crosswise. You will have 20 fairly small chicken parts. If you are starting with pieces, cut large pieces into smaller ones as above.

2. Light a direct-heat charcoal fire and let it burn down to medium (7 or 8 seconds to "ouch") or preheat a gas grill to medium. Position the grill rack about 6 inches above the heat source.

3. Meanwhile, dust the chicken pieces all over with the rub, using it all and patting it firmly to encourage it to adhere.

4. When the grill is ready, lay the chicken pieces on the rack. Cover and grill, turning once, until the rub is blackened in spots and the chicken has firmed slightly, about 10 minutes. Brush generously with some of the sauce, cover, and grill for 5 minutes. Continue brushing, turning, and grilling at 5-minute intervals until the sauce is used up. Grill for another 6 to 8 minutes, turning once, until the chicken is just cooked through while remaining juicy, about 30 minutes total for white meat, 35 minutes total for dark.

5. Transfer the chicken to a platter or plates, season with salt and pepper, and serve hot, warm, or at room temperature.

Rosemary Chicken with Pineapple-Orange Baste

It's almost as quick to make this easy, spicy baste as it is to open a bottle of prepared barbecue sauce, and it's far tastier. There are a few tricks to cooking bone-in chicken on the grill: Remove all visible fat, use low (or at least lower heat), move the chicken to cooler spots if flare-ups do occur, and, on charcoal grills, keep the vents closed. All this takes a little extra tending (as so much that's worth grilling does), but the succulent, flavorful results are worth it. Serve the chicken with Grilled Calabacitas Salad (page 202) and Ranchero Potato Salad with Double Olive Dressing (page 207).

SERVES 4 TO 6

1 (12-ounce) can frozen pineapple-orange juice concentrate, thawed
⅓ cup dry white wine
⅓ cup smooth honey mustard
2 tablespoons minced fresh rosemary
4 teaspoons soy sauce
2 teaspoons hot pepper sauce, such as Tabasco
2 garlic cloves, peeled and chopped
2 small (3¼-pound) chickens, or 6½ pounds chicken parts
Salt and freshly ground black pepper

SMOKING CHIP OPTION: APPLE

1. In a food processor, combine the juice concentrate, wine, honey mustard, rosemary, soy sauce, pepper sauce, and garlic. Process until smooth. Transfer the orange juice mixture to a measuring cup or a pitcher with a pouring lip.

2. If you are starting with whole chickens, cut out the chicken backbones and reserve for another purpose. Separate the chicken thighs and legs. Separate the wings from the breasts. Cut the breasts in half crosswise. You will have 20 fairly small chicken parts. If you are starting with parts, cut large pieces into smaller ones as above.

3. Meanwhile, light a direct-heat charcoal fire and let it burn down to medium (7 to 8 seconds to "ouch") or preheat a gas grill to medium. Position the rack about 6 inches above the heat source.

4. When the fire is ready, lay the chicken pieces on the rack. Cover and grill, turning once, until the chicken is golden, about 10 minutes. Baste generously with some of the sauce, cover, and continue to grill for 5 minutes. Continue grilling, basting, and turning at 5-minute intervals until the sauce is used up. Grill for another 6 to 8 minutes, turning once, until the chicken is shiny and just cooked through while remaining juicy, about 30 minutes total grilling time for white meat, 35 minutes total for dark.

5. Remove the chicken from the heat, transfer to a platter or plates, and season with salt and pepper. Serve hot, warm, or at room temperature.

Chicken on the Grill

As there are cooks who refuse to grill boneless chicken, so there are cooks who will not grill bone-in chicken. (It's a complicated world.) While a little trickier to finesse than boneless parts, bone-in, skin-on chicken is so savory and satisfying, it's worth the extra attention required. There are a few secrets to success. First, buy smaller chickens, about 3¼ pounds. (Less time on the grill, less time to burn outside before cooking inside, the most common bone-in chicken problem.) This isn't as easy as it sounds; these days, "young fryers" commonly top out at around 7 pounds, but the hunt for the right size chicken will pay off on the plate. Cut up the chickens yourself. Whole chickens cost less than parts, and when you cut up your own, you get actual anatomical pieces, not randomly sawed-up hunks of bird. Cutting the breasts, if large, in half crosswise, results in all pieces, light and dark alike, being almost of a size to come off the grill at the same time—less guesswork about doneness. I like to leave the skin on, for the deliciously crackly results, but dripping fat from the skin can cause flare-ups of flame. Avoid this by using a cooler fire and moving the chicken around on the rack to cooler spots (the edges are ideal). Spritzing water from a spray bottle can douse flames but can also douse a charcoal fire and toss ashes over everything, so proceed cautiously here. A little char, after all, is part of the essential grill taste. And, if you use a sweet glaze, don't start saucing the chicken until 10 minutes after the bird hits the rack. Partially precooking chicken in the microwave or in simmering water, then merely finishing it on the grill, is the coward's way out. Take your time, be patient and hover a little, and you'll be rewarded with chicken deliciously crisp and smoky outside, moist and tender within.

Adobo Chicken

The sweetly spiced and nicely fiery Mexican barbecue sauce known as adobo makes a satisfying and yet somewhat offbeat glaze for grilled chicken. While it looks like the familiar red American supermarket BBQ sauce, it tastes subtly exotic and is a very nice change of pace. Thin the adobo with a little frozen orange or apple juice concentrate and sweeten it if you like (it's not necessary) with a dollop of molasses. Good go-withs include Black Pot Beans (page 199) and Grilled Polenta with Green Chiles and Corn (page 213). Save any leftover chicken for use in the grill-baked adobo chicken pizza (recipe follows).

1. If you are starting with whole chickens, cut out the chicken backbones and reserve for another purpose. Separate the chicken thighs and legs. Separate the wings from the breasts. Cut the breasts in half crosswise. You will have 20 fairly small chicken parts. If you are starting with parts, cut the large pieces into smaller ones as above.

2. Meanwhile, light a direct-heat charcoal fire and let it burn down to medium (7 to 8 seconds to "ouch") or preheat a gas grill to medium. Position the rack about 6 inches above the heat source.

3. In a bowl, stir together the barbecue sauce, juice concentrate, and molasses.

4. When the grill is ready, oil the rack. Lay the chicken pieces on the rack. Cover and grill, turning once, until the chicken is golden, about 10 minutes. Brush with some of the adobo mixture, turn, cover, and grill for 5 minutes. Continue grilling, brushing and turning at 5-minute intervals, until the adobo is used up. Grill for another 6 to 8 minutes, or until the chicken is just cooked through while remaining juicy, about 30 minutes total grilling time for white meat, 35 minutes total for dark.

5. Transfer the chicken to a platter or plates and season with salt and pepper. Serve hot, warm, or at room temperature.

SERVES 4 TO 6

2 small (3¼-pound) chickens or 6½ pounds chicken parts
1½ cups Mexican Barbecue Sauce (Adobo) (page 277)
½ cup frozen orange or apple juice concentrate, thawed
1 tablespoon unsulphured molasses (optional)
Salt and freshly ground black pepper

SMOKING WOOD OPTION: MESQUITE

Chicken, Turkey, and Other Poultry

Grill-Baked Adobo Chicken
and
Blue Corn Pizza

SERVES 4 AS A MAIN COURSE,
8 AS AN APPETIZER

BLUE CORNMEAL PIZZA CRUST
1½ cups warm (105° to
   115°F) water
1 package dry yeast
2 teaspoons salt
5 tablespoons olive oil
¾ cup blue cornmeal
About 3 cups unbleached
   all-purpose flour

TOPPING
5 cups shredded leftover
   Adobo Chicken (page
   141)
½ cup Mexican Barbecue
   Sauce (Adobo) (page
   277)
½ pound shredded sharp
   cheddar cheese
½ pound shredded
   jalapeño Jack cheese
¾ cup thinly sliced green
   onions, tender tops
   included

SMOKING CHIP OPTION: MESQUITE

I first had grilled pizza at Al Forno, a spectacular restaurant in Providence, Rhode Island, but I first learned to make it from El Paso's chief food celebrity, Park Kerr. While working on a book together, we created a barbecued chicken pizza, using a grill-baking technique he had developed over several years of sweaty experimentation. It does take some hovering, but in the end it's worth it. Here is how I now make that chicken pizza, including my blue cornmeal pizza crust. Serve guests a big green salad, pull each pizza off the grill as it is ready, and enjoy a communal, sequential supper.

1. In a large bowl, whisk together the water and yeast and let stand for 5 minutes. Whisk in the salt and olive oil, then whisk in the cornmeal. Stir in about 2½ cups of the flour, until a soft dough forms. Generously flour the work surface, turn out the dough, and knead until smooth, about 5 minutes, adding additional flour if the dough is sticky. When it is smooth and elastic, coat a large bowl with the remaining oil. Form the dough into a ball and turn it in the oil to coat. Cover with a clean towel and let the dough rise until it is light and puffy, about 2 hours.

2. In a small bowl, combine the chicken and barbecue sauce and marinate at room temperature, stirring once or twice, for 1 hour.

3. Light an indirect-heat charcoal fire, banking the coals on one side of the kettle. Let it burn down to medium (7 to 8 seconds to "ouch") or preheat the front burner of a gas grill to medium. Position the rack about 6 inches from the heat source.

4. As the grill heats, divide the dough into 4 equal-size pieces. On a lightly floured surface, roll or pat one piece of dough out into a 12-inch round no more than ¼ inch thick.

5. Using a pizza peel, or a flat baking sheet dusted with additional cornmeal, or just boldly conveying the dough by hand, transfer the dough to the grill over the side of the grill that is *not* over the coals or the heat source. Cover and grill the dough until the top is puffed and the bottom is lightly marked by the rack but not at all crisp, about 4 minutes.

6. Using the peel, transfer the crust to a work surface and flip it over. Sprinkle one-fourth of each cheese evenly over the crust, leaving a ½-inch border. Spread one-fourth of the chicken over the cheese. Sprinkle with one-fourth of the onions. Return the pizza to the grill, cover, and bake, rotating the pizza once or twice on the rack to ensure even browning, until the cheese is melted, the chicken is hot, and the crust is cooked through and crisped or even lightly charred a bit, 8 to 10 minutes.

7. Transfer to a board and let rest a few minutes before cutting. Serve hot. Repeat with the remaining ingredients. (Turn the grill burners back on or add extra coals to reheat the grill if necessary, for the last two pizzas.)

Crisp Lime-Marinated Chicken Grilled Under a Brick

SERVES 4

2 young (3¼-pound) frying
chickens
1 cup fresh lime juice
8 garlic cloves, crushed
through a press
¼ cup packed light brown
sugar
Salt and freshly ground
black pepper

SMOKING CHIP OPTION: MESQUITE

This is a great argument for how good chicken grilled on the bone can be, and a fine illustration of how unfussy that can be to achieve. Modeled after a Tuscan dish, in which a butterflied chicken is grilled in a hot skillet under a weight (like a brick), the recipe produces a fragrant, slightly flattened, very crisp, and well-browned bird that is deliciously moist and tender inside—great food, and a genuine conversation piece. For a summertime feast, accompany it with Smoky Grill-Roasted Corn on the Cob (page 193) with Chipotle Mayonnaise (page 293) and Orzo, Black Bean, and Cherry Tomato Salad (page 210).

1. On a cutting board, set a chicken upright on its tail end with the back toward you. With a sharp knife, cut downward along both sides of the backbone and through the thigh joints. Reserve the backbone for another use (i.e., stock) if desired. With the knife, partially crack the breastbone from inside the chicken and then, with the palm of your hand, flatten the bird. Repeat with the second bird.

2. In a shallow nonreactive dish just large enough to hold the chickens, stir together the lime juice, garlic, and sugar. Add the chickens breast side-down, cover, and marinate at room temperature, turning several times, for 1 hour.

3. Meanwhile, light a direct-heat charcoal fire and let it burn down to medium (7 to 8 seconds to "ouch") or preheat a gas grill to medium. Position the rack about 6 inches above the heat source. Wrap 2 average-sized (3½-pound) bricks in doubled sheets of foil.

4. Lift the chickens from the marinade (reserve it) and place them on the rack, meaty sides-up. Set

the bricks atop the chickens, cover, and grill for 5 minutes. Lift the bricks, baste with some of the marinade, replace the bricks, cover, and grill for 5 minutes. Lift the bricks, baste again, turn the chickens, and replace the bricks. Cover and grill for 5 minutes. Lift the bricks, baste, turn the chickens, replace the bricks, cover, and grill for 10 minutes. Lift the bricks, baste the chickens with the last of the marinade, turn them (they should now be meaty side-down), replace the bricks, cover, and grill until the chicken skin is crisp and brown and the chicken meat at its thickest, on the thighs, is just cooked through while remaining juicy, another 10 minutes (for a total grilling time of 35 minutes). Move the chickens around on the grill at any time during the grilling process that the skin appears to be browning too quickly.

5. Transfer the chickens to a cutting board. Cut each chicken in half through the breastbone. Season with salt and pepper. Serve hot, warm, or at room temperature.

Sweet Hickory Whole Smoked Chicken

There is little work involved in smoking, and the rewards are great. Smoked turkey is relatively easy to find these days, though the quality varies, but smoked chicken is a harder thing to find, a pleasant change of pace, and reason enough to make your own. The skin is not eaten (it is too smoky and not really crisp) but the meat is succulent and sweetly perfumed by the hickory. Serve it warm, as you would any tender and juicy roast bird, or use it cold in sandwiches and salads or as the star of a hot-weather picnic.

1. Soak six 3-inch chunks of hickory wood in water for at least 24 hours.

2. Remove the giblets and any visible fat from the chicken. Rub it all over, inside and out, with the orange, squeezing the juice over the chicken as you go. Stuff the orange halves in the chicken's cavity. Set the chicken in a shallow disposable foil pan.

SERVES 4

1 large (5½-pound) chicken, brought just to room temperature
1 orange, halved

SMOKING WOOD CHUNKS: HICKORY

3. Meanwhile, ignite about 30 charcoal briquettes, preferably in a chimney starter. When the briquettes are covered with white ash and glowing orange, arrange them in a kettle grill, following the directions for indirect grilling on page 8. Drain the hickory chunks and arrange them atop the briquettes, spacing them apart. Set the grill rack in place. Set the pan with the chicken on the portion of the grill rack not over the briquettes. Cover the grill. Regulate the lower and upper vents to maintain a temperature between 230° and 250°F. (Generally, the lower vent should be about 25 percent open; the upper vent barely open, but grills vary.)

4. Smoke the chicken, rotating the pan on the grill once or twice and turning the chicken breast side-down about two-thirds through the smoking process, until the dark meat is fully cooked through while remaining juicy, about 2½ hours. Depending on your grill, you may need to ignite additional briquettes to maintain the desired temperature.

5. Discard the skin and serve the chicken hot, warm, or at room temperature.

Smoking Chicken on a Gas Grill

Chicken can also be smoked on some gas grills. Those with lava stones work best, and a grill with three separate burners is preferable to one with only two. Soak the hickory chunks as directed. Preheat one burner (in some grills, only one of the burners can operate alone; be sure to select this burner) to 250°F. Arrange the wood chunks on the lava stones and set the rack in place. Set the pan with the chicken on that portion of the rack over the cold burners. Cover the grill and lower the heat, adjusting it to maintain a steady temperature of about 250°F. Rotate the pan on the grill rack once or twice, and turn the chicken breast side-down about two-thirds through the smoking process. If you have successfully maintained the desired temperature, the chicken will be done in 2½ hours. If your grill can't maintain a temperature that low, monitor the chicken for signs of doneness and take it off when it is fully cooked but still juicy. It may be a little less smoky, simply because it has spent less time over the wood chunks. Certain grills, with v-shaped ceramic bars as part of their grilling system, are not as suitable for smoking unless they come with a separate side smoking chamber. If you use such a grill, follow the manufacturer's directions for using the side smoking chamber.

Cornish Hens with
Honeyed Margarita "Lacquer"

These little birds grill up sweetly smoky and very shiny, thanks to the honey in their margarita-derived marinade and basting sauce. (The marinade's proportions are pretty true to the classic cocktail, by the way, and it can actually be enjoyed over ice if you would like—just not after it's been on raw poultry.)

1. On a cutting board, set a hen upright on its tail end with the back toward you. With a sharp knife, cut downward along both sides of the back-bone and through the thigh joints. Repeat with the remaining hen. Reserve the backbones for another use (i.e., stock) if desired. With the knife, partially crack the breastbones from inside the hens and then, with the palm of your hand, flatten the birds. Transfer to a shallow nonreactive dish just large enough to hold the hens.

2. In a bowl, whisk together the lime juice, tequila, honey, and Triple Sec. Pour over the hens. Marinate, covered, turning once or twice, for 1 hour.

3. Meanwhile, light a direct-heat charcoal fire and let it burn down to medium (7 to 8 seconds to "ouch") or preheat a gas grill to medium. Position the grill rack about 6 inches above the heat source.

4. When the grill is ready, lightly oil the rack. Lift the hens from the marinade (reserve it) and lay them on the rack meaty side-up. Baste with some of the reserved marinade, cover, and grill for 10 minutes. Baste the birds, turn, cover, and grill for 5 minutes. Baste, turn, and grill for 10 minutes. Baste with the last of marinade, turn, and grill, moving the hens around on the rack if the skin is getting too dark, until crisp, brown, and just cooked through while remaining juicy, another 5 to 7 minutes. Total grilling time should be about 30 minutes.

5. Transfer the chicken to plates and season with salt and pepper. Serve hot or warm.

SERVES 4

4 Cornish hens
1 cup fresh lime juice
⅔ cup tequila
½ cup honey
¼ cup Triple Sec
Salt and freshly ground
   black pepper

SMOKING CHIP OPTION:
MESQUITE

Chicken, Turkey, and Other Poultry

Chipotle-Rubbed Turkey T-Bones with Salsa Verde

SERVES 4

4 teaspoons powdered
    chipotle chile
4 teaspoons granulated
    brown sugar
Salt
4 (1¼-inch-thick) bone-in
    slices of turkey breast
    (about 2 pounds)
Freshly ground black
    pepper
2 cups Salsa Verde with
    Pineapple (page 283)

SMOKING CHIP OPTION: MESQUITE

The turkey T-bone was invented by Jack McDavid, of Jack's Firehouse Restaurant in Philadelphia, I believe, and it is such a great idea, I've embraced it wholeheartedly. Imagine a fresh, bone-in turkey breast sawed crosswise into thick slices, then halved across the middle. The result is a thick steak of turkey white meat with a roughly t-shaped bone along one side—very satisfying in a knife-and-fork way and made extra juicy and flavorful by being cooked on the bone. Not a replacement for the original thing perhaps, but, for turkey, very, very good indeed. One you have the basic pattern for this recipe down, rubs, sauces, and other toppings will surely occur to you.

1. Light a direct-heat charcoal fire and let it burn down to medium-hot (5 seconds to "ouch") or pre-heat a gas grill to medium-high. Position the rack about 6 inches above the heat source.

2. Meanwhile, in a small bowl, thoroughly combine the chipotle powder, sugar, and 2 teaspoons of the salt. Dust the turkey steaks on all sides with the chipotle mixture, dividing it evenly and patting it firmly to encourage it to adhere.

3. When the grill is ready, lightly oil the rack. Lay the steaks on the rack, cover, and grill, turning once, until the steaks are nicely marked by the rack and just cooked through while remaining juicy, 8 to 9 minutes total.

4. Transfer the steaks to plates. Season with salt and pepper and serve immediately, passing the salsa at the table.

The Turkey T-Bone

Cutting the T-bones is not something easy to accomplish at home (it takes a mechanical meat saw), but the butchers I've asked to do it have always been delighted, largely, I think, because of its novelty. Pick out a small (5 or so pounds) fresh breast and describe what you want done. Save the meaty but unsteaklike trimmings for another use.

Grilled Duck Breast Fajitas
with
Mushrooms and Chiles

This is a special treat for duck-lovers and for all who would prefer using hands to utensils for eating. The oversized duck breasts, from a special breed of bird used to produce American foie gras, must be ordered by mail (see page 321), unless you live down the road from the duck farm. They are pricey, but there is little waste, and they taste terrific. They also freeze well and can be very nice to have on hand when you need a quick, casual, but still impressive meal for a few close friends. Fajitas traditionally come with flour tortillas, but these taste best, I think, on corn.

1. In a large skillet over medium heat, warm the duck fat. Add the poblanos and garlic and cook, covered, stirring occasionally, for 5 minutes. Add the mushrooms, season with ½ teaspoon salt, cover, and cook, stirring occasionally, until the mushrooms begin to give up their liquid, 8 to 9 minutes. Increase the heat to high and stir in the oregano and a generous grinding of pepper. Cook, uncovered, tossing and stirring often, until the mushroom liquid has evaporated and they are lightly browned, 4 to 5 minutes. Remove from the heat. (The mushrooms can be prepared several hours in advance. Rewarm before using.)

2. In a small bowl, stir together the chipotle powder, sugar, and 1 teaspoon of the salt. Dust the magret on all sides with the chipotle powder mixture, using it all and patting it firmly to encourage it to adhere. Set aside.

SERVES 4

3 tablespoons rendered duck fat or olive oil
3 poblano chiles, stemmed, seeded, and cut into julienne strips
4 garlic cloves, finely chopped
1 pound shiitake mushrooms, caps thinly sliced and stems discarded
Salt
2 tablespoons minced fresh oregano
Freshly ground black pepper
2 teaspoons chipotle chile powder
2 teaspoons granulated brown sugar
3 boneless magret (moulard duck breasts) (about 2½ pounds total), skin removed
16 (5-inch) yellow or blue corn tortillas
Cascabel–Roasted Garlic Salsa (page 285)

SMOKING CHIP OPTION: HICKORY

3. Wrap the tortillas tightly in several packets of foil. Preheat the oven to 400°F.

4. Light a direct-heat charcoal fire and let it burn down to medium-hot (5 seconds to "ouch") or preheat a gas grill to medium-high. Position the rack about 6 inches above the heat source.

5. When the grill is ready, set the tortillas in the oven to warm. Lightly oil the rack. Lay the magret on the rack, cover, and grill, turning once, until the breasts are nicely marked by the rack and the duck is done to your liking, about 8 minutes total for medium rare, which is how magret really should be served.

6. Transfer the duck to a cutting board and let it rest for a few minutes.

7. Carve the magret across the grain and at a slight angle to the board into thin slices. Season with salt and pepper.

8. Divide the magret and mushrooms among 4 plates and serve immediately, accompanied by the tortillas and salsa.

Note: The company that markets the magret also sells small containers of rendered duck fat. If you have some on hand (like the magret, it freezes well), this superb and flavorful sautéing medium will make the mushrooms even more delicious.

Herb-Rubbed Quail and Sausage Skewers with Beans and Salsa

Separately, grilled sausages and grilled quail are enchanting and delicious. Paired up, rubbed with a green herb-and-chile paste and grilled, they are sublime. Accompanied by spicy, smoky black beans and a good hot salsa, the sausages and little birds make a terrific plate of food—earthy and elegant at the same time.

1. Bring a saucepan of water to a simmer. Prick the sausages in several places with the tip of a knife, then add them to the simmering water. Poach the sausages in the water until they are firm but not cooked through, about 8 minutes. Drain, cool, and cut each sausage into thirds.

2. In a food processor, combine the olive oil, rosemary, sage, oregano, garlic, jalapeño, and salt. Process, stopping to scrape down the sides of the work bowl once or twice, until the mixture is fairly smooth.

3. Light a direct-heat charcoal fire and let it burn down to medium-hot (5 seconds to "ouch") or preheat a gas grill to medium-high. Position the grill rack about 6 inches above the heat source.

4. Divide the quail and sausage pieces among 4 flat metal skewers, arranging them so that the birds' wing sides and the sausages' cut sides are aligned, for maximum browning. Transfer to a sheet pan with sides. Spread the herb paste over the quail and sausage pieces.

5. When the grill is ready, lay the skewers on the rack. Cover and grill, turning twice, until the quail and sausage pieces are nicely browned and just cooked through while remaining juicy, 18 to 20 minutes total.

6. Meanwhile, heat the beans to a simmer.

Serves 4

4 sweet Italian sausage links (about 1 pound)
⅓ cup olive oil
¼ cup finely chopped fresh rosemary
¼ cup finely chopped fresh sage
¼ cup finely chopped fresh oregano
4 garlic cloves
1 fresh jalapeño, stemmed and minced
1 teaspoon salt
8 (5-ounce) farm-raised whole quail
Brothy Black Beans with Bacon and Beer (page 200)
1½ cups Chile de Arbol Salsa with Rosemary and Orange (page 288) or any hot salsa of your choice

Smoking Chip Option: Hickory

Chicken, Turkey, and Other Poultry

7. Slide the quail and sausage pieces from the skewers onto plates. Spoon the beans alongside. Top with some salsa and serve immediately, passing the remaining salsa at the table.

Note: I suggest sweet Italian sausages here primarily because of their availability. If you have access to the creative output of a gourmet sausage-maker, such as Bruce Aidells, you may find a more interesting, though still Southwest-compatible, sausage for use instead.

Carnes

Meats

Carnes
MEATS

BBQ Pork and Pineapple Skewers

Thanks to a dusting of cumin and to generous lashings of one southwestern-flavored barbecue sauce or another, these luau-sounding kebabs don't taste even remotely Hawaiian. Cut the chunks of tenderloin to the same size as much as possible, so they'll grill evenly. Good accompaniments include Ranchero Potato Salad with Double Olive Dressing (page 207), Citrus Slaw (page 212), and Texas Toast (page 217).

1. Cut the thinner, tapering third of each tenderloin off and reserve for another use. Cut the remaining thick portion of each tenderloin into 8 equal-sized chunks. Cut the pineapple into 16 chunks the same size as those of the pork. Alternate 4 pork chunks and 4 pineapple chunks on each of 4 flat metal skewers, spacing them slightly apart. Dust the pork and pineapple chunks on all sides with the cumin.

2. Meanwhile, light a direct-heat charcoal fire and let it burn down to medium-hot (5 seconds to "ouch") or preheat a gas grill to medium high. Position the rack about 6 inches above the heat source.

3. When the grill is ready, lightly oil the rack. Lay the skewers on the rack, cover, and grill for 4 minutes. Turn, cover, and grill for another 4 minutes. Generously brush the skewers with some of the barbecue sauce, turn, cover, and grill for another 4 minutes. Continue to brush the skewers with some of the sauce and turn them every 4 minutes, until the meat is crisp, well marked by the grill, and just cooked through while remaining juicy, a total grilling time of about 20 minutes.

4. Season with salt and pepper and slide the pork and pineapple chunks from the skewers onto plates. Serve hot.

SERVES 4

2 large pork tenderloins (about 2 pounds total)
½ fresh pineapple, cored and peeled
5 teaspoons freshly ground cumin (preferably from toasted seeds)
1½ cups Branding Iron Barbecue Sauce (page 279), Coffee Barbecue Sauce (page 275), or Chipotle-Peanut Barbecue Sauce (page 276)
Salt and freshly ground black pepper

SMOKING CHIP OPTION: APPLE

Meats

Is It Done?

The doneness of beef, lamb, and, to some extent, pork, is a matter of personal preference. What is certain is that no one wants to overcook an expensive cut of meat. (Undercooked meat, on the other hand, can always be returned to the grill.) The touch test used by restaurant chefs, pressing on the flesh between the base of the thumb and the forefinger and then pressing on the steak or whatever by way of comparison seems a little subjective to me. (Remember that these are the guys who also overcook or undercook your steak a goodly share of the time.) Since you're not grilling in a restaurant, you can always cut into the meat to assess doneness, or you can use an instant-read thermometer. On thicker cuts of meat, like huge steaks, chops, or pork tenderloins, the thermometer can be a valuable aid. Insert it into the meat at its thickest, avoiding bone, fat, or any stuffing. Meat is rare at 130° to 140°F, medium at 150° to 160°F and well done at 160° to 170°F. Pork tenderloins, which taper dramatically, are tricky and will be almost overcooked at the thin end while the thick end shows traces of pink. Remember that meat will continue to cook even after it comes off the grill. It's always better to err on the side of undercooking; for overcooking, there is no remedy.

Chimayo Pork Chops with Apple–Red Chile Glaze

The northern New Mexico village of Chimayo is a beautiful, magical place, with a rustic adobe sanctuary whose holy earth is said to work miracles. Also pretty wondrous are two of the area's local crops—apples and red chiles—the sweet and sweet-hot flavors of which cooks occasionally combine, as I have here, to the greater glory of both. This recipe is one of the very good reasons to have some adobo stashed in the freezer, but purchased jarred or frozen red chile paste (or your own homemade, page 305) can also be substituted. Thick-cut chops—marinated, sauced, and not grilled too long—come out moist and tender every time.

SERVES 4

1⅓ cups Mexican Barbecue Sauce (Adobo), page 277
¾ cup apple juice concentrate, thawed
Salt
4 thick (1-inch) center-cut, bone-in pork chops (about 3 pounds total)
Freshly ground black pepper

SMOKING CHIP OPTION: APPLE

1. In a shallow nonreactive dish, whisk together the barbecue sauce, juice concentrate, and ¼ teaspoon salt. Reserve ⅓ cup of the barbecue mixture. Add the chops to the remaining mixture and turn to coat. Cover and marinate, turning occasionally, for 2 hours at room temperature or overnight in the refrigerator. (Return the chops to room temperature, if chilled.)

2. Light a direct-heat charcoal fire and let it burn down to medium-hot (5 seconds to "ouch"), or preheat a gas grill to medium-high. Position the rack about 6 inches above the heat source.

3. When the grill is ready, lightly oil the rack. Lift the chops from the marinade (reserve it) and lay them on the rack. Cover and grill, turning once and basting with the marinade, until it is used up and the chops are nicely marked by the grill and done to your liking, about 9 minutes total for meat that is moist and just slightly pink at the bone.

4. Transfer the meat to plates. Season with salt and pepper. Top each chop with a dollop of the remaining ⅓ cup barbecue sauce mixture, dividing it evenly and using it all. Serve immediately.

Brined and Stuffed Double Pork Chops

SERVES 4

⅔ cup kosher salt
½ cup packed light brown
  sugar
4 center-cut double loin
  pork chops (about 4
  pounds total)
2 tablespoons unsalted
  butter
½ cup finely chopped
  onion
1 fresh jalapeño, stemmed
  and minced
1 garlic clove, minced
3 cups crumbled day-old
  cornbread (preferably
  Sour Cream Cornbread
  with Green Chiles and
  Pumpkin Seeds, page
  216)
1 large egg, beaten
¼ cup reduced-sodium
  canned chicken broth
¼ teaspoon salt
Freshly ground black
  pepper
4 teaspoons chipotle chile
  powder
4 teaspoon granulated
  brown sugar

SMOKING CHIP OPTION:
HICKORY OR APPLE

Brining pork (soaking it in a salt-and-sugar solution) transforms the meat's cell structure, rendering it tender and juicy even after grilling. The flavor is transformed, too, I think—intensified and more "porky," although not excessively salty. For this rather grand grill dish, I use double (two-bone) chops and cut a deep pocket in each, for a jalapeño-spiked cornbread stuffing. My tried-and-true chipotle rub (here made without salt, which, thanks to the brine, is not necessary) adds ruddy color and a smoky, seductive flavor. Serve the chops with Double Smoky Baked Black Beans (page 197) and Dried Apricot and Green Chile Chutney (page 304).

1. To make the brine, bring 8 cups water to a boil in a saucepan. Add the salt and sugar and stir just until dissolved. Remove from the heat and cool to room temperature. In a shallow container just large enough to hold the chops, combine them with the brine. Cover the container and refrigerate, turning the chops once or twice, for 12 hours.

2. Drain, discarding the brine. Cover the chops with fresh cold water and let stand at room temperature, turning once or twice, for 2 hours. Drain and pat dry.

3. With a thin, sharp knife, cut a deep pocket into each chop. With your fingers, gently open the pockets but do not tear the meat.

4. In a small heavy skillet over medium heat, melt the butter. Add the onion, jalapeño, and garlic. Cover and cook, stirring once or twice, until almost tender, about 6 minutes. Cool.

5. In a medium bowl, combine the cornbread, the onion mixture, egg, broth, ¼ teaspoon salt, and a generous grinding of pepper. Mix well; the stuffing should be moist but not wet. Divide the stuffing among the pockets in the chops, packing it in firmly and using it all. Secure the chops partially closed with long wooden picks, if desired.

6. In a small bowl, thoroughly mix together the chipotle powder and sugar. Sprinkle half the chipotle mixture evenly over the top sides of the chops, patting it firmly to encourage it to adhere.

7. Meanwhile, light a direct-heat charcoal fire and let it burn down to medium (7 to 8 seconds to "ouch"), or preheat a gas grill to medium. Position the rack about 6 inches above the heat source.

8. When the grill is ready, lightly oil the rack. Lay the chops rub side-down on the rack, cover, and grill for 8 minutes. Sprinkle the remaining rub over the chops, pat it in, and turn the chops. Cover and grill for another 8 minutes. Set the chops upright on their curved bony sides (the stuffing pockets will be uppermost). Cover and grill until the the stuffing is lightly browned, and the meat closest to the bone is just cooked through while remaining juicy (the brining will keep the meat slightly pink even when fully cooked), another 4 to 6 minutes.

9. Transfer the meat to plates, remove the wooden picks if you have used them, and season with pepper (no additional salt should be necessary). Serve immediately.

Note: Prepared cornmeal stuffing crumbs are not suitable here, but if you have no homemade cornbread leftovers in the refrigerator, cornbread made from a mix can be substituted.

Marinades and Bastes

When you baste meat with a marinade as it cooks, you are helping the meat to develop a delicious crust, essential for the best grill flavor. While there is a question of bacterial contamination from marinade that has been in contact with the raw meat, any potential bacterial contamination is destroyed by the heat of the grill. So my recipes require that you stop basting a few minutes before the meat is done—giving the heat of the grill enough time to work its magic. If you want to use a marinade as a table sauce, however, you should set some aside before adding the meat.

Pork Tenderloin with Mole Rapido

SERVES 4

2 teaspoons chipotle chile
  powder
2 teaspoons granulated
  brown sugar
Salt
2 pork tenderloins (about
  1½ pounds total),
  trimmed
Freshly ground black
  pepper
About 1⅓ cups Mole
  Rapido (page 271)
4 teaspoons toasted
  sesame seeds

SMOKING CHIP OPTION: MESQUITE

Since pork tenderloin is so quick and simple to grill, finding a sauce that will elevate it to greatness without actually taking longer to prepare than the meat itself is a challenge. Mole Rapido, my doctored-up sauce of dark and spicy mole poblano from a jar, is just the ticket, adding wonderfully complex flavor while taking almost no time at all to make. An easy chipotle rub adds another flavor dimension, making the pork tremendously appealing, quite an accomplishment for a dish done in well under an hour. Accompany the tenderloins with the Sweet Potato–Corn Salad (page 208) and pass warmed flour tortillas. (I like to wrap bites of well-sauced pork in the tortillas like little tacos and eat them out of hand.)

1. Light a direct-heat charcoal fire and let it burn down to medium-hot (5 seconds to "ouch") or preheat a gas grill to medium-high. Position the rack about 6 inches above the heat source.

2. In a small bowl, thoroughly mix together the chipotle powder, sugar, and 1 teaspoon salt. Sprinkle the chipotle mixture evenly over the pork tenderloins, using it all and patting it firmly into the meat to encourage it to adhere.

3. When the grill is ready, lightly oil the rack. Lay the tenderloins on the rack, cover, and grill, turning every 4 or 5 minutes, until the meat is well marked by the grill and done to your liking, about 18 minutes total for juicy, slightly pink pork. An instant-read thermometer inserted into the center of the meat should read 140° to 150°F.

4. Meanwhile, heat the mole just to a simmer.

5. Transfer the meat to a cutting board and let it rest for a few minutes.

6. Carve the tenderloins across the grain and at a slight angle to the cutting board into thin slices. Season with salt and pepper.

7. Arrange the slices on plates. Drizzle generously with the sauce, sprinkle the sesame seeds over all, and serve immediately.

Note: Toast sesame seeds in a small, heavy skillet over low heat, stirring often, until golden brown, 8 to 10 minutes. This may be easier if you toast more than the quantity of seeds called for in this recipe. Store the extra seeds airtight and use as needed. You may also use the sesame seeds untoasted, although they will not be as flavorful or colorful.

Grill-Smoked Pork Loin with Garlicky Sweet Sage Rub

This loin, brined to keep it moist and tender during smoking, is good as a warm entrée, teamed, for example, with Sweet Potato–Corn Salad with Honey Mustard Dressing (page 208) and Double-Smoky Baked Black Beans (page 197). It can also be enjoyed at room temperature as an appetizer: Slice it paper-thin and serve with a dollop of Dried Apricot and Green Chile Chutney (page 304). Or, use it as the filling for a sandwich like the torta on page 72, or on a sandwich of your own devising, preferably one including plenty of Roasted Garlic Aioli (page 294).

1. Soak six 3-inch hickory, apple, oak, or pecan wood chunks in water for at least 24 hours.

2. To make the brine, bring 8 cups water to a boil in a medium saucepan. Add the salt and sugar and stir until just dissolved. Cool to room temperature. In a shallow container, combine the brine and pork. Cover and refrigerate, turning once or twice, for 12 hours.

3. Drain, discarding the brine. Cover the loin with fresh cold water and let stand at room temperature for 2 hours. Drain and pat dry. Transfer

SERVES 6 TO 8

⅔ cup kosher salt
½ cup packed light brown sugar
1 center-cut boneless pork loin roast (about 4 pounds)
Leaves and tender stems from 2 medium bunches fresh sage
4 garlic cloves, coarsely chopped
2 tablespoons olive oil
2 teaspoons granulated brown sugar
1 teaspoon freshly ground black pepper

SMOKING WOOD CHUNKS:
HICKORY, APPLE, OAK, OR PECAN

the loin to a shallow disposable foil pan just large enough to hold it.

4. In a food processor, combine the sage, garlic, olive oil, brown sugar, and pepper. Process, stopping several times to scrape down the sides of the work bowl, until a rough green paste is formed. Spread the paste over the top of the pork loin.

5. Meanwhile, ignite about 48 charcoal briquettes, preferably in a chimney starter. When the briquettes are covered with white ash and glowing orange, arrange them in a kettle grill following the directions for indirect grilling on page 8. Drain the wood chunks and arrange them atop the briquettes, spacing them apart. Set the grill rack in place. Set the pan with the pork on the portion of the grill rack not over the briquettes. Cover. Regulate the lower and upper vents to maintain a temperature between 230° and 250°F. (Generally, the lower vent should be about 25 percent open; the upper vent barely open, but grills vary.)

6. Smoke, rotating the position of the pan on the rack once, for about 2 hours, or until an instant-read thermometer inserted into the center of the roast registers 170°F. The meat will be delicately smoky, juicy and tender but still slightly pink (due to the brine).

7. Transfer the meat to a cutting board and let it rest for a few minutes.

8. Slice the meat thin. Serve hot, warm, or at room temperature.

Smoked Pork Shoulder Adobo

The most seductive cut of meat for slow smoking has to be the pork shoulder. Well-marbled
with fat, it cooks up rich and tender, its naturally sweet flavor the perfect contrast to the sharp
wood smoke. This recipe, a hybrid of Tex-Mex and
Mexican methods, with a little touch of Carolina
barbecue tossed in, produces enough smoked pork
to transform into barbecued soft pork tacos, plus
extra to stash in the freezer for another meal. You
can use any barbecue sauce in the book, even resort
to bottled if you must, but the deeply flavorful, red
chile–based Mexican barbecue sauce called adobo
makes for sublime eating.

1. Soak 6 to 8 hickory or oak wood chunks in
water for at least 24 hours.

2. Let the pork roast come to room temperature. In a medium bowl, mix together the chile
powder, pepper, sugar, garlic powder, and salt.
Sprinkle it evenly over the pork roast on all sides,
patting it firmly to encourage it to adhere. Transfer
the pork to a shallow disposable foil pan just large
enough to hold it.

3. Meanwhile, ignite about 48 charcoal briquettes, preferably in a chimney starter. When the
briquettes are covered with white ash and glowing
orange, arrange them in a kettle grill following
the directions for indirect grilling on page 8. Drain
the wood chunks and arrange them atop the
briquettes, spacing them apart. Set the grill rack
in place. Set the pan with the pork on the portion
of the grill rack not over the briquettes. Cover.
Regulate the lower and upper vents to maintain a
temperature between 230° and 250°F. (Generally,
the lower vent should be about 25 percent open;
the upper vent barely open, but grills vary.)

SERVES 6

1 bone-in pork butt roast
  (about 6½ pounds)
¼ cup ancho chile powder
1 tablespoon freshly
  ground black pepper
1 tablespoon granulated
  brown sugar
1 teaspoon garlic powder
1 teaspoon salt
1 cup beer
½ cup Mexican Barbecue
  Sauce (Adobo) (page
  277), plus additional
  sauce for use at the
  table
12 (10-inch) flour tortillas
Guacamole (page 21)
About 1 cup chopped
  onion

SMOKING WOOD CHUNKS:
HICKORY OR OAK

Meats

4. Smoke for about 2 hours, rotating the position of the pan on the rack once.

5. After the pork has smoked for 1½ hours, position a rack in the lower third of the oven and preheat to 350°F. When the roast has smoked for 2 hours, transfer it to a large piece of doubled aluminum foil. Partially enclose the pork in the foil and transfer to a baking sheet. Pour the beer over the pork and seal the foil around it tightly. Set the baking sheet in the oven and cook until the pork is very tender and falling off the bone, about 3 hours.

Remove from the oven and cool to room temperature. (The pork can be used now or can be covered and refrigerated for up to 3 days or frozen for up to 1 month.)

6. Preheat or adjust the oven temperature to 375°F.

7. Cut several thick slices from the pork. Remove any visible fat and bone and roughly chop enough meat to yield 6 cups. Stir in ½ cup of the barbecue sauce. Wrap the meat mixture tightly in a packet of foil, set it in the oven, and bake until hot and steaming, about 25 minutes.

8. Wrap the tortillas tightly in 2 foil packets. Shortly before you estimate the meat will be hot, set the first foil packet in the oven.

9. To serve, divide the heated meat among 4 plates. Pass warmed tortillas, guacamole, onions, and additional adobo at the table, encouraging guests to fold the various components into small tortilla pieces like soft tacos. Set the second packet of tortillas in to heat while consuming the first.

Slow-Grilled Country Spareribs with Branding Iron Barbecue Sauce

This recipe gives the blueprint for grilling lusciously meaty country ribs, whether you use a homemade or purchased sauce. They take a long, slow time on the grill (but no fussy precooking or other kitchen tricks). Cooks who stay patient will be rewarded with meat that is succulent and just falling off the bone. Smoky Grill-Roasted Corn on the Cob (page 193) with Chipotle Mayonnaise (page 293) and Black-Eyed Pea Salad with Sweet Country Ham and Jalapeño Dressing (page 205) are ideal accompaniments.

1. Light a direct-heat charcoal fire and let it burn down to medium (7 or 8 seconds to "ouch") or preheat a gas grill to medium. Position the grill rack about 6 inches above the heat source.

2. When the grill is ready, lay the ribs on the rack. Cover and grill for 20 minutes. Turn, cover, and grill for another 20 minutes. Brush generously with some of the sauce, turn, cover, and grill for 5 minutes. Continue grilling, brushing the ribs with sauce and turning them every 5 minutes, until the sauce is used up and the ribs are very tender, a total cooking time of about 1 hour.

3. Remove from the grill, season with salt and pepper, and serve, accompanied by the extra sauce.

SERVES 6 TO 8

5 pounds thick-cut bone-in pork country spareribs, at room temperature
2 cups Branding Iron Barbecue Sauce (page 279), plus additional sauce for serving
Salt and freshly ground black pepper

SMOKING CHIP OPTION: HICKORY

Baby Back Ribs
with
Chipotle-Peanut Barbecue Sauce

SERVES 2 TO 4

*2 sides baby back ribs
(about 4 pounds)
Salt and freshly ground
black pepper
2½ cups Chipotle-Peanut
Barbecue Sauce (page
276)*

SMOKING CHIP OPTION: HICKORY

In my experience, the quantity of baby back ribs I can eat is directly proportional to the number of witnesses present, hence the range of possible servings given above. (Plus, witnesses always want some ribs, too.) This recipe is really my simple blueprint for grilling ribs (it's one of the few times I precook a grill ingredient). The smoky, peanutty barbecue sauce is particularly delicious, but Coffee Barbecue Sauce (page 275) and Branding Iron Barbecue Sauce (page 279) will also give terrific results.

1. Position a rack in the middle of the oven and preheat to 400°F.

2. Season the ribs lightly with salt and pepper. Tightly wrap each side of ribs in heavy-duty aluminum foil. Set the rib packets on a baking sheet and set the sheet in the oven. Bake until the ribs are very tender, about 1¼ hours. Let the ribs cool to room temperature sealed in the foil. Discard any juices from the packets. (The ribs can be prepared to this point up to 1 day in advance. Wrap tightly and refrigerate. Return to room temperature.)

3. Cut each side of ribs between the bones into thirds.

4. Light a direct-heat charcoal fire and let it burn down to medium (7 to 8 seconds to "ouch") or preheat a gas grill to medium. Position the rack about 6 inches above the heat source. If desired, reserve about ⅔ cup of the sauce for use at the table.

5. When the grill is ready, lay the rib sections on the rack. Cover and grill for 5 minutes. Brush the ribs with some of the remaining sauce, turn, cover, and grill for another 5 minutes. Repeat, turning and brushing the ribs at 4-minute intervals, until they are well-heated through, crisp, and generously glazed with the sauce, about 25 minutes total. Move the ribs to cooler spots on the grill if flare-ups occur.

6. Transfer the ribs to plates and serve hot or warm. Pass the reserved sauce at the table.

Pepper-Rubbed Beef Ribs
with
Coffee Barbecue Sauce

Beef ribs satisfy like pork ribs, only more so. With layered flavors of heat and sweet, these meaty morsels come off the grill looking rather like caveman fare—just the right tone to strike to please certain diners (and you surely know who they are). Serve the ribs with Heirloom Bean Salad (page 203) and Sweet Texas Slaw (page 212).

SERVES 4

4 sides beef baby back ribs
  (about 8 pounds)
3½ tablespoons Black
  Pepper Rub (page 266)
2 cups Coffee Barbecue
  Sauce (page 275)

SMOKING CHIP OPTION: HICKORY

1. Position racks in the upper and lower thirds of the oven, and preheat the oven to 400°F.

2. Tightly wrap each side of ribs in a separate foil packet. Lay the rib packets on two baking sheets. Set the sheets in the oven and bake, exchanging the position of the sheets on the racks from top to bottom and from front to back at the halfway point, until the meat is tender, about 1 hour and 40 minutes. Cool the ribs in the foil packets to room temperature. (The ribs can be prepared to this point a day ahead if desired. Remove the ribs from the packets, rewrap tightly in foil or plastic and refrigerate. Return to room temperature before proceeding.)

3. Light a direct-heat charcoal fire and let it burn down to medium (7 to 8 seconds to "ouch") or preheat a gas grill to medium. Position the grill rack about 6 inches above the heat source.

4. Meanwhile, cut the ribs into grilling portions. With a thin, sharp knife, cut alongside every other rib bone, resulting in some bones with no meat (discard these) and others with generous portions of meat on both sides. Arrange the latter on a sheet pan and scatter the pepper rub evenly over both sides of the ribs, using it all and patting to encourage it to adhere.

5. When the grill is ready, lay the ribs on the rack. Cover and grill, turning the ribs every 3 minutes and moving them around on the rack in case of flare-ups, until they are crisp, heated through, and sizzling, 12 to 15 minutes total.

6. Transfer the ribs to plates. Drizzle the ribs with some of the barbecue sauce (for color and effect) and serve immediately, passing the remaining sauce at the table.

Arracheras
with
Crunchy Vegetable Garnish

SERVES 4 TO 6

2 large fresh jalapeños
4 tablespoons olive oil
4 tablespoons fresh lime
    juice
4 garlic cloves, chopped
2 small skirt steaks,
    preferably prime grade
    (about 2 pounds total),
    well trimmed
12 (10-inch) flour tortillas
4 cups finely shredded
    green cabbage
8 large radishes, trimmed
    and thinly sliced
3 green onions, trimmed
    and sliced
¼ cup finely chopped
    cilantro
Salt
½ teaspoon sugar
Freshly ground black
    pepper
2 cups Cantina Red Table
    Sauce (page 290)

SMOKING CHIP OPTION: MESQUITE

Before you can appreciate (or even really understand) the fancied up version of a classic dish, it's good to be familiar with the original. Here is the simple Mexican combination of smoky grilled skirt steak and tart vegetable slaw, wrapped into soft warm tortillas, which after several generations of restaurant overachievement became fajitas, Tex-Mex style. Despite my general culinary rule that more is more, this rendition has its elemental and deeply satisfying charms. (To get even further back to basics, skip the slaw and just slather the meat with plenty of salsa before wrapping and eating.)

1. Stem and chop 1 jalapeño. In a small food processor or blender, combine the jalapeño, 2 tablespoons of the olive oil, 2 tablespoons of the lime juice, and the garlic. Puree until smooth. In a shallow nonreactive dish, spread the garlic mixture over both sides of the steaks. Cover and marinate at room temperature for 2 hours, or in the refrigerator overnight. (Return the steaks to room temperature if chilled.)

2. Position a rack in the middle of the oven and preheat to 400°F. Wrap the tortillas tightly in 3 foil packets of 4 tortillas each.

3. Stem and mince the remaining jalapeño. In a medium bowl, toss together the cabbage, radishes, green onions, jalapeño, the remaining 2 tablespoons olive oil, the remaining 2 tablespoons lime juice, the cilantro, ¾ teaspoon salt, the sugar, and a generous grinding of pepper. Adjust the seasoning. Let stand, stirring once or twice, for up to 30 minutes.

4. Meanwhile, light a direct-heat charcoal fire and let it burn down to hot (3 seconds to "ouch") or preheat a gas grill to high. Position the rack about 6 inches above the heat source.

5. When the grill is ready, put the packets of tortillas in the oven to warm. Lay the steaks on the rack. Cover and grill, turning once and basting with any garlic mixture left in the dish (there won't be much), until the steaks are done to your liking, about 10 minutes for medium rare.

6. Transfer the meat to a cutting board and let it rest for 5 minutes.

7. Carve the steaks across the grain and at an angle to the cutting board into thin slices. Season with salt and pepper.

8. Serve the meat on heated plates, accompanied by the cabbage mixture, the tortillas, and the salsa. Encourage guests to tear off small sections of tortilla and use them to enclose and roll up meat, slaw, and salsa in proportions they like.

Fiesta Beef Fajitas with All the Trimmings

SERVES 6 TO 8

¼ cup unsweetened
    pineapple juice
¼ cup fresh lime juice
4 tablespoons olive oil
8 garlic cloves, coarsely
    chopped
2 fresh jalapeños,
    stemmed and chopped
1 tablespoon packed dark
    brown sugar
1 tablespoon soy sauce
1 tablespoon
    Worcestershire sauce
2 skirt steaks, preferably
    prime grade (about
    2¼ pounds total)
16 to 18 (10-inch) flour
    tortillas
2 medium-large onions,
    thinly sliced
3 bell peppers, preferably
    1 each of red, yellow
    and green, stemmed,
    cored, and cut into
    julienne strips
Salt
Freshly ground black
    pepper
Guacamole (page 21) or
    Avocado-Tomatillo
    Salsa (page 284)
2½ cups Cantina Red
    Table Sauce (page 290)
    or Cascabel–Roasted
    Garlic Salsa (page 285)

For a party on your plate, this is truly the way to go. Communal, messy, and completely self-indulgent, these kitchen-sink fajitas are as big and bold as the Lone Star State itself. For the true carnivore, the sautéed vegetable accompaniment is more than a little optional, but most people who've enjoyed fajitas in a restaurant lately are going to feel cheated if you don't serve up a sizzling pile of onions and peppers alongside. Others—die-hard meat-eaters—can just think of the veg as parsley—pretty, but not actually for eating.

1. In a food processor, combine the pineapple juice, lime juice, 2 tablespoons of the olive oil, 4 garlic cloves, the jalapeños, sugar, soy sauce, and Worcestershire sauce. Process until smooth.

2. In a shallow nonreactive dish, pour the pureed mixture over the steaks. Cover and marinate, turning occasionally, for 3 hours at room temperature or overnight in the refrigerator. (Return the steaks to room temperature if chilled.)

3. Position a rack in the middle of the oven and preheat to 400°F. Wrap the tortillas tightly in 4 foil packets of 4 to 6 tortillas each.

4. In a large skillet over medium heat, warm the remaining 2 tablespoons olive oil. Add the remaining 4 garlic cloves and cook uncovered, stirring once or twice without browning, for 5 minutes. Add the onions and bell peppers and season with ¾ teaspoon salt and ½ teaspoon pepper. Increase the heat to high and cook, tossing and stirring occasionally, until the vegetables are lightly browned while retaining some crunch, about 5 minutes. Remove from the heat and keep warm.

5. Meanwhile, light a direct-heat charcoal fire and let it burn down to hot (3 seconds to "ouch")

or preheat a gas grill to high. Position the rack about 6 inches above the heat source.

6. When the grill is ready, put the packets of tortillas in the oven. Lift the steaks from the marinade (reserve it) and lay them on the rack. Cover and grill, turning once and basting with the reserved marinade, until the steaks are done to your liking, about 10 minutes for medium rare.

7. Transfer the meat to a cutting board and let it rest for 5 minutes.

8. Carve the steaks across the grain and at an angle to the cutting board into thin slices. Season with salt and pepper.

9. Serve the meat on heated plates, accompanied by the tortillas, guacamole, sautéed vegetables, and salsa. Encourage guests to tear off small sections of tortilla and use them to enclose and roll up meat, guacamole, vegetables, and salsa in proportions they like.

Note: Because the salsa is a lesser player among the crowd of embellishments, a good, purchased salsa can easily be substituted here, without reducing the quality of the fajitas at all.

Slow and Smoky Beef Brisket
from the Grill

SERVES 8, WITH LEFTOVERS

1 packer-trimmed whole
  beef brisket, about 10
  pounds
14 tablespoons (4 batches)
  Quick Red Rub (page
  266)
1 (12-ounce) bottle beer

SMOKING WOOD CHUNKS:
HICKORY OR OAK

Though this is technically a grill book, it's hard
not to occasionally celebrate a few of the other
things the grill can do, chief among them
smoking. This recipe, like the one for pork shoulder
on page 165, is divided into two parts. First, the
meat smokes and partially cooks on the grill, then
gets moistened with beer, wrapped in foil, and
slow-finished in the oven until falling-off-the-bone
tender. Slice the finished brisket, slather it with
Branding Iron Barbecue Sauce (page 279), and
serve it with sides that recall its smokeshack
origins—Sweet Texas Slaw (page 212), Double-
Smoky Baked Black Beans (page 197), and Plain
Cornbread (page 215).

1. Soak 6 to 8 hickory or oak wood chunks in
water for at least 24 hours.

2. Let the brisket come to room temperature.
Sprinkle the rub evenly over the brisket on all sides,
patting it firmly to encourage it to adhere. Transfer
the meat to a shallow disposable foil pan just large
enough to hold it.

3. Meanwhile, ignite about 48 charcoal briquettes, preferably in a chimney starter. When
the briquettes are covered with white ash and
glowing orange, arrange them in a kettle grill following the directions for indirect grilling on page
8. Drain the wood chunks and arrange them atop
the briquettes, spacing them apart. Set the grill rack
in place. Set the pan with the pork on the portion
of the grill rack not over the briquettes. Cover.
Regulate the lower and upper vents to maintain a
temperature between 230° and 250°F. (Generally,
the lower vent should be about 25 percent open;
the upper vent barely open, but grills vary.)

About Briskets

I find whole, untrimmed briskets (the packer's cut) in many supermarkets, but depending on where you live, you may need to order it specially from the butcher. It's the complete hunk of meat, with all its fat intact—necessary for proper succulence, though much of it cooks away. The brisket will come conveniently sealed in heavy plastic wrap, which will allow you to store it, well-refrigerated, for at least 2 weeks, giving you plenty of time to invite a crowd over for the big feast.

4. Smoke, rotating the position of the pan on the rack once, for 2 hours for moderately smoky meat, 3 hours for very smoky meat.

5. About 30 minutes from the estimated end of the smoking period, position a rack in the lower third of the oven and preheat to 350°F. When the brisket has smoked to the level you desire, transfer it to a large piece of doubled aluminum foil. Partially enclose the brisket in the foil and transfer to a baking sheet. Pour the beer over the pork and seal the foil around it tightly. Set the baking sheet in the oven and cook until the brisket is very tender and falling off the bone, 2 to 3 hours, depending on how long it spent being smoked.

6. Remove the brisket from the oven. Let the meat rest in its cooking juices for 20 minutes.

7. Transfer the brisket to a cutting board, discarding any juices and fat remaining in the foil packet. Cut away any obvious fat, and slice it thickly across the grain. Or cool the meat to room temperature, cover, and refrigerate for up to 3 days or freeze for up to 1 month. (Rewarm chilled brisket by slicing it, then enclosing tightly in foil and warming it in a 350°F oven until steamy hot, about 25 minutes.)

Peppery Poblano-Stuffed Rib Eye Steaks

SERVES 4

4 *fresh poblano chiles*
4 *large, thick (1½-inch) rib eye steaks (about 3 pounds total)*
4 *garlic cloves, crushed through a press*
Salt and freshly ground black pepper
⅔ *cup Southwestern Herb and Spice Butter (page 299), at room temperature*

SMOKING WOOD OPTION: HICKORY

There's no steak quite like a grilled rib eye, at least in my book. Here this Cadillac of all steaks gets stuffed with poblanos, easily the aristocrat of chiles. Together the rich, meaty steak and spicy, meaty chile make a combination that's hard to beat. And never content to leave well enough alone, I've also added a compound butter to melt luxuriously over all. For maximum tenderness as well as flavor, buy well-marbled, prime beef for this recipe. Lesser grades of rib eye will be as tasty, but on the chewy side.

1. In the open flame of a gas burner, under a preheated broiler, or on a hot grill rack, roast the poblanos, turning them occasionally, until the peels are lightly but evenly charred, 8 to 10 minutes total. Transfer to a paper bag, close the bag, and steam the chiles until cool. Rub away the burnt peel, and stem and seed the chiles. (The poblanos can be roasted up to 1 day ahead. Wrap well and refrigerate, returning them to room temperature before proceeding.)

2. With a sharp knife, cut a pocket into each steak (the butcher will do this if asked). Open the poblanos out flat and cut each into 2 pieces that will fit in the pockets in the steaks. Spread the garlic evenly over the poblano pieces. Season lightly with salt and pepper. Tuck two garlic-coated poblano slices into each steak pocket and press gently to close. (The steaks can be stuffed several hours before grilling. Cover and hold at room temperature.)

3. Light a direct-heat charcoal fire and let it burn down to medium-hot (5 seconds to "ouch"), or preheat a gas grill to medium-high. Position the grill rack about 6 inches above the heat source.

4. When the grill is ready, lay the steaks on the rack. Cover and grill, turning once, until the steaks are done to your liking, about 8 minutes total for rare.

5. Remove the steaks from the heat, season with salt and pepper, and spread the butter over the steaks. Serve immediately.

Grilled Porterhouse Steaks with Roquefort–Toasted Pecan Butter

Even a great steak can pall after a while, which is why I offer the choice of splitting these monster porterhouses among four diners. (There is a nutritional angle to be considered as well, I guess, but you know what that is and we needn't go into it any further here.) Should you decide to subdivide, rather than try to grill a thin steak properly—never very successful—it's always preferable to select the thickest you can find and slice it for serving after it's cooked. Such a steak is then properly seared outside, for maximum flavor, while remaining moist and juicy within.

1. Light a direct-heat charcoal fire and let it burn down to medium-hot (5 seconds to "ouch") or preheat a gas grill to medium-high. Position the grill rack about 6 inches above the heat source.

2. When the grill is ready, lay the steaks on the rack. Cover and grill, turning once, until the steaks are well browned and done to your liking, about 9 minutes total for very rare.

3. Transfer the steaks to a cutting board and let them rest for a few minutes.

4. To serve whole, transfer the meat to plates, spread the butter over each steak and serve immediately. To divide the steaks among four diners, cut the bones out of the steaks with a sharp knife. Carve the meat across the grain and at a slight angle to the cutting board into thin slices. Arrange the slices on heated plates (this is especially important with very rare steak, which will not even be warm inside) and season lightly with salt. Spread the butter over the steak and serve immediately.

SERVES 2 TO 4

4 (1¼-inch-thick) porter-
house steaks, preferably
prime grade (about 3½
pounds total), at room
temperature
Salt
⅔ cup Roquefort–Toasted
Pecan Butter (page
302), at room
temperature

SMOKING CHIP OPTION: HICKORY

Spice-Rubbed T-Bones

SERVES 4

4 (1¼-inch-thick) T-bone steaks, preferably prime grade, at room temperature
3½ tablespoons Quick Red Rub (page 266)
⅔ cup Chile de Arbol, Grilled Green Onion, and Sun-Dried Tomato Butter (page 303), at room temperature

The average T-bone is not quite as massive as the average porterhouse, and so I typically serve each person a whole steak. If you prefer to subdivide, however, consider serving three steaks to four diners, rather than two to four. Not enough steak can make people cranky.

1. Light a direct-heat charcoal fire and let it burn down to medium-hot (5 seconds to "ouch") or preheat a gas grill to medium-high. Position the grill rack about 6 inches above the heat source.

2. Meanwhile, dust the steaks with the rub (it will not coat them heavily), patting to encourage it to adhere.

3. When the grill is ready, lay the steaks on the rack. Cover and grill, turning once, until the steaks are well browned and cooked to your liking, about 9 minutes total for very rare.

4. Transfer the steaks to heated plates, spread the butter on top of the steaks, and serve immediately.

Chipotle-Rubbed Filet Mignon with Bourbon-Mustard Sauce

Beef and bourbon—a time-tested manly combination. Here the duo appears as a tender but subtle fillet, sitting in a puddle of bourbon-spiked mustard cream sauce—easy, but restaurant elegant. A quick little chipotle rub adds additional firepower to the plate. Serve the steak with Portobello Mushroom and Bell Pepper Salad with Rosemary Vinaigrette (page 201) and (naturally) Texas Toast (page 217).

1. Light a direct-heat charcoal fire and let it burn down to medium-hot (5 seconds to "ouch") or preheat a gas grill to medium-high. Position the rack about 6 inches above the heat source.

2. In a small bowl, thoroughly combine the chipotle powder, sugar, and 2 teaspoons salt. Sprinkle half the chipotle mixture over the tops of the steaks, dividing it evenly and patting it firmly into the meat to encourage it to adhere.

3. When the grill is ready, lightly oil the rack. Invert the steaks onto the rack, rub side-down. Cover and grill for 5 minutes. Sprinkle the remaining chipotle mixture over the steaks, dividing it evenly and patting it firmly into the meat. Turn the steaks, cover, and grill until the meat is done to your liking, another 4 minutes or so for rare fillets.

4. Transfer the meat to plates. The bacon should be cooked and edible, but if it is not, remove and discard it. Season the steaks with salt and pepper. Spoon the bourbon sauce around the steaks, dividing it evenly and using it all. Serve immediately.

Note: You should be able to purchase fillet steaks already wrapped in bacon. But if not, you can wrap the steaks with standard-cut bacon yourself, and secure with toothpicks.

SERVES 4

4 teaspoons chipotle chile powder

4 teaspoons granulated brown sugar

Salt

4 (1¼-inch-thick) bacon-wrapped fillet steaks (about 3 pounds total) (see Note)

Freshly ground black pepper

1⅓ cup Bourbon-Mustard Sauce (page 274), heated just to a simmer

SMOKING CHIP OPTION: HICKORY

Marinated Flank Steak with Cilantro-Parsley Vinaigrette

SERVES 4 TO 6

2 tablespoons olive oil
1 tablespoon sherry wine
    vinegar
1 garlic clove, crushed
    through a press
½ teaspoon dried oregano,
    crumbled
½ teaspoon freshly ground
    cumin (preferably from
    toasted seeds)
Freshly ground black
    pepper
1¾-pound flank steak,
    preferably prime grade
Salt
⅔ cup Cilantro-Parsley
    Vinaigrette (page 298)

SMOKING CHIP OPTION: MESQUITE

Short-term marinating does little for flank steak except coat the outside with liquid that caramelizes to a tasty brown crust. Long-term marinating, on the other hand, can give the meat a pickled flavor and make it mushy, rather than tender. My preference here, as always with flank steak, is to marinate it no longer than is convenient to whatever else I am doing in the kitchen, and to grill it hot and briefly—only long enough to render it rare. This method results in tender, juicy, and flavorful meat that tastes like meat, not marinade. The thick and deliciously herbal green vinaigrette that is drizzled over the steak after it is sliced is a southwestern version of the Argentine classic, chimichurri.

1. In a shallow nonreactive dish, stir together the oil, vinegar, garlic, oregano, cumin, and ½ teaspoon pepper. Add the steak and let it marinate at room temperature, turning occasionally, for up to 2 hours.

2. Meanwhile, light a direct-heat charcoal fire and let it burn down to hot (3 seconds to "ouch") or preheat a gas grill to high. Position the rack about 6 inches above the heat source.

3. When the grill is ready, lift the steak from the marinade (reserve it) and lay the steak on the rack. Cover and grill, turning once and basting occasionally with the marinade, until the steak is done to your liking, about 9 minutes for rare, which is recommended.

4. Transfer the steak to a cutting board and let it rest for 5 minutes.

5. Carve the steak across the grain and at a slight angle to the cutting board into very thin slices. Season to taste with salt and pepper and arrange the steak slices on heated plates. Serve immediately, passing the vinaigrette at the table.

Sherry-Marinated
Lamb and Mushroom Kebabs

Savory and satisfying, these kebabs, with their simple marinade, let the flavor of the lamb shine through. If you like tomatoes with your shish kebab, don't mingle them on the same skewers with the lamb and mushrooms, or they'll overcook. Instead, slide large cherry tomatoes onto separate skewers, brush them with some of the marinade (or just a little roasted garlic oil) and grill them alongside the lamb until heated through and juicy but not bursting, about 4 minutes total.

1. In a shallow nonreactive dish, whisk together the sherry, oil, sugar, garlic, chile powder, cumin, oregano, and ½ teaspoon pepper. Add the lamb, cover, and marinate, turning occasionally, at room temperature for 2 hours or overnight in the refrigerator. (Return the lamb to room temperature if chilled.)

2. Light a direct-heat charcoal fire and let it burn down to medium-hot (5 seconds to "ouch), or preheat a gas grill to medium-high. Position the rack about 6 inches above the heat source.

3. Lift the lamb cubes from the marinade (reserve it) and divide them and the cremini among 4 flat metal skewers, alternating meat and mushrooms.

4. When the grill is ready, lay the lamb skewers on the rack. Cover and grill, turning once or twice and basting the lamb and the mushrooms with the reserved marinade, until it is used up. Continue grilling until the lamb is done to your liking, about 8 minutes total for rare meat.

5. Remove the skewers from the grill and season with salt and pepper. If you like the idea, serve the lamb and mushrooms on the skewers on plates (warning guests the metal will be hot). Or, using the tines of a fork, slide the lamb and mushrooms off the skewers onto the plates. Either way, serve immediately.

SERVES 4

½ cup dry sherry
3 tablespoons olive oil
3 tablespoons packed
    dark brown sugar
4 garlic cloves, crushed
    through a press
4 teaspoons medium-hot
    unblended chile powder
    (preferably from
    Chimayo)
2 teaspoons freshly
    ground cumin (prefer-
    ably from toasted seeds)
2 teaspoons dried
    oregano, crumbled
Freshly ground black
    pepper
2 pounds lamb sirloin, in
    well-trimmed 2-inch
    cubes
12 medium-large cremini
    (brown) mushrooms,
    stems trimmed flat with
    the caps
Salt

SMOKING CHIP OPTION: MESQUITE

Lamb Chop and Potato Skewers with Red Wine Adobo

SERVES 4

Salt

16 very small (1-inch) red-skinned potatoes, trimmed

¾ cup Mexican Barbecue Sauce (Adobo) (page 277)

¾ cup dry red wine

4 garlic cloves, crushed through a press

12 well-trimmed loin lamb chops (about 3 pounds total)

Freshly ground black pepper

SMOKING CHIP OPTION: MESQUITE

Grilled on a skewer and served that way as well, lamb chops and potatoes automatically become something a little more festive: Skewered food is just more fun than the unskewered kind. This also makes things easier for the grill chef, who simply has fewer things to get onto and off the fire. A touch of fragrant mesquite smoke and a glazing with the richly flavored Mexican barbecue sauce called adobo complete a very satisfying picture. Even in these days of casual dining, you may need to (and should) give guests permission to pick up and gnaw on the savory bones.

1. Over high heat, bring a medium pot of salted water to a boil. Add the potatoes and cook uncovered, stirring occasionally, until the potatoes are tender, about 12 minutes. Drain and cool.

2. In a shallow nonreactive dish, whisk together the barbecue sauce, wine, and garlic. Add the lamb chops, cover, and marinate, turning them once or twice, for 1 hour at room temperature or overnight in the refrigerator. (Return the chops to room temperature if chilled.)

3. Light a direct-heat charcoal fire and let it burn down to medium-hot (5 seconds to "ouch") or preheat a gas grill to medium-high. Position the rack about 6 inches above the heat source.

4. Lift the chops from the marinade (reserve it) and divide them and the potatoes among 4 flat metal skewers, alternating the meat and potatoes.

5. When the grill is ready, lightly oil the rack. Lay the skewers on the rack, cover, and grill, turning once and basting the chops and potatoes with the reserved marinade, until they are lightly marked by the grill and the meat is done to your liking, about 9 minutes total for medium-rare lamb.

6. Transfer the skewers to plates (or remove the chops and potatoes and arrange them on plates), season with salt and pepper, and serve immediately.

Loin Lamb Chops with Blackberry-Habanero Glaze

This dish's terrific combination of flavors resulted from a refrigerator clean-out session in which a couple of ungrilled chops got marinated in leftover blackberry salsa (which was first cooked a little to mellow and mingle its flavors). The result was so appealing and tasty that I now make it on purpose. Good accompaniments include Heirloom Bean Salad (page 203) and Smoky Grill-Roasted Corn on the Cob (page 193) with Chipotle Mayonnaise (page 293).

SERVES 4

2 tablespoons corn oil
1¼ cups Blackberry Salsa
  (page 282)
2 tablespoons honey
2 garlic cloves, crushed
  through a press
12 well-trimmed loin lamb
  chops (about 3 pounds
  total)
Salt and freshly ground
  black pepper

SMOKING CHIP OPTION: MESQUITE

1. In a small heavy saucepan over low heat, warm the oil. When it is hot, add the salsa (it may splatter slightly). Stir in the honey and garlic. Simmer, uncovered, stirring often, until the salsa has thickened slightly and looks more cooked than raw, about 7 minutes. Remove from the heat and cool. Reserve ½ cup of the blackberry mixture.

2. In a shallow nonreactive dish, combine the remaining blackberry mixture and the chops. Cover and marinate, turning once or twice, for 1 hour at room temperature or overnight in the refrigerator. (Return the chops to room temperature if chilled).

3. Light a direct-heat charcoal fire and let it burn down to medium-hot (5 seconds to "ouch") or preheat a gas grill to medium-high. Position the rack about 6 inches above the heat source.

4. Lift the chops from the marinade and, if desired for easier handling, divide them among 3 or 4 flat metal skewers.

5. When the grill is ready, lay the chops on the rack. Cover and grill, turning the chops once and basting them with the marinade, until it is used up and the meat is done to your liking, about 9 minutes total for medium-rare lamb.

6. Transfer the chops to a platter or to individual plates. Season with salt and pepper and spoon the reserved blackberry sauce on top of the chops, dividing it evenly and using it all. Serve immediately.

Cumin-Grilled Butterflied Leg of Lamb

SERVES 8

5- to 6-pound butterflied
leg of lamb
6 tablespoons freshly
ground cumin (prefer-
ably from toasted seeds)
2 tablespoons dried
oregano, crumbled
1 teaspoon garlic powder
Salt
Freshly ground black
pepper
2½ cups Cascabel–Roasted
Garlic Salsa (page 285)
or Coffee Barbecue
Sauce (page 275)
(optional)

SMOKING CHIP OPTION: MESQUITE

A boneless leg of lamb grills up looking fairly unlovely, but provides meat ranging from fully cooked but juicy to rare—something, in other words, for everyone. From the cook's standpoint, there is only one big thing to monitor on the grill, rather than dozens of little things, but the process still requires a certain vigilance. Even the best-trimmed legs of lamb will have some fat, and flare-ups, especially when the lamb is skin side-down on the grill, are inevitable. Leftover lamb is terrific in sandwiches and salads (see page 105) so you may want to make that happen by inviting fewer guests or by ordering a larger piece of meat. (If you choose the latter, grill the lamb at a slightly lower heat for a little longer, and watch very closely for flare-ups and charring.)

1. Trim off and discard any visible fat from the lamb. Let the meat come to room temperature.

2. In a small bowl, thoroughly mix together the cumin, oregano, garlic powder, 1 teaspoon salt, and 1 teaspoon pepper. Sprinkle half the cumin mixture evenly over the meaty side of the lamb, using it all and patting it firmly into the meat to encourage it to adhere.

3. Light a direct-heat charcoal fire and let it burn down to medium (7 to 8 minutes to "ouch") or preheat a gas grill to medium. Position the grill rack about 6 inches above the heat source.

4. When the grill is ready, lay the meat on the rack, skin side up. Cover and grill, watching for flare-ups and moving the meat around on the rack as necessary to avoid overcooking, for 10 minutes. Scatter the remaining cumin mixture over the meat and pat it firmly in. Turn the meat, cover, and grill, watching closely for flare-ups, until the meat is done to your liking, another 10 minutes for lamb that ranges from just done through to medium rare. An instant-read thermometer inserted into the meat at its thickest point should read 130° to 140°F.

5. Transfer the meat to a cutting board and let it rest for 5 minutes.

6. Separate the lamb along the natural muscle divisions and carve each piece across the grain and at a slight angle to the cutting board into thin slices. Arrange the slices on a heated platter as you go, grouping them according to doneness. Season lightly with salt and pepper and serve immediately, accompanied by one of the sauces at the table, if desired.

Note: Some butchers are better at butterflying leg of lamb than others. Be certain when you order the butterflied leg that the butcher knows you will be using it for grilling, not for stuffing and reassembling, and that you would like it as flat and as much of an even thickness as is possible.

Pecan-Grilled Rack of Lamb with Mustard Crust

This is pretty fancy eating for grill food, but rack of lamb is nothing more than a row of dressy little loin chops, joined together, and, to be honest, the best way to eat them is with your fingers, so why not put them on a backyard menu? Pecan wood chips, if you can find them, make a smoke that is particularly compatible with the mustard crust, but mesquite can also be used with fine results. Good accompaniments would be Pasta and Grilled Vegetable Salad with Cilantro Dressing (page 209) and Texas Toast (page 217).

1. Position a rack in the middle of the oven and preheat to 400°F.

2. Remove most of the loose papery outside peel from the garlic bulbs. Cut the top one-quarter off each head, exposing the cloves inside. Partially enclose each garlic bulb in a packet of heavy-duty foil. Drizzle each with 1 tablespoon of olive oil and 1 tablespoon of sherry. Seal the packets tightly, place in the oven, and bake until the garlic cloves are very soft and brown, about 1 hour. Remove from the oven and cool to room temperature in the foil.

SERVES 4

4 large bulbs regular (not elephant) garlic
6 tablespoons olive oil
4 tablespoons dry sherry
½ cup Dijon mustard
2 tablespoons packed light brown sugar
2 tablespoons minced fresh rosemary
Salt
Pepper
2 (8-chop) racks of lamb (about 2½ pounds total), rib bones frenched by the butcher

SMOKING CHIP OPTION:
PECAN OR MESQUITE

3. Scoop or squeeze the softened garlic out of the peels into a food processor. Add the mustard, the remaining 2 tablespoons olive oil, the sugar, rosemary, ½ teaspoon salt and ½ teaspoon pepper. Process, stopping several times to scrape down the sides of the work bowl, until the mixture is fairly smooth. (This paste can be prepared up to 1 day ahead. Cover well and refrigerate.)

4. Divide each rack of lamb in half between the fourth and fifth ribs. Wrap the exposed bones in foil to prevent their burning. Spread the mustard paste over the meaty portion of the lamb racks, including the ends, dividing it evenly and using it all. Let stand at room temperature for 1 hour.

5. Meanwhile, light an indirect-heat charcoal fire using the method described on page 8, banking the coals on one side of the kettle, and let it burn down to medium-hot (about 5 seconds to "ouch") or preheat a gas grill to medium-high. Position the rack about 6 inches above the heat source.

6. When the grill is ready, lightly oil the rack. If you are using a gas grill, shut off the middle burner. Set the lamb, meaty side up, on the grill rack above the side without coals or over the turned-off burner. Cover and grill for 15 minutes. Turn, cover, and continue to grill until the crust is marked by the rack and the meat is done to your liking, another 5 to 7 minutes for rare lamb (which is really how it should be served). An instant-read thermometer inserted into the meat at its thickest point should read 130° to 140°F.

7. Transfer the meat to a cutting board and let it rest for a few minutes.

8. Remove the foil. Cut the lamb between the bones into chops, season with salt and pepper, and serve immediately.

Spice-Rubbed Venison Tenderloin with Dried Blueberry Sauce

Mildly gamy farm-raised venison is a fine meat for grilling, requiring only that you not over-cook it, since it is lean and dries out easily. A rub adds additional flavor, while an elegantly meaty sauce, studded with tequila-plumped dried blueberries, makes this elegant enough for a fine dinner party.

1. In a small bowl, combine the blueberries and tequila. Cover and let stand at room temperature until the berries have absorbed most of the tequila and are plump, about 2 hours.

2. In a small heavy saucepan over low heat, warm the olive oil. Add the shallot, garlic, and thyme. Cover and cook, stirring once or twice, for 5 minutes. Add the beef stock, ¼ teaspoon salt, and a generous grinding of black pepper. Bring to a simmer. Cook uncovered, skimming the stock as needed, until it is reduced by one-quarter, about 15 minutes. Add the blueberries, any unabsorbed tequila, and the vinegar and simmer for 5 minutes. Remove from the heat.

3. In a small bowl, stir together the chipotle powder, ½ teaspoon black pepper, the sugar, corian-der, ½ teaspoon salt, and the cinnamon. Sprinkle the spice mixture evenly over all sides of the veni-son, patting it firmly to encourage it to adhere.

4. Meanwhile, prepare a direct-heat charcoal fire and let it burn down to medium-hot (5 seconds to "ouch") or preheat a gas grill to medium-high. Position the rack about 6 inches above the heat source.

5. When the grill is ready, lightly oil the rack. Lay the tenderloins on the rack, cover, and grill,

SERVES 4

⅓ cup dried blueberries
⅓ cup tequila
1 tablespoon olive oil
2 tablespoons minced
 shallot
1 garlic clove, minced
Pinch dried thyme,
 crumbled
2 cups beef stock
Salt
Freshly ground black
 pepper
1 tablespoon sherry wine
 vinegar
1 teaspoon chipotle chile
 powder
½ teaspoon granulated
 brown sugar
¼ teaspoon ground
 coriander
Pinch ground cinnamon
4 venison tenderloin
 steaks (about 2 pounds
 total)
2 tablespoons chilled
 unsalted butter, cut into
 small pieces

SMOKING CHIP OPTION:
APPLE OR CHERRY

turning once, until done to your liking, about 9 minutes for medium-rare meat, which is preferable.

6. Transfer the meat to a cutting board and let it rest for a few minutes.

7. Meanwhile, set the pan with the sauce over low heat and bring to a simmer. One at a time, whisk the pieces of butter into the simmering sauce, always adding a fresh piece before the previous piece is completely absorbed. The sauce will thicken. Remove from the heat and adjust the seasoning.

8. Carve the tenderloins across the grain and at a slight angle to the cutting board into thin slices.

9. Arrange the slices on heated plates. Spoon the sauce around them, dividing it evenly and using it all. Serve immediately.

*Ensaladas,
Frijoles, y
Verduras*

Salads,
Beans, and
Vegetable
Side Dishes

Smoky Grill-Roasted Corn on the Cob

Ⓞne of the most sublime things to come off a grill is sweet corn. Especially when cooked as it is here—husks pulled back, corn lightly oiled and grilled just until the juicy kernels are lightly caramelized—it's revolutionary: Corn as you've never enjoyed it before. The first time or two or ten, that corn, plus a little sweet butter and a bit of salt and pepper, may be enough. Eventually, though, you may seek other options, and so I also suggest a couple of compound butters and a smoky chipotle mayonnaise. Mayo on corn, you ask? It's popular in Mexico, where they have a thing for mayonnaise that I attribute to that period when Mexico was under French rule. Don't scoff until you've tried it—it's delicious.

1. Light a direct-heat charcoal fire and let it burn down to medium-hot (5 seconds to "ouch") or preheat a gas grill to medium-high. Position the rack about 6 inches above the heat source.

2. Meanwhile, pull back the cornhusks, leaving them attached at the stem end. Remove and discard the silks. With twine, tie the husks together at their ends, forming a kind of handle. Brush the corn kernels with the oil.

3. When the grill is ready, lay the corn on the rack. Cover and grill, turning occasionally, until the corn is lightly but evenly browned, 8 to 10 minutes.

4. Leave the husks still attached if desired, or remove them. Serve the corn hot, accompanied by salt, pepper, and one of the butters or the mayonnaise.

Note: This recipe works best with the new supersweet corn varieties, bred to be tender and stay sweet days after picking. If in doubt, ask your produce person, or buy your corn from a farm stand, where the grower can vouch for the type of corn you are buying.

SERVES 2 TO 4

*4 large ears sweet,
    tender corn (preferably
    just-picked)*
2 tablespoons olive oil
*Salt and freshly ground
    black pepper*
*Unsalted butter, Green
    Chile–Cheese Butter
    (page 300), South-
    western Herb and Spice
    Butter (page 299), or
    Chipotle Mayonnaise
    (page 293)*

SMOKING CHIP OPTION: MESQUITE

Salads, Beans, and Vegetable Side Dishes

Steamy Husk-Grilled Corn on the Cob

SERVES 2 TO 4

*4 large ears sweet,
tender corn, preferably
just-picked*

*6 tablespoons unsalted
butter, Green Chile–
Cheese Butter (page
300) or Southwestern
Spice and Herb Butter
(page 299), plus addi-
tional plain or flavored
butter for serving,
softened*

*Salt and freshly ground
black pepper*

This other best way to grill corn is borrowed from my Tucson friend Michael Honstein. For this method, the husks are pulled back, the silks removed, the corn lavished with plain or flavored butter, then the husks are tied back in place. On the grill for at least 20 minutes, the corn steams inside the husks and is basted with the butter. The charred and very rustic looking ears are served (preferably outdoors) as is, for guests to peel back, experiencing a cloud of sweet corn-scented steam akin to uncovering something cooked "under glass." Neither smoky (no chips are called for), nor caramelized, the corn is nevertheless sweetly tender and very seductive. Again, plain butter may do you for a while, but future options are suggested.

1. Light a direct-heat charcoal fire and let it burn down to medium-hot (5 seconds to "ouch") or preheat a gas grill to medium-high. Position the rack about 6 inches above the heat source.

2. Meanwhile, pull back the husks, leaving them attached at the stem ends. Remove and discard the silks. Brush each ear of corn with about 1½ tablespoons of butter. Pull the husks back up over the ears and tie them in place with twine.

3. When the grill is ready, lay the ears on the rack. Cover and grill, turning occasionally, until the peels are fairly well charred, about 20 minutes. Check inside one ear, if desired, to determine doneness, though most truly sweet, tender corn virtually can be eaten raw.

4. This is outdoor food. Despite their charred and messy appearance, serve the ears in the husks, letting guests experience the pleasure of uncovering the sweet steamy corn inside. Pass additional butter, salt, and pepper at the table.

Sweet and Smoky Corn Relish

Somewhere between a salad and a condiment, this colorful concoction goes nicely with grilled pork, chicken, shellfish, and even some finfish, such as salmon. It's a bit sweet, a bit hot, a little tangy, and a touch smoky—a terrific combination of flavors. The relish freezes well, if you want to "put some up" during prime corn season, and can then be enjoyed year-round. It's wonderful with a Thanksgiving turkey.

1. In a small bowl, combine the vinegar and mustard seeds, cover, and let stand at room temperature until softened, about 2 hours.

2. Light a direct-heat charcoal fire and let it burn down to medium-hot (5 seconds to "ouch") or preheat a gas grill to medium-high. Position the rack about 6 inches above the heat source.

3. Brush the corn and the green onions with 1½ tablespoons of the oil. When the grill is ready, lay the onions, corn, and the pepper on the rack. Cover and grill, turning the onions once, until they are well marked by the grill, about 5 minutes total. Transfer the onions to a cutting board. Continue to grill the corn and the pepper, turning occasionally, until the corn kernels are lightly browned and caramelized and the pepper skin is lightly but evenly charred, another 8 to 10 minutes. Transfer the corn to a cutting board. Transfer the pepper to a paper bag, close the bag, and steam the pepper until cool.

4. Slice the green onions. Cut the corn kernels off the ears. Scrape any juices off the ears; you should have 3 cups kernels and juices. Rub the burnt peel off the bell pepper, stem and seed it, and dice the flesh.

5. In a medium bowl, combine the corn, bell pepper, onions, the cider vinegar mixture, the remaining 3 tablespoons oil, chipotle chile, maple syrup, ½ teaspoon salt, and a generous grinding of pepper. Adjust the seasoning.

6. Serve immediately, or cover and refrigerate for up to 2 days or freeze for up to 2 months.

SERVES 6 (MAKES ABOUT 3½ CUPS)

3 tablespoons cider vinegar

2 teaspoons whole yellow mustard seeds

8 ears fresh, sweet corn, husks and silks removed

5 large green onions, tops trimmed to no more than 2 inches

4½ tablespoons corn oil

1 large red bell pepper

1 tablespoon minced canned chipotle chile en adobo

1 tablespoon maple syrup

Salt

Freshly ground black pepper

SMOKING CHIP OPTION: APPLE

Chipotle-Glazed Vegetable Kebabs

SERVES 6

2 medium-large zucchini,
   trimmed
18 small white mush-
   rooms, stems trimmed
   flat with the caps
18 large cherry tomatoes,
   stemmed
¾ cup Chipotle Vinaigrette
   (page 298)
Salt and freshly ground
   black pepper

SMOKING CHIP OPTION: MESQUITE

Colorful and quick, these mixed vegetable kebabs are also very tasty, thanks to a steady basting as they grill with my trusty, all-purpose chipotle salad dressing. Be sure to pick out small mushrooms and large cherry tomatoes and cut the zucchini cubes to the same size as the other vegetables, to ensure even cooking. The tomatoes will be done first in any case; when they're hot, tender, and juicy but not yet falling to mush, the kebabs are done.

1. Cut each zucchini crosswise into 9 equally thick slices. Trim the slices to form cubes. Divide the vegetables, alternating them, among 6 flat metal skewers. Be certain to arrange the flat sides of the zucchini cubes and the stems ends of the mushrooms so they will get the maximum exposure to the fire.

2. Light a direct-heat charcoal fire and let it burn down to medium-hot (5 seconds to "ouch") or preheat a gas grill to medium-high. Position the rack about 6 inches above the heat source.

3. When the grill is ready, lightly brush the kebabs with some of the vinaigrette. Lay the kebabs on the rack, cover, and grill, turning every 2 minutes and basting often with the vinaigrette, until it is used up and the vegetables are lightly colored by the grill, 6 to 8 minutes total.

4. Season with salt and pepper and slide the vegetables off the skewers onto plates. Serve hot or warm.

Double-Smoky
Baked Black Beans

To save kitchen time in the summer, this zesty side dish uses convenient canned beans. If you're a purist and want to soak and simmer your own, start with 2¾ cups dried beans.

1. In a medium heavy skillet over low heat, cook the bacon until it is almost crisp, about 10 minutes. Remove from the pan and chop. Reserve the drippings.

2. Position a rack in the middle of the oven and preheat to 350°F.

3. In a large bowl, stir together the bacon, bacon drippings, beans, onions, barbecue sauce, beer, molasses, mustard, chipotles, sugar, Worcestershire sauce, and soy sauce. Spoon into a 9-by-13-inch glass baking dish. Bake, uncovered, until the beans are bubbling and the sauce has thickened slightly, about 55 minutes.

4. Serve warm or at room temperature.

SERVES 8 TO 10

6 thick-cut bacon strips

8 cups cooked drained black beans or 6 (15-ounce) cans black beans, rinsed and drained

1½ cups chopped onions

1¼ cups prepared thick and smoky barbecue sauce, homemade or store-bought

¾ cup dark beer

¼ cup unsulphured molasses

3 tablespoons Dijon mustard

3 tablespoons minced canned chipotle chiles with clinging sauce

3 tablespoons packed dark brown sugar

2 tablespoons Worcestershire sauce

1 tablespoon soy sauce

Pot Beans

SERVES 12

2 pounds dried pinto
  beans, picked over
About 3 quarts water
1 onion, finely chopped
¼ pound salt pork,
  trimmed and finely
  chopped
⅓ cup Mixed Dried Red
  Chile Puree (page 305),
  or frozen or jarred red
  chile puree, or 2 tablespoons unblended
  medium-hot chile
  powder
4 garlic cloves, minced
Salt

The Spanish name—*frijoles de la olla*—translates as beans of the pot, a bare-bones description that badly fails to do them justice. Few
dishes are easier to put together than this, and
none, I think, smell as good while cooking or taste
as delicious when done. That the result of this
modest effort is also one of the foundations of
southwestern cookery says volumes about how
simple the best of this food can be. The recipe
makes a lot, because that's no more work than
making a little, and because the beans are so versatile. Serve half of them in bowls (plain or with
chopped onions, shredded cheese and/or salsa
added) as a side dish at one meal to appreciate
how good beans plain can be. Then, cook the other
half into the most delicious refried beans ever for
another (see Refried Beans, next page). Or stash
them in the freezer and use them as the basis for a
terrific bean dip when next the grill is hot (see page
27). Try this recipe once, and you'll never think of
beans in quite the same way again.

1. In a large bowl, cover the beans with tepid
water and let for stand 10 minutes. Drain and
repeat. Drain again.
2. In a large (at least 6-quart) tall pot, combine
the beans with enough water to cover them by
about 4 inches. Set over medium heat. Add the
onion, salt pork, chile puree, and garlic and bring
to a simmer. Partially cover the pan, decrease the
heat, and cook, stirring occasionally, for 2 hours.
Add 1 tablespoon salt and continue to cook, adding
a little additional water if the beans seem too dry,
until the beans are tender but still slightly brothy,
another hour or so. Adjust the seasoning.
3. The beans can be eaten immediately but will
improve with an overnight rest. Cool completely,

then cover and refrigerate. Rewarm over low heat, thinning with additional water as needed, until hot. (You can freeze the beans for up to 2 months.)

VARIATION: Black beans can be substituted, to make Black Pot Beans *(Frijoles Negros de la Olla)*. Follow the basic pot bean recipe, but use black beans and substitute a smoked ham hock simmered in the pot instead of the salt pork. Discard the ham hock when the beans are done. Along with the salt, for the final hour's simmering, add 2 teaspoons dried epazote.

Refried Beans
(FRIJOLES REFRITOS)

In a large, preferably nonstick skillet over medium heat, warm 2 tablespoons bacon drippings or olive oil. Add 1 cup pinto or black pot beans with their liquid. With a potato masher, roughly crush the beans, then simmer them uncovered, stirring occasionally, for 5 minutes. Repeat 5 times more with 5 more cups of beans and broth, adding the beans 1 cup at a time, mashing them and then simmering them for 5 minutes before adding the next cup. After all the beans are in and mashed, simmer, stirring often, until the beans are thick and creamy, a final 5 minutes or so. The beans can be served immediately or reheated later in the skillet or in a microwave oven. (Add a few tablespoons of water if the beans have become dry.)

Brothy Black Beans with Bacon and Beer

SERVES 4 TO 6

4 thick-cut bacon strips,
 chopped
¾ cup chopped onion
3 garlic cloves, chopped
1 small fresh jalapeño,
 stemmed and minced
1 teaspoon dried oregano,
 crumbled
½ teaspoon freshly ground
 cumin (preferably from
 toasted seeds)
½ teaspoon freshly ground
 black pepper
4 cups Black Pot Beans
 with cooking liquid
 (page 199)
¾ cup reduced-sodium
 canned chicken broth
¾ cup amber beer, such as
 Dos Equis

Plain pot beans are delicious comfort food, but definitely designed to be supporting players. These beans, boosted with bacon, beer, and other bold flavors, approach star status and can certainly hold their own alongside bold southwestern grilled main courses. They are brothy by intent and should be served in bowls, so that every drop can be savored. Pintos work just as well here as black beans, by the way, they're just not as trendy.

1. In a medium heavy saucepan over low heat, cook the bacon, stirring occasionally, until it is almost crisp, about 10 minutes. Add the onion, garlic, jalapeño, oregano, cumin, and black pepper. Cook, covered, stirring occasionally, for 5 minutes.

2. Add the beans, broth, and beer and bring to a simmer. Cook, uncovered, stirring occasionally, until liquid on the beans is reduced by about half, about 20 minutes.

3. Adjust the seasoning and serve hot.

Portobello Mushroom and Bell Pepper Salad with Rosemary Vinaigrette

Vividly flavored and colored, this is one of my favorite grill menu side dishes. It's especially nice with lamb. Serve it alongside the meat, or slice the meat thinly and fan it over the salad. (The vinaigrette mixed with lamb juices is delicious.)

1. Light a direct-heat charcoal fire and let it burn down to medium-hot (5 seconds to "ouch"), or preheat a gas grill to medium-high. Position the grill rack about 6 inches above the heat source.

2. Meanwhile, brush the mushroom caps with ⅓ cup of the oil. When the grill is ready, lay the mushroom caps and peppers on the rack. Cover and grill, turning the mushroom caps once and the peppers occasionally, until the mushrooms are tender and lightly marked by the grill, about 8 minutes total, and the pepper peels are lightly but evenly charred, about 12 minutes. Transfer the mushrooms to a cutting board. Transfer the peppers to a paper bag, close the bag, and steam the peppers until cool.

3. Slice the mushrooms ½-inch thick. Rub away the burnt peel, stem and core the peppers, and cut them lengthwise into ¼-inch strips.

4. In a small food processor or blender, combine the vinegar, rosemary, garlic, ¼ teaspoon salt, and a generous grinding of pepper. Process to blend. Scrape down the sides of the work bowl. With the motor running, gradually add the remaining ⅓ cup oil through the feed tube; the dressing will thicken. Adjust the seasoning.

5. Line a platter with the greens. Arrange the mushroom slices over the greens. Mound the pepper strips over the mushrooms. Drizzle everything with dressing and serve immediately.

SERVES 6

2 pounds (6 large) portobello mushrooms, stems discarded
⅔ cup olive oil
2 large red bell peppers
1 tablespoon red wine vinegar
1 tablespoon minced fresh rosemary
1 garlic clove, chopped
Salt
Freshly ground black pepper
About 5 ounces mixed baby salad greens (mesclun)

SMOKING CHIP OPTION: MESQUITE

Grilled Calabacitas Salad

SERVES 6 TO 8

3 medium-large zucchini
(about 1½ pounds total),
trimmed and quartered
lengthwise

4 large ears supersweet
corn, husks and silks
removed

¼ cup corn oil

3 long green chiles, such
as Anaheim or Hatch,
or 2 large poblano chiles

1 large red bell pepper

⅓ cup sour cream

⅓ cup mayonnaise

4 teaspoons fresh lime
juice

2 garlic cloves, crushed
through a press

Salt

Freshly ground black
pepper

SMOKING CHIP OPTION: MESQUITE

*C*alabacitas is both the Spanish name for small squash varieties, especially zucchini, and for a homey side dish combining zucchini with corn and green chiles: It's a kind of southwestern succotash, in effect. Come summer, the general idea also translates nicely into a salad of grilled zucchini and corn, in a cool sour cream dressing. As usual, the hotter the chile, the more interesting the salad. It sounds unlikely, but chopped fresh basil is very nice in this, one of my most relied-upon grill meal side dishes.

1. Light a direct-heat charcoal fire and let it burn down to medium-hot (5 seconds to "ouch") or preheat a gas grill to medium-high. Position the rack about 6 inches above the heat source.

2. Brush the zucchini and corn all over with the corn oil.

3. When the grill is ready, lay the zucchini, corn, green chiles, and red pepper on the rack. Cover and grill, turning occasionally, until the zucchini and corn are lightly but evenly browned, about 8 minutes, and the peels of the green chiles and red pepper are lightly but evenly charred, about 8 minutes for the green chiles and about 10 minutes for the pepper. Transfer the zucchini and corn to a cutting board. Transfer the chiles and pepper to a paper bag, close the bag, and steam until cool.

4. Cut the zucchini into 1-inch pieces and transfer to a large bowl. Cut the corn kernels off the cobs and transfer to the bowl with the zucchini. Rub the burnt peels off the chiles and pepper and stem and core them. Dice the green chiles. Cut the red pepper into long, thin strips; add both to the large bowl.

5. In a medium bowl, whisk together the sour cream, mayonnaise, lime juice, garlic, and ¼ teaspoon salt.

6. Pour the dressing over the vegetables in the bowl, season generously with pepper, and toss. Adjust the seasoning and toss again.

7. Serve within an hour or so of making.

Heirloom Bean Salad

Here is a salad that celebrates the return of lost or heirloom beans to the American market-place. The three varieties of dried beans called for are those that New Mexico grower Elizabeth Berry recommends as being particularly suitable for salads, but substitutions can be made (see Note). I include the fresh green beans for color and because I like the contrast of textures. Elizabeth's other bean salad advice: Use orange juice. If you know her, you know enough not to argue, so here it is, with plenty of orange juice, also roasted garlic, rosemary, and sherry wine vinegar. This is particularly delicious alongside plain (or plainer) grilled red meats, whose juices mingle nicely with the salad's dressing.

1. In separate bowls, cover the three dried bean varieties with cold water and let soak for 12 hours or overnight.

2. Position a rack in the middle of the oven and preheat to 400°F. Remove most of the papery outer peels of the garlic. Cut off the top quarter of the garlic bulb, exposing the cloves within. Partially enclose the garlic in a doubled piece of foil. Drizzle with the sherry and 1 tablespoon of the olive oil and enclose tightly. Bake until the garlic inside the peels is tender and brown, about 1 hour. Cool the garlic to room temperature in the foil.

3. Drain the soaked beans. Transfer them to 3 medium saucepans and cover with fresh cold water, lightly salt the water in each pan, set each over medium heat, and bring to a simmer. Partially cover and cook, stirring occasionally, until the beans are just tender, about 50 minutes, but bean cooking times vary widely with the age of the beans and the altitude at which you are cooking. Persevere until the beans are individually tender and creamy; undercooked beans are difficult to digest. Drain the beans and transfer them to a large bowl. Pour the orange juice over the hot beans. Cool to room temperature, stirring occasionally.

4. Meanwhile, bring a large pan of salted water to a boil. Add the green beans

SERVES 6 TO 8

⅔ cup dried calypso beans, picked over
⅔ cup dried painted pony beans, picked over
⅔ cup dried flageolet beans, picked over
Salt
1 large bulb regular (not elephant) garlic
1 tablespoon dry sherry
5 tablespoons olive oil
⅓ cup fresh orange juice
¾ pound green beans, trimmed and cut into ¾-inch lengths
¼ cup sherry wine vinegar
2 teaspoons sugar
1 teaspoon hot pepper sauce, such as Tabasco
½ teaspoon freshly ground black pepper
½ cup diced red onion
2 teaspoons minced orange zest
2 teaspoons minced fresh rosemary

and cook, partially covered, stirring once or twice, until they are just tender, about 6 minutes. Drain and transfer to a bowl of iced water. As soon as the beans are cool, drain them and pat dry.

5. Squeeze or spoon the softened garlic out of the peels into a small food processor. Add the vinegar, the remaining 4 tablespoons olive oil, the sugar, 1 teaspoon salt, the Tabasco, and pepper. Process until fairly smooth.

6. Pour the garlic mixture over the cooled beans. Add the onion, orange zest, and rosemary and toss. Adjust the seasoning. (The salad can be prepared to this point several hours in advance. Cover and hold at room temperature.)

7. Just before serving, mix in the green beans and adjust the seasoning. Serve at room temperature.

Note: The beans are simmered separately so that each retains its distinctive color and can be cooked to its ideal stage of doneness.

Heirlooms

Heirloom beans are those varieties that, for various reasons—disease susceptibility, low yields, sometimes sheer neglect—have fallen out of commercial favor. They are often sold in the company of "boutique" beans, not really lost but not produced in any significant commercial quantities either. But, thanks to the efforts of people like New Mexico's Elizabeth Berry, who specializes in rescuing forgotten beans and growing them out into quantities that then become commercially viable, there are more beans to be had than ever before—good news for southwestern cooks, who have relied on them for centuries as a primary food source. Richly colored and uniquely shaped, these rediscovered beans range from one tiny type that resembles wild rice grains to a huge white, marble-sized variety. They taste good, too, at least as good as supermarket varieties and often better. Even more importantly, however, returning these beans to production increases the world's genetic diversity, ever more essential as mainstream farmers put more of their efforts into growing fewer varieties. But the good thing about vanished beans is that only a few beans are needed to revive an entire variety. One of Elizabeth's beans, Oklahoma Cave, for example, came to her as a mere five specimens. After years of patiently growing out this low-yield bean, replanting each year's entire crop as next season's seeds, she now has enough to offer the rarity for sale— very good news for bean lovers. To mail-order Elizabeth Berry's heirloom beans, contact Ronniger's Organic Farm (see page 321).

Black-Eyed Pea Salad with
Sweet Country Ham and Jalapeño Dressing

The robust flavors of black-eyed peas, smoke, and chiles, plus a garlicky sweet-and-sour dressing, mark this salad as harking from the farthest eastern point of the Southwest, along about Texarkana, perhaps, or even Port Arthur. It's great alongside so many foods—a big old steak, great BBQ chicken, pork ribs, even (or maybe especially) smoky grilled shrimp—it should be in everyone's summer repertoire.

1. In a large pan, cover the beans with cold water. Bring to a brisk simmer and cook, partially covered, stirring occasionally, for 30 minutes. Salt the water and continue to cook the beans, stirring occasionally, until tender while still holding their shape, another 20 to 30 minutes, but bean cooking times vary widely. Taste before removing from the heat; undercooked beans are hard to digest. When the beans are done, drain and cool to room temperature.

2. In a medium skillet over moderate heat, warm the olive oil. Add the ham and cook, stirring occasionally, until lightly browned, about 6 minutes. Remove from the heat and add the onion, garlic, and jalapeño. Return the skillet to the burner, decrease the heat, and cook, stirring often without browning, for 2 minutes.

3. Meanwhile, in a small bowl, stir together the vinegar, sugar, and ¾ teaspoon salt. Add the vinegar mixture to the skillet. Increase the heat to high and bring to a boil, stirring often. Boil hard for 30 seconds, then pour the hot dressing over the beans. Stir in ½ teaspoon fresh black pepper and cool to room temperature.

4. Adjust the seasoning before serving.

SERVES 6 TO 8

2 (1-pound) bags frozen black-eyed peas, thawed and drained
Salt
5 tablespoons olive oil
6 ounces lean and smoky good-quality ham, in ¼-inch dice
¾ cup diced onion
3 garlic cloves, minced
1 fresh jalapeño, stemmed and minced
5 tablespoons cider vinegar
3 tablespoons sugar
Freshly ground black pepper

Potato Salad with Roasted Garlic Aioli

SERVES 6 TO 8

3 pounds well-scrubbed, small red-skinned potatoes, quartered
Salt
1½ cups Roasted Garlic Aioli (page 294)
½ cup thinly sliced green onions, tender tops included
Freshly ground black pepper

It's not a grill meal without potato salad, and so I offer up a trio here, just to be on the safe side. While not playing favorites, I confess to finding this garlicky concoction very satisfying indeed, and particularly well suited to plating up beside any number of southwestern-style main courses. Sometimes I cook the potatoes whole, slide them onto the grill and let them get crisp and smoky before quartering them—a nice touch but not a necessary one.

1. In a large pan, cover the potato quarters with salted cold water. Bring to a boil over medium-high heat. Partially cover, decrease the heat slightly, and simmer the potatoes, stirring them occasionally, until they are just tender while still holding their shape, about 12 minutes. Drain and cool to room temperature. (The potatoes can be prepared several hours in advance. Cover tightly and hold at room temperature.)

2. Shortly before serving, toss the potatoes with the aioli and onions in a large bowl. Adjust the seasoning and toss again.

3. Serve at room temperature.

Ranchero Potato Salad with Double Olive Dressing

Olives play an important part in the Spanish-derived ranchero cooking tradition of California, hence this loosely inspired but otherwise entirely fanciful salad. California's olives have improved in flavor in recent years, but so has the supply of gutsy Mediterranean imports, so no one need resort to using bland and flabby impostors here. Good beside many grilled southwestern entrées, this goes especially well with lamb and chicken dishes.

1. In a large pan, cover the potato quarters with salted cold water. Bring to a boil over medium-high heat. Partially cover, decrease the heat slightly, and simmer the potatoes, stirring them occasionally, until they are just tender while still holding their shape, about 12 minutes. Drain and cool to room temperature. (The potatoes can be prepared several hours in advance. Cover tightly and hold at room temperature.)

2. In a large bowl, whisk together the green and black olives, olive oil, vinegar, and ¼ teaspoon salt. Add the potatoes, onion, parsley, and a generously grinding of pepper and toss well. Adjust the seasoning and toss again.

3. Serve shortly after making the salad.

SERVES 6 TO 8

3 pounds well-scrubbed, small red-skinned potatoes, quartered
Salt
⅓ cup finely chopped pitted green olives
⅓ cup finely chopped pitted brine-cured black olives, such as Kalamata
3 tablespoons olive oil
2 tablespoons sherry wine vinegar
⅓ cup diced red onion
¼ cup finely chopped flat-leaf parsley
Freshly ground black pepper

Salads, Beans, and Vegetable Side Dishes

Sweet Potato–Corn Salad with Honey Mustard Dressing

SERVES 6 TO 8

1 large red bell pepper
3 pounds (4 large) sweet
   potatoes, peeled and cut
   into ¾-inch chunks
Salt
¾ cup mayonnaise
3 tablespoons hot honey
   mustard
1 teaspoon hot pepper
   sauce, such as Tabasco
¾ teaspoon salt
½ teaspoon freshly ground
   black pepper
1 (1-pound) bag frozen
   supersweet corn,
   thawed and drained
½ cup thinly sliced green
   onions, tender tops
   included

Here is a colorful summer salad, full of sweet and tangy flavors. It goes very nicely with pork, chicken, and even some fish—exactly the kinds of things you are going to be grilling. One useful rule of salad making is illustrated here: However good and sweet the fresh corn of the season is, frozen kernels work better in nearly all salads using corn. Recently I have seen frozen supersweet corn—just the kind to use here.

1. In the open flame of a gas burner, under a preheated broiler, or on the grill, roast the bell pepper, turning it occasionally, until the peel is lightly but evenly charred. Transfer to a paper bag, close the bag, and steam the pepper until cool. Rub away the burnt peel, stem, core, and dice the pepper.

2. In a large pot, cover the potatoes with salted cold water. Bring to a simmer over medium heat. Partially cover and cook until the potatoes are just tender while still holding their shape, about 8 minutes. Drain.

3. In a large bowl, whisk together the mayonnaise, mustard, pepper sauce, salt, and pepper. Add the potatoes, corn, bell pepper, and green onions. Stir gently but thoroughly. Adjust the seasoning.

4. Serve the salad at room temperature, within an hour or two of completion.

Pasta and Grilled Vegetable Salad with Cilantro Dressing

Colorful but uncomplicated, this bright salad is just right beside any number of grilled main courses. It's flexible, too, and such compatible ingredients as tomatoes, chickpeas, olives, roasted peppers and chiles, or grilled mushrooms can join the party. Gas grillers can fire up and cook the vegetables at their convenience. Charcoalers may want to grill the vegetables in advance, at another, earlier, grill meal, and hold them until assembling the salad.

1. In a food processor, combine the cilantro, vinegar, garlic, ½ teaspoon salt, and ½ teaspoon pepper. Process, scraping down the sides of the work bowl once or twice, until fairly smooth. With the motor running, gradually add the ½ cup oil through the feed tube. The dressing will thicken slightly. Adjust the seasoning.

2. Over high heat, bring a large pot of salted water to a boil. Add the pasta, partially cover, and cook, stirring occasionally, until the pasta is just tender, according to the package directions. Drain, rinse well, and drain again.

3. Meanwhile, light a direct-heat charcoal fire and let it burn down to medium-hot (5 seconds to "ouch") or preheat a gas grill to medium-high. Position the grill rack about 6 inches above the heat source.

4. Brush the corn, zucchini, and onion slices with the remaining 3 tablespoons oil. When the grill is ready, lay the vegetables on the rack. Cover and grill, turning once or twice, until the vegetables are cooked through and well marked by the grill on all sides, 10 to 12 minutes total. Transfer to a cutting board and cool. (The salad can be pre-

SERVES 6 TO 8

1 cup finely chopped cilantro leaves and tender stems
3 tablespoons sherry wine vinegar
2 garlic cloves, chopped
Salt
Freshly ground black pepper
½ cup plus 3 tablespoons olive oil
¾ pound dried imported semolina fusilli
2 large ears sweet, tender corn (preferably just-picked)
2 large zucchini, trimmed and halved lengthwise
1 large red onion, cut into 3 thick slices

SMOKING CHIP OPTION: MESQUITE

pared up to this point several hours in advance. Wrap the ingredients separately and hold at room temperature.)

5. Cut the corn kernels off the cobs. Cut the zucchini and onion into ½-inch pieces.

6. In a large bowl, combine the pasta and vegetables. Add the dressing, season generously with pepper, and toss well. Adjust the seasoning and toss again.

7. Serve more or less immediately.

Orzo, Black Bean, and Cherry Tomato Salad

SERVES 6 TO 8

*12 ounces imported
   semolina orzo
About 20 ripe, juicy cherry
   tomatoes, halved
1 (15-ounce) can black
   beans, rinsed and well
   drained
⅔ cup diced red onion
¼ cup olive oil
2½ tablespoons sherry
   wine vinegar
½ teaspoon salt
½ cup finely chopped
   cilantro leaves and
   tender stems
Freshly ground black
   pepper*

This is another good, all-purpose salad, one that incorporates enough different and colorful starches and vegetables, that it can accompany the entrée all by itself.

1. Over high heat, bring a large pot of salted water to a boil. Add the orzo, partially cover, and cook, stirring occasionally, until the orzo is just tender while still holding its shape, according to the package directions. Drain, rinse well, and drain again.

2. Shortly before serving time, toss together the orzo, tomatoes, beans, onion, oil, vinegar, and salt in a large bowl. Add the cilantro and a generous grinding of pepper and toss again.

3. Serve more or less immediately.

Jicama and Grilled Red Pepper Slaw

Crunchy and sweet-tart, this slaw has a slight but intriguing smoky flavor, thanks to the grilled vegetables. (You don't have to grill the vegetables; you'll still have a nice slaw that will go well beside a grilled main course, it just won't be quite as interesting.) The vegetables and the dressing can be prepared several hours in advance, but they should be combined shortly before serving.

1. Light a direct-heat charcoal fire and let it burn down to medium-hot (5 seconds to "ouch") or preheat a gas grill to medium-high. Position the rack about 6 inches above the heat source.

2. Brush the green onions with 1½ tablespoons of the oil.

3. When the grill is ready, lay the onions and peppers on the rack. Cover and grill, turning the onions once and the peppers occasionally, until the onions are marked by the grill and tender, about 6 minutes total, and the peppers are lightly but evenly charred, 10 to 12 minutes total. Transfer the onions to a cutting board. Transfer the peppers to a paper bag, close the bag, and steam the peppers until cool.

4. Slice the onions into ¼-inch pieces. Rub away the burnt peel from the peppers, stem and core them, and cut them lengthwise into ¼-inch strips.

5. In a large bowl, whisk together the orange juice, lime juice, honey, cumin, and ½ teaspoon salt. Gradually whisk in the remaining 3 tablespoons oil; the dressing will thicken. Add the pepper strips, onion slices, and jicama to the dressing. Season generously with pepper and toss. Adjust the seasoning and toss again.

6. Serve within 30 minutes of making the salad.

SERVES 6

8 large green onions, tops trimmed to no more than 3 inches long
4½ tablespoons corn oil
3 large red bell peppers
⅓ cup fresh orange juice
1½ tablespoons fresh lime juice
1 tablespoon honey
¾ teaspoon freshly ground cumin (preferably from toasted seeds)
Salt
Freshly ground black pepper
1 (18-ounce) jicama, peeled and cut into matchstick-size pieces

SMOKING CHIP OPTION: HICKORY

Salads, Beans, and Vegetable Side Dishes

Citrus Slaw

SERVES 4

3 tablespoons fresh
    orange juice
1 tablespoon fresh lime
    juice
1 tablespoon finely
    minced orange zest
Salt
3 tablespoons corn oil
5 cups thinly sliced red
    cabbage
Freshly ground black
    pepper

Though originally conceived to top the fish tacos on page 65, this slaw is good enough to serve on other sandwiches (the pork tortas on page 74, for example) or to stand alone as a crunchy accompaniment to many grilled main courses. The quantity produced here will top 12 tacos, 4 tortas, or provide a side dish for 4.

1. In a large bowl, whisk together the orange juice, lime juice, orange zest, and ¼ teaspoon salt. Gradually whisk in the oil; the dressing will thicken. Add the cabbage, season generously with pepper and toss. Adjust the seasoning.

2. Let the slaw stand at room temperature for up to 30 minutes to soften and blend the flavors.

Sweet Texas Slaw

SERVES 6

6 tablespoons cider vinegar
¼ cup corn oil
3 tablespoons sugar
1 tablespoon honey
    mustard
¾ teaspoon celery seed
½ teaspoon salt
8 cups thinly sliced cab-
    bage (about 1 pound)
1 large green bell pepper,
    stemmed, cored, and cut
    into matchstick pieces
½ cup chopped onion
Freshly ground black pepper

Things are, indeed, bigger in Texas, also frequently sweeter. That's how they like it and the preference extends to slaws. Other parts of the country like sweet slaws, too, though, which is why people are so happy when I serve this. You can make it a little less sweet, if you like, but then you'll have to call it something else.

1. In a large bowl, whisk together the vinegar, oil, sugar, mustard, celery seed, and salt. Add the cabbage, green pepper, and onion and toss well. Season generously with pepper and toss again.

2. Serve immediately, for a crunchy slaw. Or let stand, covered, at room temperature, stirring occasionally, for 1 hour, for a more tender slaw.

Grilled Polenta with
Green Chiles and Corn

Corn, the great staple of the Southwest, eventually charmed much of the world, no place more so than Italy. Polenta, the seductive mush Italians make of ground corn, was ultra-trendy for a while, but now seems to have settled down to quiet classic status, joining the formerly overexposed likes of crème brûlée and mashed potatoes—foods so good they're never truly out of style. Since this is a grill book, we will grill our polenta, producing a very different kettle of fish from the soft and creamy kind. Corn kernels and green chiles are stirred into it also, and when the mush has chilled and set, it is cut into interesting shapes, and grilled to a crisp and smoky turn.

1. In the open flame of a gas burner, under a preheated broiler, or on the grill if desired, roast the poblanos, turning them occasionally, until the peels are lightly but evenly charred. Transfer to a paper bag, close the bag, and steam the chiles until cool. Stem and core them and chop the flesh fairly fine.

2. Measure the cornmeal into a heavy medium pot. Gradually whisk the water into the cornmeal. Whisk in the salt. Set the pan over medium heat and bring to a simmer, whisking constantly. Decrease the heat slightly, partially cover the pan, and cook, stirring occasionally, until the polenta pulls away from the side of the pan and is very thick, about 25 minutes. Remove from the heat and stir in the poblanos, corn and pepper.

3. Brush an 8-inch square pan with 1 tablespoon of the oil. Add the polenta mixture and, with

SERVES 6 TO 8

2 poblano chiles
1½ cups yellow cornmeal
4 cups water
1¼ teaspoons salt
¾ cup frozen corn kernels,
    thawed and well drained
½ teaspoon freshly ground
    black pepper
2½ tablespoons olive oil

SMOKING CHIP OPTION: MESQUITE

Grilled Polenta with Green Chiles and Corn

Corn, the great staple of the Southwest, eventually charmed much of the world, no place more so than Italy. Polenta, the seductive mush Italians make of ground corn, was ultra-trendy for a while, but now seems to have settled down to quiet classic status, joining the formerly overexposed likes of crème brûlée and mashed potatoes—foods so good they're never truly out of style. Since this is a grill book, we will grill our polenta, producing a very different kettle of fish from the soft and creamy kind. Corn kernels and green chiles are stirred into it also, and when the mush has chilled and set, it is cut into interesting shapes, and grilled to a crisp and smoky turn.

1. In the open flame of a gas burner, under a preheated broiler, or on the grill if desired, roast the poblanos, turning them occasionally, until the peels are lightly but evenly charred. Transfer to a paper bag, close the bag, and steam the chiles until cool. Stem and core them and chop the flesh fairly fine.

2. Measure the cornmeal into a heavy medium pot. Gradually whisk the water into the cornmeal. Whisk in the salt. Set the pan over medium heat and bring to a simmer, whisking constantly. Decrease the heat slightly, partially cover the pan, and cook, stirring occasionally, until the polenta pulls away from the side of the pan and is very thick, about 25 minutes. Remove from the heat and stir in the poblanos, corn and pepper.

3. Brush an 8-inch square pan with 1 tablespoon of the oil. Add the polenta mixture and, with

SERVES 6 TO 8

2 poblano chiles
1½ cups yellow cornmeal
4 cups water
1¼ teaspoons salt
¾ cup frozen corn kernels,
    thawed and well drained
½ teaspoon freshly ground
    black pepper
2½ tablespoons olive oil

SMOKING CHIP OPTION: MESQUITE

the back of a spoon dipped into water, smooth the top. Cool completely, then cover, and chill until very firm, about 24 hours.

4. Light a direct-heat charcoal fire and let it burn down to medium-hot (5 seconds to "ouch") or preheat a gas grill to medium-high. Position the rack about 6 inches above the heat source.

5. Invert the polenta pan onto a cutting board. The chilled polenta will drop out. With a thin, sharp knife, wiped clean between cuts, slice the polenta into triangles (or use round cookie cutters or form another shape of your own choosing).

6. When the grill is ready, brush the tops of the polenta pieces with half of the oil. With a spatula, invert the polenta pieces onto the rack. Cover and grill for 5 minutes. With the spatula, carefully release the polenta pieces from the rack. Brush the tops with the remaining oil, invert the polenta, cover, and grill until well marked by the rack and heated through, another 4 to 5 minutes.

7. Transfer to plates or a platter. Serve hot.

Cornbread with Red Chile–Pecan Streusel

SERVES 9

STREUSEL
½ cup unbleached
  all-purpose flour
½ cup pecans (about 2
  ounces)
¼ cup packed light brown
  sugar
2 tablespoons medium-
  hot red chile powder
  (preferably from
  Chimayo)
6 tablespoons unsalted
  butter

Cornbread is very accommodating stuff, welcoming a host of add-ons that only seem to make it more satisfying, without making it too much more work. Among my latest tamperings is this one. Imagine a crunchy pecan topping, like that on an apple crumble, but spiked with sweet-hot red chile and baked atop a pan of moist buttermilk cornbread. Sound tempting? It is, and, for the moment at least, it ranks with my friends and family as the most-requested recipe in my repertoire. The streusel not only can, but must, be made ahead, in order to chill, while the cornbread itself takes almost no time at all.

1. To make the streusel, combine the flour, pecans, sugar, chile powder, and butter in a food processor. Coarsely chop together with short bursts of power. With the motor running, process until a damp cookie-style dough forms. Do not over-process; leave some texture. Cover tightly and chill until firm, at least 2 hours.

2. To make the cornbread, position a rack in the middle of the oven and preheat to 400°F. Lightly coat a 9-by-13-inch metal baking pan with shortening. (If you are using a glass pan, reduce the oven temperature to 375°F.)

3. In a large bowl, thoroughly stir together the cornmeal, flour, sugar, baking powder, and salt. In a medium bowl, thoroughly whisk the eggs. Whisk in the buttermilk and melted butter. Add the egg mixture all at once to the dry ingredients and stir just until combined; do not overmix. Spread the batter in the prepared pan.

4. With a fork, crumble any large pieces of chilled streusel into chunks no larger than a grape. Scatter all of the streusel evenly over the top surface of the cornbread.

5. Bake until the edges of the cornbread are just beginning to pull away from the sides of the pan and a tester inserted into the center of the bread comes out almost clean, about 20 minutes.

6. Cool in the pan on a rack for 5 minutes. Serve hot or warm.

VARIATION: For plain cornbread, simply omit the streusel topping. Prepare and bake the cornbread as directed; the baking time is the same.

CORNBREAD

*2 cups yellow cornmeal
(preferably stone-ground)*

*1 cup unbleached
all-purpose flour*

⅓ cup sugar

*4 teaspoons baking
powder*

1 teaspoon salt

2 large eggs

*1½ cups buttermilk, at
room temperature*

*½ cup unsalted butter,
melted and cooled
slightly*

Sour Cream Cornbread with Green Chiles and Pumpkin Seeds

SERVES 9

½ cup raw pumpkin seeds
2 cups yellow cornmeal
   (preferably stone-
   ground)
1 cup unbleached
   all-purpose flour
⅓ cup sugar
4 teaspoons baking
   powder
1 teaspoon salt
2 large eggs
½ cup sour cream, at room
   temperature
½ cup canned cream-style
   corn
½ cup chopped roasted hot
   green chiles
½ cup unsalted butter,
   melted and slightly
   cooled

Here is another currently popular cornbread variation, one that not only pleases at grill suppers, but works for southwestern breakfasts and brunches as well. Pine nuts can replace the pumpkin seeds; use the same quantity.

1. Position a rack in the middle of the oven and preheat to 400°F. In a shallow metal pan, like a cake tin, toast the pumpkin seeds, stirring occasionally, until they are crisp, brown, and puffed, about 12 minutes. Cool and coarsely chop.

2. Lightly coat the inside of a 9-by-13-inch metal baking pan with solid vegetable shortening. (If you are using a glass pan, reduce the oven temperature to 375°F.)

3. In a large bowl, thoroughly stir together the cornmeal, flour, sugar, baking powder, and salt. In a medium bowl, whisk the eggs. Whisk in the sour cream, corn, chiles, and melted butter. Add the sour cream mixture all at once to the dry ingredients. Stir until almost combined. Add the pumpkin seeds and stir until just incorporated. Do not overmix. Spread the batter in the prepared pan.

4. Bake until the edges of the cornbread are just beginning to pull away from the sides of the pan and a tester inserted into the center comes out clean, about 20 minutes.

5. Let cool in the pan on a rack for 5 minutes. Serve hot.

Texas Toast

The chain restaurant versions of the uniquely rectangular slabs of squishy bread known as Texas toast have a certain charm. Made with good, gusty bread, spread with fresh garlic butter and toasted over a smoky grill fire, however, Texas toast makes sublime eating and a fine accompaniment to many a grilled entrée, especially when that entrée is spelled s-t-e-a-k. The hopelessly nostalgic (like me) may perhaps wish to whittle a larger loaf of bread into the right shape if crustless thick rectangular slices are desired.

1. In a small bowl, combine the butter, garlic, pepper, and salt. Mix well.

2. Light a direct-heat charcoal fire and let it burn down to medium-hot (5 seconds to "ouch") or preheat a gas grill to medium-high. Position the rack about 6 inches above the heat source.

3. Brush the bread slices all over with the oil.

4. When the grill is ready, lay the bread on the rack. Cover and grill, turning once, until the bread is crisp and brown, 2 to 3 minutes per side.

5. Remove from the heat. Working quickly, spread both sides of the bread slices with the butter, dividing it evenly and using it all. Serve immediately.

SERVES 6

¼ cup unsalted butter, softened
2 garlic cloves, crushed through a press
½ teaspoon freshly ground black pepper
Pinch salt
6 (2-inch-thick) slices firm, country-style bread
¼ cup olive oil

SMOKING CHIP OPTION: MESQUITE

Postres

Desserts

Postres
DESSERTS

Glazed Peach and Pineapple Skewers

Not many fruits grill successfully, but these two do. My usual advice is to select firm but ripe fruit; the grill doesn't cook it much but does make it juicy and the caramelization adds a welcome edge of burnt sugar flavor. Be sure the grill is scrupulously clean and free from flavors of the main course. Naturally, smoking chips are not used.

SERVES 4

½ cup bourbon
⅓ cup honey
4 tablespoons unsalted butter, melted
12 (1½-inch) chunks fresh pineapple
3 medium peaches, pitted and quartered
Vanilla Bean Ice Cream (page 238) or purchased premium vanilla ice cream, softened

1. Light a direct-heat charcoal fire and let it burn down to medium-hot (5 seconds to "ouch") or preheat a gas grill to medium-high. Position the rack about 6 inches above the heat source.

2. Meanwhile, stir together the bourbon, honey, and butter in a small bowl. Divide the fruit pieces among 4 skewers, alternating them.

3. When the grill is ready, lightly oil the rack. Lay the skewers on the rack, brush with some of the bourbon mixture, and cover. Grill, brushing with more bourbon mixture and turning the skewers once or twice, until the glaze is used up and the fruit is lightly marked by the grill, 6 to 8 minutes total.

4. Slide the fruit off the skewers into shallow dessert bowls. Top each portion with a scoop of ice cream and serve immediately.

Tequila–Mixed Berry Compote with Dulce de Leche

SERVES 6

1 unopened (14-ounce) can sweetened condensed milk
½ teaspoon vanilla extract
1 pound strawberries, hulled and coarsely chopped
12 ounces fresh blueberries, picked over
⅓ cup sugar
¼ cup tequila
3 tablespoons Triple Sec
2 tablespoons fresh lime juice

Dulce de leche is a comfort staple consisting of sweetened condensed milk, heated in the unopened can until it caramelizes into a butterscotch-like sauce. It's homey and satisfying on spoons, fingers, cakes, and cookies, but turns almost elegant when served atop tequila-marinated fresh berries.

1. Set the unopened can of condensed milk in a small heavy saucepan. Add water to come about three-quarters of the way up the sides of the can. Set over medium heat and bring to a gentle simmer. Partially cover and cook, turning the can over at the halfway point, for 1 hour.

2. Remove from the heat and cool the can in the pan of water to room temperature. Open the can only when cool.

3. Spoon the dulce de leche into a storage container and stir in the vanilla. Cover and refrigerate. (The dulce de leche can be prepared up to 3 days ahead. Return almost to room temperature before using.)

4. In a large bowl, combine the strawberries, blueberries, sugar, tequila, Triple Sec, and lime juice. Let stand at room temperature, stirring once or twice, for 30 minutes.

5. To serve, divide the berries and their juices among 6 dessert dishes. Top each portion with a generous dollop of dulce de leche and serve immediately.

Warm Mango Betty à la Mode

Apple brown Betty is a homey and frugal dessert, consisting mostly of diced apples baked with bread crumbs that thicken the fruit's juices, forming what is sometimes referred to as a pudding. Pretty much the same process happens here, with golden mangoes standing in for the apples, but the results, somehow, seem exciting and tropical, not homey at all. A scoop of some kind of ice cream makes this creation even more special, and while vanilla (homemade or store-bought) is classic, for a real flavor and color thrill, try topping the Betty with Avocado-Buttermilk Ice Cream (page 236) instead.

1. Position a rack in the upper third of the oven and preheat to 375°F.

2. In a bowl, toss together the mangoes, sugar, lime juice, and vanilla. Let stand, stirring once or twice, for 15 minutes.

3. In a medium bowl, thoroughly toss together the bread crumbs and melted butter. Lightly butter an 8-inch square baking dish. Spread half the mango mixture in the dish. Sprinkle with half the bread crumbs. Spread the remaining mango mixture in the dish; top with the remaining bread crumbs.

4. Bake until the fruit is bubbling and the top bread crumb layer is lightly browned, 30 to 40 minutes. Cool slightly in the dish on a rack.

5. Divide among serving dishes. Top each portion with a scoop of ice cream and serve immediately.

SERVES 4

5 cups diced mangoes (about 6 large mangoes)
6 tablespoons sugar
1 tablespoon fresh lime juice
1 teaspoon vanilla extract
2 cups fine fresh white bread crumbs
6 tablespoons unsalted butter, melted and cooled slightly, plus softened butter for the baking dish
Avocado-Buttermilk Ice Cream (page 236), Vanilla Bean Ice Cream (page 238), Canela–Black Pepper Ice Cream (page 237) or purchased premium vanilla ice cream, softened slightly

Mango, Peach, and Strawberry Shortcakes

SERVES 6

FRUIT FILLING

2 cups diced mangoes
    (2 large mangoes)
2 cups diced peaches
    (2 large peaches)
2 cups strawberry chunks
    (1 pint berries)
½ cup sugar
3 tablespoons fresh lime
    juice
1 tablespoon minced lime
    zest

SHORTCAKES

2½ cups unbleached all-
    purpose flour, plus flour
    for the work surface
3 tablespoons plus
    2 teaspoons sugar
4 teaspoons baking
    powder
¼ teaspoon salt
½ cup solid vegetable
    shortening, well chilled,
    cut into small pieces
7 tablespoons chilled
    unsalted butter, cut into
    small pieces
1 large egg
⅔ cup chilled buttermilk

1 cup whipping cream

Shortcake is the essence of summer. Here, mango adds a lush tropical note to the all-American favorite, making it an ideal southwestern grill menu dessert. The fruit filling can be combined and left to macerate for an hour or so, but the short-cakes should be mixed up and baked just before serving. Whipped cream is the good and tradition-al accompaniment here, but if you want to go to the trouble, homemade Vanilla Bean Ice Cream (page 238) is sublime.

1. To make the fruit filling, combine the mangoes, strawberries, peaches, sugar, lime juice, and lime zest in a large bowl. Cover and let stand at room temperature, stirring once or twice, for at least 30 minutes and up to 1½ hours.

2. To make the shortcake, position a rack in the upper third of the oven and preheat to 450°F.

3. Into a large bowl, sift together the flour, 3 tablespoons of the sugar, the baking powder, and salt. Cut the vegetable shortening and butter into the dry ingredients with a vegetable cutter until bits the size of corn kernels are formed.

4. In a small bowl, thoroughly whisk the egg. Whisk in the buttermilk. With as few strokes as possible, stir in the buttermilk mixture until a soft, crumbly dough is formed.

5. Flour the work surface. Turn out the dough and gather and briefly knead it into a ball until it just holds together. Roll out the dough into a 9-by-3-inch rectangle about ¾-inch thick. Trim the edges. Cut the dough into six 3-inch squares. Transfer the squares to an ungreased, preferably insulated, baking sheet. Sprinkle the shortcakes with the remaining 2 teaspoons sugar.

6. Bake the shortcakes until they are puffed and golden, and the bottoms are crisp, 12 to 14 minutes.

7. Meanwhile, whip the cream to stiff peaks.

8. Let the shortcakes rest on the sheet on a rack for 2 minutes.

9. Split the shortcakes in half horizontally, setting a bottom half on each of 6 dessert plates. Spoon about ½ cup of the fruit mixture, juices included, over each shortcake bottom. Top each with a small dollop of the cream. Set the shortcake tops in place. Spoon the remaining fruit and juices over and around the short-cakes. Top each with a large dollop of whipped cream and serve immediately.

Tropical Fruit Soup

This cool, tart, and very pretty soup is an easy way to conclude a summertime grill meal. The coconut-flavored base, which needs thorough chilling, can be prepared well in advance, while the last-minute serving details are minimal, thus keeping the chef cool, too. For a more elaborate presentation, suitable for a dressy dinner party, float a scoop of mango or raspberry sorbet in the soup, along with the fruit.

1. In a bowl, stir together the orange juice, pineapple juice, coconut milk, honey, and lime juice. Skim any foam from the surface, cover, and refrigerate until very cold, at least 5 hours and preferably overnight.

2. To serve, stir to recombine the juice mixture, if separated. Ladle into chilled wide bowls. Divide the diced fruit among the bowls, mounding it in the center of each. Scatter the raspberries around, garnish each bowl with a sprig of mint, and serve immediately.

SERVES 4

1 cup fresh orange juice
1 cup unsweetened
   pineapple juice
¾ cup unsweetened
   canned Thai-style
   coconut milk
6 tablespoons honey
1 tablespoon fresh lime
   juice
1 teaspoon vanilla extract
2½ cups assorted diced
   fresh tropical fruit, such
   as mango, pineapple,
   and papaya
Fresh raspberries
Sprigs of mint

Rustic Dixon Apple Tart with Red Chile Glaze

SERVES 4

CRUST

1 cup unbleached all-
    purpose flour
2 tablespoons sugar
2 tablespoons whole
    wheat flour
Pinch salt
4 tablespoons chilled
    unsalted butter, cut into
    small pieces
4 tablespoons chilled solid
    vegetable shortening,
    cut into small pieces
3 to 4 tablespoons ice
    water

FILLING

4 medium-large apples,
    such as Granny Smith,
    peeled, cored, and thinly
    sliced
3 tablespoons packed light
    brown sugar
1 tablespoon fresh lemon
    juice
1 tablespoon unbleached
    all-purpose flour
1 teaspoon medium-hot
    unblended chile powder
    (preferably Chimayo)
1 teaspoon white sugar
2 tablespoons unsalted
    butter, melted

This free-form tart is easy to make and very forgiving if your pastry-handling skills are minimal. It celebrates the apples of Dixon, a small community north of Santa Fe famed for its crops of fall fruit, although any good, not-too juicy apple will work fine here. The apple compatibility of the crackly glaze demonstrates once again that, though picante, chiles are indeed fruit. Canela–Black Pepper Ice Cream (page 237) makes an intriguing and delicious accompaniment, but then so does (less labor-intensive) Honey and Spice Whipped Cream (page 229), spiked with a cross-cultural touch of Chinese five-spice powder.

1. To make the crust, combine the white flour, sugar, whole wheat flour, and salt in a food processor. Pulse to blend. Add the butter and shortening and pulse until bits the size of corn kernels form. With the motor running, add enough of the ice water through the feed tube to form a granular, cornmeal-like dough. Turn it out onto a work surface, gather it into a ball, flatten into a disk, wrap in plastic, and chill for at least 1 hour.

2. Soften the dough for a few minutes at room temperature if it seems hard to roll. Dust the work surface with flour and roll the dough out into an 11-inch round. Transfer the round to a baking sheet with sides. (The dough can be prepared up to this point 24 hours in advance. Cover tightly and refrigerate, returning the dough almost to room temperature before proceeding.)

3. Position a rack in the upper third of the oven and preheat to 450°F.

4. To make the filling, combine the apples, brown sugar, lemon juice, and 1 tablespoon flour in a medium bowl. Let stand at room temperature, stirring once or twice, until juicy, about 15 minutes.

5. In a small bowl, stir together the chile powder and 1 teaspoon white sugar.

6. Spoon the apples and any juices into the center of the round of dough, mounding the fruit and leaving a 2-inch border of dough exposed. Fold the exposed dough border up over the fruit, pleating it, to make a rough edge. Brush the edge and the top of the exposed apple filling with the melted butter. Sprinkle the buttered crust edge filling evenly with the sugar-chile mixture.

7. Set the baking sheet in the oven. Decrease the heat to 400°F and bake until the filling is bubbling and the crust is golden and crisp, about 25 minutes.

8. Briefly cool the tart on the baking sheet on a rack. Cut into wedges and serve warm, topped with a scoop of ice cream or a dollop of whipped cream.

Honey and Spice Whipped Cream

Any fruit dessert that welcomes spices (most would qualify) will welcome this just slightly zippier whipped cream topping. Red chile honey is delicious—try it also on cornbread. It can be ordered from Coyote Café General Store (see Mail-Order Sources, page 321) but plain honey can be used.

1. In a medium bowl, whip the cream until fairly stiff peaks form. Add the honey, sour cream, and five-spice powder and beat until well combined.

2. Store the whipped cream, covered, in the refrigerator and use it within 30 minutes or so.

MAKES ABOUT 1 CUP

½ cup whipping cream
1 tablespoon honey
1 tablespoon sour cream
½ teaspoon Chinese five-
spice powder

Strawberry-Rhubarb Upside-Down Cake

SERVES 8

12 tablespoons unsalted butter, softened
¾ cup packed light brown sugar
1 cup diced rhubarb (½-inch pieces) (see Note)
2½ cups chunked fresh strawberries
1¾ cups unbleached all-purpose flour
1 teaspoon baking powder
1 teaspoon baking soda
¼ teaspoon salt
¾ cup plus 2 tablespoons white sugar
2 tablespoons minced orange zest
3 large eggs, separated
1 tablespoon fresh lemon juice
1 teaspoon vanilla extract
⅔ cup buttermilk, at room temperature
Unsweetened whipped cream
Small whole strawberries (optional)

Serve this rustic, easy-to-make cake still warm from the oven if you can, when the flavor and texture are at their best. In my book, whipped cream is the best accompaniment, but those who like ice cream with cake will definitely like it with this one. Serve homemade Vanilla Bean Ice Cream (page 238) if you like, or buy a premium strawberry ice cream at the store.

1. Position a rack in the middle of the oven and preheat to 350°F.

2. In a 9-inch round cake pan with 2-inch-high sides, combine 6 tablespoons of the butter, the brown sugar, and rhubarb. Set in the oven and heat, stirring once or twice, until the mixture bubbles, about 10 minutes. Remove from the oven, stir in the chunked strawberries and set aside.

3. In a medium bowl, sift together the flour, baking powder, baking soda, and salt, then sift again.

4. In a large bowl, mash together ¾ cup of the white sugar and the orange zest with the back of a wooden spoon, until the sugar is moist and fragrant. Add the remaining 6 tablespoons butter and, using the spoon or a hand-held mixer, cream well. Add the egg yolks one at a time, beating well after each addition. Beat in the lemon juice and vanilla. Add the dry ingredients and the buttermilk by thirds to the egg mixture, beating just to blend after each addition; do not overmix.

5. Using a whisk or an electric mixer with clean beaters, whip the egg whites in a clean bowl until soft peaks form. Sprinkle the remaining 2 tablespoons white sugar over the egg whites and continue to whip until stiff and glossy. Add about one-third of the whites to the cake batter and fold in well. Add the remaining whites and fold in until just combined; a few streaks of white may remain.

6. Spoon the batter over the fruit in the pan and spread it to the edges.

7. Bake until the cake is lightly browned and springs back when lightly pressed, about 40 minutes. A tester inserted into the center of the cake should come out clean.

8. Let the cake rest in the pan on a rack for 5 minutes. Invert a serving plate over the cake pan. Flip the cake pan and plate over together, then lift the pan away.

9. To serve, cut the still-warm cake into wedges. Top each wedge with a dollop of whipped cream and a whole strawberry. Serve immediately.

Note: Frozen rhubarb, already softened by its freezing, works best here, though fresh can be used.

Cajeta Caramel-Pecan Bars

MAKES ABOUT 18 BARS

1½ cups pecans (about
  6 ounces)
1¾ cups unbleached
  all-purpose flour
1 teaspoon baking powder
½ teaspoon baking soda
½ teaspoon salt
¾ cup unsalted butter,
  softened
¾ cup packed light brown
  sugar
¾ cup white sugar
2 large eggs, at room
  temperature
2 teaspoons vanilla
  extract
⅓ cup cajeta, preferably
  made of goats' milk

*C*ajeta is a thick Mexican caramel sauce some-times based on goats' milk, although the common brand available here in jars seems to be made with cows' milk instead (at least it lacks a distinctive goaty tang). Either version, when drizzled over a fairly traditional pan of blondie batter and baked, transforms those bake-sale staples into treats with gooey, toffee-like veins running throughout—a distinct improvement over the original, to my way of thinking.

1. Position a rack in the middle of the oven and preheat to 400°F. In a metal pan, like a cake tin, toast the pecans, stirring them once or twice, until they are crisp, lightly browned, and fragrant, 8 to 10 minutes. Remove and cool. Coarsely chop the pecans.

2. Decrease the oven temperature to 350°F. Coat a 9-by-13-inch metal pan lightly with solid vegetable shortening. (If you are using a glass pan, lower the oven temperature to 325°F.)

3. Sift together the flour, baking powder, baking soda, and salt, then sift again.

4. In a large bowl, cream the butter. Add the brown and white sugars and cream until light. One at a time, beat in the eggs. Mix in the vanilla. Add the dry ingredients and mix until almost combined. Add the pecans and stir until just combined; do not overmix.

5. Spread the batter in the prepared pan. Drizzle the cajeta evenly over the batter.

6. Bake until the edges are just beginning to pull away from the sides of the pan and a tester inserted into the center comes out almost clean, about 25 minutes.

7. Let cool completely in the pan on a rack. Cut into bars to serve.

Espresso-Piñon Brownies with Kahlua-Chocolate Glaze

Deliciously rich and complexly flavored, these are aristocratic brownies, worthy of concluding a great meal. Enjoy them plain, with a cup of coffee, or accompany them with a big scoop of Vanilla Bean Ice Cream (page 238).

1. Position a rack in the middle of the oven and preheat to 375°F. Spread the pine nuts in a shallow metal pan, like a cake tin, and roast, stirring once or twice, until crisp and golden brown, about 10 minutes. Remove from the pan and cool.

2. Decrease the oven temperature to 325°F. Butter a 9-by-13-inch metal baking pan.

3. In a large bowl, cream together the butter and both sugars until fluffy. Whisk in the eggs, one at a time, beating just to combine after each addition. Stir in the cocoa, 4 teaspoons of the espresso powder, the vanilla, and salt. Add the flour and pine nuts. Mix just to combine. Spread the batter in the prepared pan.

4. Bake the brownies until a tester inserted into the center comes out clean, about 30 minutes.

5. Cool completely in the pan on a rack.

6. Cut the brownies into sixteen 3- by 2-inch bars. Set the bars, spacing them apart, on a large piece of foil or waxed paper.

7. In the top of a double boiler over simmering water, combine the chocolate, Kahlua, and remaining 1 teaspoon espresso powder. Stir occasionally until smooth, then remove from the heat. Dip the tines of a fork into the chocolate mixture and decoratively drizzle it over the brownies, using it all.

8. Let the glaze cool and set, then store the brownies in an airtight container at room temperature until serving.

MAKES 16 BROWNIES

½ cup pine nuts (piñon nuts)
1 cup unsalted butter, softened
1¼ cups white sugar
½ cup firmly packed dark brown sugar
4 large eggs
½ cup unsweetened cocoa powder
5 teaspoons instant espresso powder
1 teaspoon vanilla extract
¼ teaspoon salt
1¼ cups unbleached all-purpose flour
4 ounces bittersweet chocolate, chopped
3 tablespoons Kahlua

Four "P" Nut Harvest Bars

MAKES 24

CRUST
2 cups unbleached
  all-purpose flour
⅔ cup confectioners' sugar
1 cup unsalted butter,
  softened

TOPPING
10 tablespoons unsalted
  butter, melted and
  slightly cooled
½ cup dark corn syrup
½ cup packed dark brown
  sugar
2 tablespoons dark rum,
  such as Myers's
1 teaspoon vanilla extract
Pinch salt
1 cup lightly salted
  roasted peanuts (about
  5 ounces)
1 cup shelled roasted
  pistachios (about 5
  ounces)
1 cup chopped pecans
  (about 4 ounces)
½ cup pine nuts (about
  2½ ounces)

Various nuts are important crops throughout the Southwest, where the hot, dry climate is conducive to their growth. For these rich, little, easy-to-make, easy-to-like bars—more candy than cookie—I've combined the four principal nut crops of the region into one nutty extravaganza. I especially like these slightly warm, alongside a big bowl of Vanilla Bean Ice Cream (page 238).

1. Position a rack in the middle of the oven and preheat to 350°F.

2. To make the crust, sift together the flour and confectioners' sugar into a medium bowl. Cut the butter into the flour with a pastry cutter. Knead the dough with your knuckles until it is smooth. Pat the dough evenly into a 9-by-13-inch metal baking pan (if you are using glass, reduce the oven temperature to 325°F).

3. Bake until the crust is set and no longer raw looking and is golden brown around the edges, about 15 minutes.

4. Let the crust cool in the pan on a rack for 5 minutes.

5. Meanwhile, make the topping. In a large bowl, stir together the melted butter, corn syrup, brown sugar, rum, vanilla, and salt. Add the nuts and mix well. Spread the nut mixture evenly over the warm crust.

6. Return the pan to the oven and bake until the filling is lightly browned, bubbling, and set at the edges, another 20 to 25 minutes.

7. Cool completely on a rack before cutting into bars. Stored airtight at room temperature, the bars will keep for at least a week. They can be frozen for up to 1 month.

Mexican-Chocolate Shortbread Cookies

Among the cookie recipes I have developed over the years, these remain the most popular. Lately I have been adding a bit of ancho chile powder, along with the cinnamon and black pepper, which makes the cookies even tastier. (The flavor of anchos is sometimes described as "chocolaty.") Serve these with plain ice cream, simple fruit desserts, or just a cup of coffee or hot chocolate.

1. Sift together the flour, cocoa, ancho powder, cinnamon, salt, and pepper, then sift again. In a medium bowl, cream together the butter and the 10 tablespoons sugar until light. Mix in the vanilla, then add the flour mixture. Stir and knead the dough (it will be dry and crumbly at first) until it is smooth and supple.

2. Between 2 sheets of waxed paper, roll the dough out as evenly as possible to a thickness of ¼ inch. Chill for 30 minutes.

3. Meanwhile, position racks in the upper and lower thirds of the oven and preheat to 275°F. Lightly coat two cookie sheets with solid vegetable shortening.

4. Cut out the cookies with a 2-inch round cutter. Pierce each cookie twice with the tines of a fork. Spread the coating sugar on a small plate. Lightly press the top of each cookie into the sugar, so that the sugar clings to the dough. Arrange the cookies, sugar side-up, on the prepared sheets, spacing them about 1 inch apart.

5. Bake the cookies, exchanging the position of the sheets on the racks from top to bottom and from front to back, until the cookies are crisp and firm, about 40 minutes.

6. Remove from the oven and cool the cookies on the sheets on racks for 5 minutes. Transfer to paper towels and cool completely.

7. Store the cookies airtight at room temperature. They will be better the day after they are baked and will keep for about 1 week.

MAKES ABOUT 24 COOKIES

2 cups unbleached all-purpose flour

⅔ cup lightly packed unsweetened cocoa powder

1 tablespoon pure ancho chile powder

½ teaspoon ground cinnamon

½ teaspoon salt

¼ teaspoon freshly ground black pepper

1 cup unsalted butter, softened

10 tablespoons sugar, plus additional sugar for coating the cookies

2 teaspoons vanilla extract

Desserts

Avocado-Buttermilk Ice Cream

MAKES ABOUT 1½ QUARTS

3 large eggs
1⅓ cups sugar
3 cups buttermilk
1 cup whipping cream
½ teaspoon vanilla extract
Pinch salt
3 black-skinned buttery-
    ripe California (Hass)
    avocados

This wonderful ice cream is subtle but delicious, the avocados giving it a mysteriously nutty flavor and rich texture, not to mention a stunning celadon color. It's best on its own, as a hot-day cooler, the way you might enjoy a gelato in Italy, or paired with delicately flavored fruit desserts, such as the Warm Mango Betty on page 225.

1. In a large bowl, thoroughly whisk the eggs. Gradually whisk in the sugar. Whisk in the buttermilk, cream, vanilla, and salt. Cover and chill until very cold, at least 5 hours and preferably overnight.

2. Halve and pit the avocados and scoop the flesh from the peels into a food processor. Add about 3 cups of the chilled egg mixture to the food processor. Process, stopping several times to scrape down the sides of the work bowl, until the mixture is smooth.

3. Combine the pureed avocado mixture with the remaining egg mixture and transfer to the canister of an ice cream maker. Churn according to the manufacturer's directions.

4. Transfer to an airtight container and store in the freezer. The texture of the ice cream will be best in the first 48 hours after it is frozen.

5. Before scooping, soften slightly in the refrigerator, if necessary.

Canela–Black Pepper Ice Cream

Canela is also called Mexican cinnamon. Softer than regular cinnamon bark, its flavor is more subtle and yet more aromatic at the same time. Paired with a bit of black pepper, for an intriguing taste and the slightest touch of heat, it makes a most unusual and tasty ice cream. Try this with any warm apple dessert (like the tart on page 228) for a heaven-made combination.

MAKES ABOUT 1½ QUARTS

4 egg yolks
¾ cup sugar
1 teaspoon freshly ground
    canela
½ teaspoon freshly ground
    black pepper
Pinch salt
2½ cups half-and-half
1½ cups whipping cream
½ teaspoon vanilla extract

1. In a large bowl, whisk together the egg yolks, sugar, canela, pepper, and salt.

2. In a heavy 3-quart saucepan, combine the half-and-half and whipping cream and bring just to a simmer. Gradually whisk the hot cream into the egg mixture. Return the mixture to the pan and set over low heat. Cook, stirring constantly, until the mixture thickens slightly and leaves a track on the back of a spoon when a fingertip is drawn across it, about 4 minutes.

3. Strain the mixture into a bowl, whisk in the vanilla, cover, and chill until very cold, for at least 5 hours and preferably overnight.

4. Transfer the cold custard to the canister of an ice cream maker and churn according to the manufacturer's directions.

5. Store the ice cream, covered, for up to 2 days in the freezer.

6. Before scooping, soften slightly in the refrigerator, if necessary.

Note: To experience the unique flavor of canela, you will need to grind your own. It is commonly found in health food stores or in good spice shops. Use an electric spice mill to grind 3 or 4 pieces of the fairly soft bark to a powder, then measure out what you need. Regular cinnamon, if that is all you find, still makes good ice cream; you may want to use a little less.

Vanilla Bean Ice Cream

MAKES ABOUT 1½ QUARTS

4 large egg yolks
⅔ cup sugar
Pinch salt
2½ cups half-and-half
1½ cups whipping cream
1 vanilla bean

Vanilla was discovered in Mexico centuries ago, and its powerful lure soon captured the world. Though most vanilla is now grown elsewhere (and much of what passes for vanilla in Mexico is fake and potentially poisonous), its flavor still runs through sweets of the Southwest like a brown, fragrant stream. Vanilla really shines in simple desserts of cream, egg, and sugar, and this ice cream—the ultimate garnish to many southwestern desserts, as well as one of the world's great comfort dishes on its own—is no exception. Make it in an old-fashioned salt-and-ice-type machine, if you can, for the best texture.

1. In a medium heatproof bowl, whisk together the egg yolks, sugar, and salt.

2. In a medium heavy saucepan, combine the half-and-half and cream. Split the vanilla bean lengthwise. Scrape the tiny seeds out of the bean halves into the cream. Add the bean halves to the cream as well and set the pan over medium-low heat. Bring the cream mixture very slowly to a simmer, stirring often, to infuse it with the vanilla flavor.

3. Gradually whisk the hot cream into the egg mixture. Pour the mixture back into the saucepan and set it over low heat. Cook, stirring constantly, until the mixture thickens into a custard that will coat the spoon heavily and will leave a clear track when a finger is drawn across it, about 4 minutes.

4. Immediately transfer the custard (along with the vanilla bean halves) to a heatproof bowl and cool to room temperature. Cover the custard with plastic wrap, pressing it onto the surface to prevent formation of a skin. Refrigerate until very cold, at least 5 hours and preferably overnight.

5. Discard the vanilla bean halves. Pour the chilled custard into the canister of an ice cream maker and churn according to the manufacturer's directions.

6. Transfer the finished ice cream to a storage container, cover tightly, and store in the freezer. The ice cream will be best if eaten within 48 hours.

7. Before scooping, soften slightly in the refrigerator, if necessary.

Mexican-Chocolate Ice Cream

Inspired by the distinctive flavors of Mexican chocolate (most often used in making a foamy and delicious hot drink), this ice cream uses premium Belgian chocolate, toasted almonds, and plenty of real vanilla—a deluxe treat. It's so rich, good, and intensely flavored, a serving needs little more by way of embellishment than a single, perfect strawberry.

MAKES ABOUT 1½ QUARTS

1 cup whole unblanched almonds (about 4 ounces)
½ pound imported premium dark chocolate, chopped (Callebaut is recommended)
4 egg yolks
¾ cup sugar
1 teaspoon ground cinnamon
Pinch salt
3 cups half-and-half
1 cup whipping cream
1 tablespoon vanilla extract

1. Position a rack in the middle of the oven and preheat to 400°F. In a shallow metal pan, like a cake tin, toast the almonds, stirring them once or twice, until they are crisp, lightly browned and fragrant, about 10 minutes. Remove from the pan, cool, and coarsely chop.

2. In the top of a double boiler over gently simmering water, melt the chocolate, stirring occasionally. Remove the double boiler from the heat, but leave the chocolate sitting over the hot water.

3. In a large bowl, whisk the egg yolks thoroughly. In a small bowl, combine the sugar, cinnamon, and salt. Gradually whisk into the yolks.

4. In a heavy medium saucepan over moderate heat, combine the half-and-half and whipping cream. Bring to a simmer. Gradually whisk the hot cream into the egg yolk mixture. Return this mixture to the saucepan, set over low heat and cook, stirring constantly, until the mixture forms a custard thick enough to heavily coat the back of a spoon, about 4 minutes.

5. Remove from the heat and immediately transfer to a bowl. Scrape the melted chocolate into the custard. Stir in the vanilla and whisk to combine; the custard may appear grainy. Cover, pressing plastic wrap onto the surface of the custard to prevent formation of a skin, and refrigerate until very cold, at least 5 hours.

6. Pour the chilled mixture into the canister of an ice cream maker and churn according to the manufacturer's directions. Coarsely chop the almonds and add them to the ice cream near the end of the churning period.

7. Transfer to an airtight container and store the ice cream in the freezer for up to 2 days.

8. Before scooping, soften slightly in the refrigerator, if necessary.

Pineapple-Coconut Ice Cream Pie
with
Hot Fudge Sauce

SERVES 6

CRUST
1 cup finely and evenly
   crushed chocolate wafer
   cookies (such as
   Nabisco Famous)
¼ cup sugar
4 tablespoons unsalted
   butter, melted and
   slightly cooled

FILLING
3 pints Häagen-Dazs
   pineapple-coconut ice
   cream, softened slightly

SAUCE
1 (12-ounce) bag genuine
   semisweet chocolate
   chips
½ cup unsalted butter, cut
   into small pieces
⅓ cup whipping cream
⅓ cup coconut-flavored
   rum, such as Malibu
⅓ cup superfine sugar
½ teaspoon vanilla extract
Pinch salt

¾ cup sweetened flaked
   coconut

An interesting sign of the times is the increased availability of southwestern and Latino ingredients in supermarkets all over the U.S. Among the most telling are a couple of new ice cream flavors from Häagen-Dazs: dulce de leche, modeled on the caramelized condensed milk treat (see page 224) and pineapple-coconut. The latter finds its way into this easy frozen dessert, which waits for up to a week in the freezer for just the right occasion. Homemade fudge sauce, spiked with a little coconut-flavored rum, hardens into chewy bliss as it hits the frozen pie.

1. To make the crust, stir together the crumbs and sugar in a medium bowl. Add the butter and stir and mash together until the crumbs are evenly moistened. Transfer to a 9-inch pie pan and pat the crumb mixture firmly onto the bottom and up the sides of the pan. Chill for 30 minutes.

2. Spread the softened ice cream into the prepared pie crust, mounding it in the center. Freeze until solid, at least 2 hours. Wrap the pie well and store in the freezer for up to 1 week.

3. To make the sauce, combine the chocolate chips, butter, cream, rum, and sugar in a medium heavy saucepan over low heat. Cook, stirring often, until smooth. Remove from the heat and stir in the vanilla and salt. (The sauce can be cooled, covered, and refrigerated for up to 10 days. Rewarm over low heat or in a microwave oven before using.)

4. To toast the coconut, position a rack in the middle of the oven and preheat to 350°F. Spread the coconut in a shallow metal pan, like a cake tin, and toast, stirring often, until golden, 8 to 10 minutes. (The coconut can be prepared up to a week in advance. Store airtight at room temperature.)

5. To serve, let the pie stand at room temperature for 10 minutes. With a knife dipped into hot water and wiped dry between cuts, divide the pie into wedges. Transfer the wedges to dessert plates. Pour about ¼ cup of sauce over and around each piece of pie. Sprinkle each piece of pie with about 3 tablespoons coconut and serve immediately.

Frozen Raspberry Margarita Pie

SERVES 6

CRUST

1 cup finely and evenly
   crushed graham crackers
¼ cup sugar
4 tablespoons unsalted
   butter, melted and
   slightly cooled

FILLING

2 large eggs, separated
1 (14-ounce) can sweet-
   ened condensed milk
½ cup fresh lime juice
1 tablespoon minced lime
   zest
1 tablespoon tequila
1 tablespoon Triple Sec or
   other orange liqueur
¼ teaspoon cream of tartar

SAUCE

12 ounces fresh
   raspberries, picked over
¼ cup sugar
2 tablespoons tequila
1 tablespoon Triple Sec or
   other orange liqueur
1 tablespoon fresh lime
   juice

The sharp-eyed will recognize this pie's origins in the traditional key lime pie. The kitchen wisdom that such a pie could survive freezing comes from Eleanor Klivan's wonderful book, *Bake and Freeze Desserts*. The margarita adaptation and the tequila-raspberry sauce are my own additions. The result is a breathtakingly frosty, remarkably easy, and utterly delicious do-ahead hot-weather dessert, the perfect antidote for palates recovering from a zippy southwestern grill meal.

1. To make the crust, stir together the crumbs and sugar in a medium bowl. Add the butter and stir and mash together until the crumbs are evenly moistened. Transfer to a 9-inch pie pan and pat the crumb mixture firmly onto the bottom and up the sides of the pan. Chill for 30 minutes.

2. To make the filling, whisk the eggs yolks in a large bowl. Add the condensed milk and whisk to blend. Add the lime juice, zest, tequila, and Triple Sec. Whisk no more than necessary to combine. In a medium bowl, beat the egg whites until foamy. Add the cream of tartar and continue to beat until stiff peaks form. Evenly fold the whites into the filling.

3. Spoon the filling into the prepared piecrust and freeze until solid, at least 2 hours. Wrap tightly and freeze overnight.

4. To make the sauce, combine the raspberries, sugar, tequila, Triple Sec, and lime juice in a food processor. Process until smooth. (The sauce can be prepared up to 1 day ahead, if desired. Cover tightly and refrigerate.)

5. To serve, let the pie stand at room temperature for 10 minutes. Using a knife dipped into hot water and wiped clean between cuts, divide the pie into wedges. Transfer the wedges to plates, pour or spoon the sauce over and around each wedge, and serve immediately.

Vanilla-Lime Flans

A touch of lime transforms the traditional south-western caramel custard dessert known as flan, lightening it without reducing the comfort factor. For color (plus great flavor), scatter a few whole fresh raspberries around the flans after they are unmolded.

SERVES 8

1⅓ cups plus ½ cup sugar
½ cup water
4 teaspoons minced lime
 peel
3 large eggs
5 large egg yolks
2 cups whipping cream
1½ cups milk
2½ teaspoons vanilla
 extract
¼ teaspoon salt

1. Position a rack in the middle of the oven and preheat to 325°F. Place eight ¾-cup ramekins or custard cups on a work surface.

2. In a heavy medium saucepan over low heat, stir together 1⅓ cups of the sugar and the ½ cup water until the sugar dissolves. Increase the heat and boil without stirring, brushing down the sides of the pan with a wet pastry brush and swirling the pan to promote even cooking, until the syrup turns a deep amber, about 8 minutes. Immediately divide the caramel among the ramekins. Using kitchen mitts to protect your hands, and working quickly, pick up, tilt and rotate each ramekin to coat the sides with caramel. Transfer the ramekins to a roasting pan.

3. In a large bowl, use the back of a spoon to mash together the remaining ½ cup sugar and the lime zest until the sugar is moist and fragrant. Add the eggs and yolks and whisk to blend.

4. In a heavy medium saucepan over moderate heat, combine the cream and milk. Bring just to a boil. Gradually whisk the hot cream mixture into the egg mixture. Whisk in the vanilla and salt. Ladle the custard into the prepared ramekins, dividing it evenly and using it all. Add enough hot water to the roasting pan to come halfway up the sides of the ramekins.

5. Set the roaster in the oven and bake the flans until they are just set and beginning to color on top, about 45 minutes. Remove from the roaster and cool for 45 minutes. Cover and refrigerate overnight.

6. To serve, let the flans stand at room temperature for 15 minutes. Carefully cut around the sides of the flans with a knife to loosen. Invert the flans onto plates, drizzling them with any liquid caramel remaining in the ramekins. Serve immediately.

Cocktails and Coolers

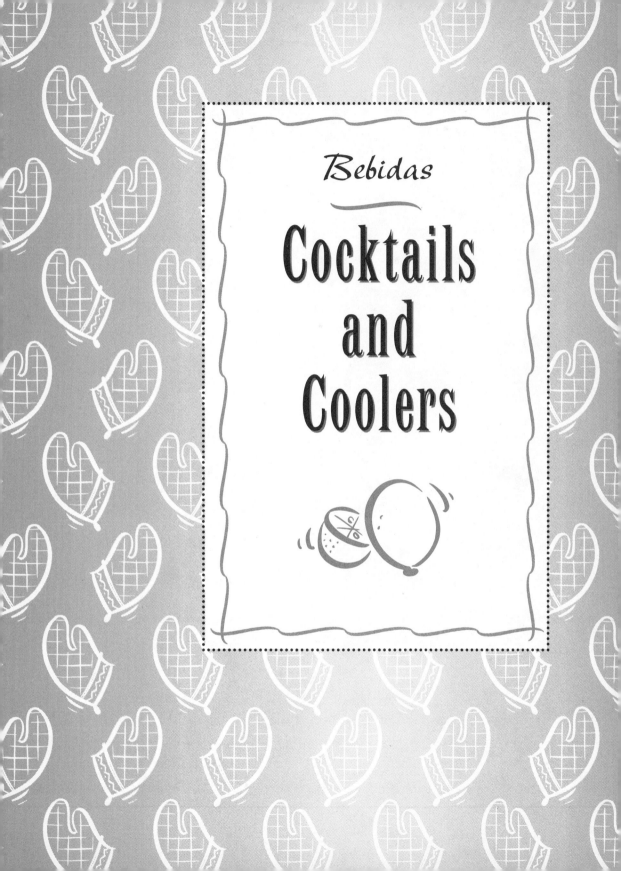

Bebidas

COCKTAILS AND COOLERS

Classic Fresh Lime Margarita with Tequila Plata

I had to type this recipe title three times before I stopped making "margarita" plural—it's that hard for me to think of this ultimate southwestern party cocktail in the singular. When properly made, as it is here, with little more than fresh lime juice and a distinctively flavored 100 percent blue agave-based silver tequila, it's so delicious you'll definitely want to enjoy more than one. (It's almost as powerful as a martini, and so it should be enjoyed in moderation.) This is a long way from slushy, machine-extruded tourist Margaritas or sloppy, happy-hour twofers based on artificially flavored sweet-and-sour mix. Try one—it will revolutionize what you think of margaritas.

1. Run the lime wedge around the rim of a stemmed cocktail glass to moisten it; reserve the lime wedge. Dip the moistened glass rim in the salt to coat it. Set aside.

2. In a cocktail shaker, combine the tequila, Cointreau, and lime juice. Add 5 cubes from a household ice tray. Shake until very cold.

3. For a margarita "up," strain into the prepared glass; for on the rocks, strain over fresh ice cubes. Squeeze the lime wedge into the glass and serve immediately.

MAKES 1 COCKTAIL

1 lime wedge
Kosher salt, on a small
*   plate*
2 ounces (¼ cup) tequila,
*   preferably 100 percent*
*   blue agave tequila plata*
1½ ounces (3 tablespoons)
*   Cointreau or another*
*   orange liqueur*
1½ ounces (3 tablespoons)
*   fresh lime juice*
Ice

Clearing Up Tequila

Tequila is a distilled spirit, based partially or wholly on the fermented fruits of a plant called the blue agave. Produced in a legally defined area of Mexico, largely in the state of Jalisco, tequila is a particularly distinctive and pure example of the larger class of distilled spirits known as mescals (some of which, but never tequila, include a worm in the bottle). There is much cheap, bad tequila, but then there is also much good tequila, for those willing to shop for it, pay the necessary price, and open themselves up to enjoy a vigorously flavored though smooth and elegant spirit. The best tequilas (the so-called superpremiums) are made from 100 percent blue agave sugars, bottled at the distillery and frequently sold in individually numbered bottles. The worst contain the minimum amount of blue agave and may well be transported over the border in tanker trucks to be bottled in the U.S. One hundred percent blue agave silver (or "plata") tequila is the drink of true tequila lovers, the shimmering spirit full of the taste of the agave fruits. Some of these silver tequilas are aged, transforming them into cognaclike sipping liquors. (Gold tequila, elevated by advertising into something special, is nothing more than lesser silver tequila, colored and flavored by the addition of caramel. Smoother, less vegetal-tasting than all-agave platas, better gold tequilas are a good place for tequila beginners to start.) Among those brand names that tequila lovers love to see are Herradura, El Tesoro, Patron, and Centinela. But go beyond the name and read the label to be sure you are getting the best of the best. Sample your superpremium plata tequila in a straight shot, if desired, or shake up a genuine, fresh lime margarita. *¡Salud!*

Frozen Watermelon–Prickly Pear Margaritas

The crimson fruit of the prickly pear cactus is what gives the plant its name. The oval, sometimes spiny fruits don't much resemble pears either in appearance or flavor. They look more like large red hen's eggs and they taste, to me, like strawberries diluted with watermelon, hence this cocktail pairing. Since that is all the dilution one drink can stand, I use frozen melon cubes rather than ice. The cocktail that results is slushy, not all that frozen, and packed with crimson color and fruity flavor.

1. Transfer the watermelon cubes to a plastic storage bag and freeze until solid.

2. Trim the ends off the prickly pears (wear gloves if they seem at all spiny). Remove and discard the thick peels and cut the flesh into chunks. Transfer to a food processor and puree. Pour the pureed prickly pear into a sieve set over a bowl. With a rubber scraper, push the juice and any pulp through the sieve; discard the small black seeds. Measure out 1 cup prickly pear juice.

3. Combine the juice, tequila, Triple Sec, and lime juice. Cover and chill until cold, at least 2 hours.

4. Shortly before serving, moisten the rims of 2 large stemmed glasses with one of the lime wedges. Dip the rims in the salt.

5. In a blender, combine the frozen melon cubes and the prickly pear mixture. Blend on high until smooth and slushy. Divide the mixture between the two prepared glasses. Squeeze a lime wedge into each glass and serve immediately.

MAKES 2 GENEROUS COCKTAILS

2 cups seedless red-ripe watermelon, cut in 1-inch chunks

6 large prickly pear fruits

4 ounces (½ cup) gold tequila

4 ounces (½ cup) Triple Sec or other orange liqueur

1 ounce (2 tablespoons) fresh lime juice

2 lime wedges

Kosher salt, on a small plate

Tunas

The fruits of the prickly pear cactus are called tunas. Inside the thick peel of a tuna (which may be armed with a few stickers and which is always removed for eating) is a juicy crimson flesh, studded with small black seeds. Puree the peeled tunas in a food processor, then sieve to get the juice. The tunas are not as common around the country as the pads, but can be ordered by those who want a unique southwestern experience. The fruits keep well, a couple of weeks perhaps in the refrigerator, or the juice can be frozen, in ice cube tray compartments if desired, and used when needed.

Chimayo Cocktail

SERVES 4

Ice
6 ounces (¾ cup) tequila, preferably 100 percent blue agave tequila plata
4 ounces (½ cup) fresh, unfiltered apple juice or cider
1 ounce (2 tablespoons) fresh lime juice
1 ounce (2 tablespoons) crème de cassis (black currant liqueur)
Fresh apple wedges (optional)

Rancho de Chimayo is one of the best-known restaurants in northern New Mexico. Located in the rustic and beautiful village of Chimayo, on the road from Santa Fe to Taos, it specializes in red chile–fired local cuisine, although it may well be this delicious house signature cocktail that has spread its reputation across the country. The cider will cause you to think of this as an autumn drink (and indeed it's delicious with a whiff of fall in the air), but I think it's good whenever the urge for tequila strikes. This is about as strong as a genuine margarita, so proceed with caution.

1. In a cocktail shaker half-filled with ice, combine the tequila, apple juice, lime juice, and cassis. Shake until very cold.

2. Strain over fresh ice in 4 cocktail glasses. Garnish each with an apple slice, if desired, and serve immediately.

Baja Breeze

A southwestern rum cocktail? Of course. Rum, the most widely enjoyed spirit on the planet, is no stranger to spicy foods, warm weather, or to Mexico, where rum far outsells tequila. (Think of that long eastern Caribbean coast and you get the general idea of how and where rum made its Mexican invasion.) Strong and thirst-quenching, this tall, tropical cooler is a favorite around my Santa Fe grill, and while it can be very successfully made with tequila, it's with rum that my guests like it best. Guava nectar makes the drink uniquely delicious (and faintly pink) and is easy to locate in most supermarkets these days, but mango nectar can be substituted.

1. In a tall glass, stir together the white and dark rums, pineapple juice, guava nectar, Cointreau, and lime juice.

2. Fill the glass about three-quarters full of ice. Add a splash of soda, if desired, and serve immediately.

MAKES 1 COCKTAIL

2 ounces (4 tablespoons) white rum
½ ounce (1 tablespoon) dark rum, such as Myers's
1 ounce (2 tablespoons) unsweetened pineapple juice
1 ounce (2 tablespoons) guava nectar
1 tablespoon Cointreau or other orange liqueur
1 tablespoon fresh lime juice
Ice
Club soda (optional)

"Sour Orange" Tequila Driver

A frequently suggested replacement for sour orange, popular in southern Mexico but difficult to find here, is a combination of regular OJ and lime juice. Using that as my basis for this tequila-based cousin of the more prosaic screwdriver produced an astonishingly tasty cocktail. This isn't some wimpy little brunch drink—it's good enough for your next southwestern-style

MAKES 1 COCKTAIL

⅓ cup fresh orange juice
2 ounces (¼ cup) tequila
1 ounce (2 tablespoons) fresh lime juice
Ice
1 lime wedge

backyard grill party. You don't need an all-agave silver tequila for this to succeed, but it will add an extra touch of flavor and class.

1. In a tall glass, combine the orange juice, tequila, and lime juice. Add 5 or 6 cubes from a home-style ice tray and stir to blend.

2. Squeeze the lime wedge into the cocktail and serve immediately.

Pineapple-Tequila Spritzer

MAKES 1 COCKTAIL

⅓ cup chilled pineapple
  juice
1½ ounces (3 tablespoons)
  tequila, preferably 100
  percent blue agave
  tequila plata
½ ounce (1 tablespoon)
  Triple Sec or other
  orange liqueur
Club soda
Lime wedge

Lighter and more refreshing than a margarita, this tropical cooler nevertheless will get the party off to a great start. Just a splash of soda is all that's required—don't drown your drink!

In a tall cocktail glass, stir together the pineapple juice, tequila, and Triple Sec. Fill the glass with ice. Add a splash of soda, squeeze the lime wedge into the glass, and serve immediately.

Bloody Maria

ere's another ordinary brunch quaff, transformed by tequila into something far more festive. In addition to good tequila, buy good (thick, flavorful, not too salty) tomato juice for this, and chill the juice, to prevent drink dilution. I'm not much for horseradish in my bloody Marias, but if you like the idea, use about half a teaspoon.

1. In a shaker, combine the tomato juice, tequila, lime juice, pepper sauce, Worcestershire, and soy sauce. Add 5 or 6 cubes from a home-style ice tray. Shake until very cold.

2. Strain into a stemmed cocktail glass (over fresh ice cubes if you must, but I don't condone this), squeeze the lime wedge into the cocktail, and serve immediately.

Note: You may wish to coat the rim of the glass with kosher salt, as for a margarita. This looks great (and tastes great, too); you may then wish to omit the soy sauce from the drink.

MAKES 1 COCKTAIL

4 ounces (½ cup) chilled tomato juice
2 ounces (¼ cup) tequila
½ ounce (1 tablespoon) fresh lime juice
¼ teaspoon hot pepper sauce, such as Tabasco
¼ teaspoon Worcestershire sauce
¼ teaspoon soy sauce
Ice
1 lime wedge

Sangrita Cocktail

MAKES 1 COCKTAIL

2 ounces (¼ cup) tequila
1½ ounces (3 tablespoons)
   chilled tomato juice
1½ ounces (3 tablespoons)
   chilled orange juice
½ ounce (1 tablespoon)
   lime juice
½ teaspoon grenadine
¼ teaspoon (or a bit more)
   hot pepper sauce
¼ teaspoon soy sauce
1 lime wedge

In Jalisco, where much tequila is produced, the ritual of the lick of salt, shot of tequila, and lime squeeze is replaced by the sangrita ritual. For this you are issued, along with your shot of tequila, a jigger of red-orange liquid that typically contains sour orange juice, lime juice, hot sauce, grenadine, and sometimes tomato juice. It's sweet-hot and, once you've tried it, seems the only logical accompaniment to tequila shots. But, since we're talking backyard barbecues here, not bachelor parties, a cocktail based upon the general sangrita idea seems more civilized than shots, so here is my very good rendition, with a little tomato juice thrown in for good measure.

In a tall glass, combine the tequila, tomato juice, orange juice, lime juice, grenadine, pepper sauce, and soy sauce. Add 5 or 6 cubes from a home-style ice tray and stir to blend. Squeeze the lime wedge into the cocktail and serve immediately.

El Suero

SERVES 1

1 lime wedge
Coarse (kosher) salt on a
   small plate
1 (12-ounce) bottle
   well-chilled beer

It's a popular idea throughout the Southwest, and once I got over my general shock at the notion, I've enjoyed beer over ice from Oaxaca to El Paso. When the food is hot and the weather is hotter, few things are as refreshing. Start with well-chilled beer (to avoid dilution), drink it quickly (not a problem), and use a lesser beer (Corona and Tecate are ideal), rather than some modern artisanal example of the brewmaster's art. I probably should say the salt is optional, except, for me, it isn't—it's essential.

Run the wedge of lime around the rim of a tall cocktail glass; reserve the wedge. Dip the moistened glass rim in the salt to coat. Fill the glass about three-quarters full of ice. Gradually pour the beer over the ice. Squeeze the lime wedge into the glass and serve immediately.

Oaxacan Agua Fresca of Melon, Pineapple, and Cucumber

*A*guas frescas (or "fresh waters") are drinks based on pureed fresh fruit, sometimes thinned with water, and typically without the addition of dairy products. At their best, they are made from very ripe fruit, are lightly sweetened (if at all), and taste refreshingly and intensely of their main ingredients. On first swallow, this drink from the southwestern Mexican state of Oaxaca seems merely cool and green, but then the separate fruit and vegetable flavors sort themselves out in a most satisfying and intriguing way. Some versions include a bit of finely chopped celery, pureed along with the melon and cucumber, then strained for a smoother texture.

1. In a blender, combine the melon, cucumber, pineapple juice, lime juice, and sugar. Blend, first on low, then on a higher speed, until the mixture is smooth.

2. The agua fresca can be served immediately, but it will be better if it is covered and refrigerated until cold, about 2 hours. This will prevent dilution when the ice is added.

3. To serve, fill tall glasses about three-quarters full of ice. Pour the agua fresca over the ice, garnish with mint, if desired, and serve immediately.

SERVES 4 TO 6

*3 cups cubed ripe
 honeydew melon
 (1-inch pieces)*
*1½ cups cubed cucumber
 (1-inch pieces)*
*1½ cups unsweetened
 pineapple juice*
*1½ tablespoons fresh lime
 juice*
*1½ tablespoons packed
 light brown sugar*
Ice
Sprigs of mint (optional)

Prickly Pear–Hibiscus Tea

SERVES 4 TO 6

4 cups water
9 Red Zinger tea bags
⅓ cup sugar
8 large prickly pear cactus
  fruits
1 tablespoon fresh lime
  juice
Ice

This brisk concoction owes its existence to the charming theory that ingredients of the same color taste good together. The only thing redder than the juice of the prickly pear cactus fruit is the tea Mexicans make from the hibiscus or jamaica flower. You can buy pure hibiscus in some health food stores, but since it is the main ingredient in Red Zinger Tea, I find it easier just to use the commercially packed leaves, which already come in tea bags. If you can find a big glass barrel-shaped jar, serve the tea from it, just as they would in Mexico.

1. In a medium saucepan, bring the water to a boil. Add the tea bags, remove from the heat, cover, and let stand, stirring once or twice, for 6 minutes. Remove and discard the bags. Stir in the sugar and cool the tea to room temperature.

2. Trim the ends off the prickly pears (wear gloves if they seem at all spiny). Remove and discard the thick peels and cut the flesh into chunks. Transfer to a food processor and puree. Pour the pureed prickly pear into a sieve set over a bowl. With a rubber scraper, push the juice and any pulp through the sieve; discard the small black seeds. There should be about 1½ cups juice.

3. Stir the prickly pear juice and lime juice into the cooled tea. Cover and chill.

4. Serve the tea the same day it is brewed, over ice in tall glasses.

Really Good Iced Tea

MAKES 3 QUARTS

5 quarts water
7 tea bags
Ice

In many parts of the Southwest, restaurant waitresses set a glass of iced tea on the table in front of you just as they do iced water—both fundamental additions to any good meal. To make really good tea, use good-quality tea leaves, avoid boiling water (despite what you've heard about the proper way to make a cup of tea) and dilute the resulting infusion to drinking strength with warm, not cold water, which ensures clarity. I also think most problems with tea happen in the refrigerator, so cool it just to room temperature, then ice and drink from there. I don't believe in sweetened tea, but I do offer superfine sugar, so those who do can count on it dissolving, not laying in a layer at the bottom of the glass.

1. In a small saucepan, bring 1 quart of the water almost to a boil. Add the tea bags, remove from the heat, and let steep for 4 minutes. Remove the tea bags (don't squeeze them out) and discard. Stir in 4 quarts warm water. Cool the tea to room temperature.

2. Serve within a few hours, without refrigerating, over ice in tall glasses.

Triple-Citrus-Ade

Limeade is one of the Southwest's great thirst-quenchers, second only to iced tea. Here, in the spirit of excess, is an "ade" that combines three citrus juices, in what I think is an even better cooler. I confess to a certain laziness, especially when the weather is hot (and this is a hot-weather drink), and so I don't hesitate to purchase freshly squeezed orange and grapefruit juices from a gourmet health food supermarket. Try this also as the mixer for an especially terrific tequila cocktail.

1. In a tall pitcher, combine the orange, grapefruit, and lime juices. Add the sugar and stir until dissolved.

2. Cover and refrigerate until serving over ice in tall glasses.

Note: Superfine sugar, available in most large supermarkets along with the regular kind, dissolves more readily in cold liquid. Regular sugar can be substituted, you'll just have to stir longer to get it to completely dissolve.

SERVE 4

2 cups fresh orange juice
2 cups fresh pink
  grapefruit juice
½ cup fresh lime juice
½ cup superfine sugar
Ice

Low-Fat Cantaloupe Liquado
with Honey and Lime

SERVES 4

3 cups cubed ripe
   cantaloupe (1-inch
   pieces)
1¾ cups low-fat milk
3 tablespoons honey
2 tablespoons fresh lime
   juice
Ice
Sprigs of mint (optional)

Liquados are close cousins of aguas frescas, composed of fresh fruits alone or in combination, but with the addition of a dairy product of one kind or another. Here the dairy is low-fat milk, which, along with the incorporation of honey, makes this very much like a breakfast smoothie. Enjoy it that way if you like, as a quaff on a hot day, or with food, especially something light but spicy from the grill. Some of the cantaloupe can be replaced with chopped ripe strawberries.

1. In a blender, combine the melon, milk, honey, and lime juice. Blend, first on low, then on a higher speed, stopping once or twice to scrape down the sides of the blender jar and to be sure the honey is incorporated. The blender will be full.

2. The liquado can be served immediately, but it will be better if it is covered and refrigerated until cold, about 2 hours. This will prevent dilution when the ice is added.

3. To serve, fill tall glasses about three-quarters full of ice. Pour the liquado over the ice, garnish with mint if desired, and serve immediately.

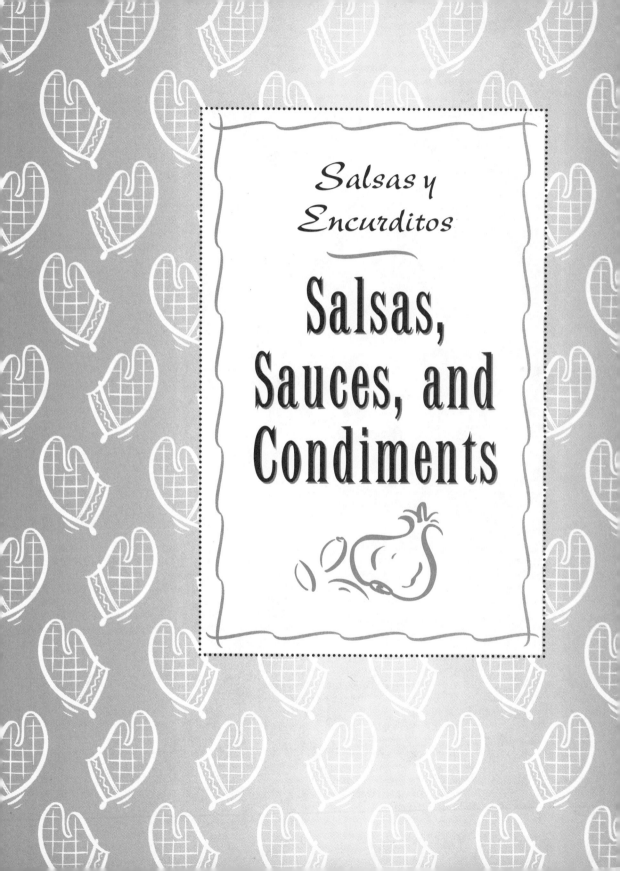

Salsas y Encurditos

Salsas, Sauces, and Condiments

Salsas y Encurditos
SALSAS, SAUCES, AND CONDIMENTS

Rubs the Right Way

Like mops, rubs represent grilling finesse—an extra length the master griller goes to in the pursuit of ultimate flavor and succulence. Rubs confuse many cooks, who assume there is some arcane formula for success, but in truth, simpler is better. Most of us have experienced rubs in at least one form—as the charred and fiery crust on Cajun blackened fish. That emblematic dish provides all the information the insecure need regarding rubs: they coat only the outside of the food, they are meant to be at least partially burned, and subtlety is not the name of the game. A rub provides a hit of flavor that is perceived first, before that which it coats is tasted, and it may (I stress may) help seal in juices. Although moist herb pastes fall into the general category, and although some rare rubs combine dried spices and fresh herbs, the best rubs are of dried ingredients whose similarity of texture makes for through blending and even coating. Something boldly flavored (chile powder or paprika), something hot, something sweet (which rounds the flavor and helps the rub brown nicely), a touch of garlic if you like, and some salt are really all it takes. Rubs are the perfect place to use onion and garlic powder (not salt) as well as granulated brown sugar, since they mix so well with dried herbs and spices.

Simple Rub for Fish

This rub's title says it all. Though a snap to prepare, it does, in fact, produce a tasty and slightly shiny crust that makes the fish especially attractive. The result doesn't taste sweet but the fish tastes better. The secret is the granulated brown sugar—check your supermarket's baking aisle, you may be surprised to find it there.

1. In a small bowl, mix together the sugar, pepper, and salt.

2. Use immediately or transfer to an airtight container and store at room temperature.

MAKES ABOUT 1 TABLESPOON (ENOUGH FOR ABOUT 2 POUNDS FISH)

2 teaspoons granulated brown sugar
½ teaspoon freshly ground black pepper
¼ teaspoon salt

Black Pepper Rub

MAKES ABOUT 3½ TABLESPOONS
(ENOUGH FOR ABOUT 8 POUNDS
MEAT)

*2 tablespoons coarsely
  ground black pepper
1 tablespoon granulated
  brown sugar
½ teaspoon salt
¼ teaspoon garlic powder*

This is powerful stuff, so a little goes a long way. It's best on red meat, especially beef, and essential on beef ribs.

1. In a small bowl, mix together the pepper, sugar, salt, and garlic powder.

2. Use immediately or transfer to an airtight container and store at room temperature.

Quick Red Rub

MAKES ABOUT 3½ TABLESPOONS
(ENOUGH FOR ABOUT 2 POUNDS
MEAT, POULTRY, OR FISH)

*2 tablespoons medium-
  hot unblended red chile
  powder (preferably from
  Chimayo)
2 teaspoons freshly
  ground cumin (prefer-
  ably from toasted seeds)
1 teaspoon freshly ground
  black pepper
1 teaspoon granulated
  brown sugar
¼ teaspoon garlic powder
¼ teaspoon salt*

When it comes to rubs, usually less is more. This easy all-purpose rub is one I use extensively, and it does the job of coloring and flavoring food as well as one with three times as many ingredients. If you find yourself using it as often as I do, make up a large batch and store it airtight in the spice cupboard. Then, when you need a pinch or a lot, you'll have a great flavor-booster on hand.

1. In a small bowl, combine the powdered chile, cumin, pepper, sugar, garlic powder, and salt; mix well.

2. Use immediately or transfer to an airtight container and store at room temperature.

Cumin-Oregano Rub

This robust rub seems particularly good on chicken, though I've used it with good results on various other meats, even some seafood (fresh tuna, for example).

1. In a small bowl, combine the cumin, oregano, sugar, garlic powder, salt, and pepper. Mix well.
2. Use immediately or transfer to an airtight container and store at room temperature.

MAKES ABOUT ¼ CUP
(ENOUGH FOR 2½ POUNDS POULTRY,
MEAT, OR SEAFOOD)

3 tablespoons ground
  cumin (preferably from
  toasted seeds)
1 tablespoon dried
  oregano, crumbled
2 teaspoons granulated
  brown sugar
½ teaspoon garlic powder
½ teaspoon salt
½ teaspoon freshly ground
  black pepper

Salsas, Sauces, and Condiments

Mastering Mops

One of those things seasoned grill cooks can do to ensure they've gone all out for the food they're cooking is to mop it. The term is a literal one, derived from the early days of pit barbecue when the pit master repeatedly sloshed the whole hog, quarter of a cow, or whatever with a mixture of water and vinegar, using a (clean!) cotton floor mop. Mops should be simple to make (since they mostly run off) but should be flavorful, since they do contribute a light coating of flavor (less than a glaze or full-fledged barbecue sauce). They may also flavor the grill smoke as they vaporize on the hot coals and thus contribute flavor that way, too. Recipes are hardly necessary, since mops are readily improvised from what is at hand—beer, frequently, as well as lemonade, fruit juice, or wine. Vinegar with some honey mustard stirred in or cider mixed with ketchup also work well. The point, mostly, is to keep mopping—the effort pays off in moister, tastier food.

Achiote Paste

Recados are seasoning pastes that are fundamental to the cooking of the Yucatan. Achiote paste, or *recado rojo* (red paste), is the best known in this country and the most readily available. It is commonly sold in a small block in Latin groceries and some gourmet shops. The main ingredient of achiote paste is the seed of the annatto (also called achiote) tree. These seeds supply brick-red color (annatto is also used to makes cheeses like cheddar orange) as well as a subtle flavor. Most of what makes achiote paste taste so distinctive, however, are the other ingredients, chiefly garlic, vinegar, oregano, and spices, including black pepper, cloves, cumin, and cinnamon. The commercial paste lacks the punch of homemade, but is convenient and fairly widely available. If you use it, do what I do and add a pinch of the other various spices to boost the total impact. Store the paste airtight (I keep it in a tightly covered jar), to prevent flavor loss. It's not particularly pricey, so if you think yours is over the hill, buy a new package.

Chipotle-Orange Mop

MAKES ABOUT 1⅓ CUPS
(ENOUGH FOR ABOUT 2 POUNDS
POULTRY, MEAT, OR SEAFOOD)

1 cup fresh orange juice
2 canned chipotles en
   adobo, with clinging
   sauce
3 tablespoons packed light
   brown sugar
1 tablespoon fresh lime
   juice
1¼ teaspoons salt

This mop has a citrus sweetness that soon reveals a powerfully smoky heat. I like it best on the turkey burgers on page 71 or on other poultry, but it's also good on pork and on seafood, like shrimp.

1. In a blender, combine the orange juice, chipotles, sugar, lime juice, and salt. Blend until smooth.

2. Use immediately or cover and refrigerate for up to 3 days. Bring to room temperature before using.

Rosemary-Achiote Mop

This mop is not authentic, but it is delicious and a good way to begin to understand the potential of achiote as a seasoning. The touches of orange, rosemary, and habanero make it particularly good on seafood and chicken, but it is great on pork as well. Like most mops, it's thin, but with frequent basting, it will leave behind a tasty and slightly spicy coating you'll come to love.

1. In a blender, combine the orange juice, lime juice, achiote paste, rosemary, sugar, habanero, and salt. Add oregano, black pepper, cumin, cinnamon, and cloves to taste. Process until fairly smooth.

2. Use within an hour or so of making.

MAKES ABOUT 1¼ CUPS
(ENOUGH FOR 2 POUNDS OF MEAT, POULTRY, OR SEAFOOD)

1 cup fresh orange juice
1 tablespoon fresh lime juice
2 teaspoons achiote paste
1 teaspoon minced fresh rosemary
1 teaspoon packed light brown sugar
1 habanero chile, finely chopped
¾ teaspoon salt
Pinch dried oregano (optional)
Pinch freshly ground black pepper (optional)
Pinch ground cumin (optional)
Pinch ground cinnamon (optional)
Pinch ground cloves (optional)

Salsas, Sauces, and Condiments

Tamarind-Honey Glaze

MAKES ABOUT 1½ CUPS
(ENOUGH FOR 2 POUNDS MEAT)

*1 cup tamarind water
(see box below)*
⅓ cup honey
*2 tablespoons fresh lime
juice*
*2 teaspoons freshly
ground black pepper*
¼ teaspoon salt

Once you get used to working with tamarind, an odd but not a difficult process, it's no big deal to whip up a batch of this sweet-tart glaze. I especially love it on pork tenderloin, whether I'm making the Grilled Tamarind Pork and Noodle Salad on page 99 or just serving the meat plain. It's also good on chicken and terrific on shellfish like shrimp and spiny lobster tail.

1. In a bowl, whisk together the tamarind water, honey, lime juice, pepper, and salt.

2. Use the glaze immediately or cover and refrigerate it for up to 3 days.

Tamarind

Tamarind is an evergreen tree found growing in Asia and West Africa, but is now also grown in Mexico. Its seeds come inside pods, surrounded by a very tart, sticky pulp, which is used as the basis for a refreshing drink or as a fruity addition to sauces and glazes. In this country, one does occasionally see the pods, particularly in exotic produce stores, but they are often too dried out to be of use. Latin markets and some gourmet shops stock what is called seedless tamarind paste and that is what you want to use. The brown sticky block, which resembles some terrible chewing tobacco, is actually full of seeds.

To make 1 cup tamarind water *(agua de tamarindo)*, pull off a 6-ounce blob (roughly ¾ cup) of the paste. In a blender, combine the paste with 1½ cups very hot tap water. Pulse several times, then let the pulp and water stand in the blender, pulsing it occasionally, for 10 minutes. Try not to break up the seeds, which can make the water bitter. Pulse several more times, then transfer the contents of the blender to a sieve set over a bowl. With a rubber scraper, force the puree through the sieve into the bowl (be sure to scrape off any puree clinging to the underside of the sieve. Discard the seeds. Stir the tamarind water to combine. The water can be used immediately or it can be refrigerated for up to 3 days or frozen for several months.

Mole Rapido

Mole poblano, one of the greatest Mexican sauces, is most often prepared for special feast days and frequently requires the efforts of all the cooks (read: women) in the village spread over several painstaking days, utilizing something like twenty-six ingredients. Mole from a jar is naturally a convenience, not a culinary triumph, but for that essential chile-chocolaty flavor, a craving that must be answered, my doctored mole "rapido" is more than acceptable. It keeps well in the fridge and is great on pork and, surprisingly, grilled shrimp (especially when thinned with a little cream), as well as chicken enchiladas.

MAKES ABOUT 3 CUPS
(6 TO 8 SERVINGS)

4 Italian plum tomatoes
   (about ¾ pound)
1½ cups reduced-sodium
   canned chicken broth
1 (8¼-ounce) jar prepared
   mole
1 tablespoon packed dark
   brown sugar
1 tablespoon smooth
   peanut butter (any
   supermarket brand)
½ teaspoon salt

1. Position the rack about 6 inches from the heat source and preheat the broiler. In a shallow metal pan, like a cake tin, broil the tomatoes, turning them once, until the peels are charred and the tomatoes are soft, about 14 minutes total. Cool.

2. In a food processor, combine the tomatoes, broth, mole, sugar, peanut butter, and salt. Process, stopping several times to scrape down the work bowl, until fairly smooth.

3. Transfer to a small, heavy saucepan and set over low heat. Bring just to a simmer, stirring often.

4. Use immediately or cool, cover, and refrigerate for up to 1 month. Rewarm over low heat, thinning with additional broth as needed, before using.

Red Pipian

MAKES ABOUT 3 CUPS

2 large bulbs regular (not elephant) garlic
2 tablespoons dry sherry
3 tablespoons olive oil
⅓ cup raw pumpkin seeds
4 plum tomatoes (about 12 ounces)
½ onion
2 ancho chiles
1 slice firm white bread, crusts removed
⅓ cup unsalted skinless roasted peanuts
1 canned chipotle chile en adobo, minced
½ teaspoon ground allspice
½ teaspoon ground cinnamon
½ teaspoon freshly ground black pepper
¼ teaspoon dried thyme, crumbled
⅛ teaspoon ground cloves
1 teaspoon sugar
Salt
About 4½ cups reduced-sodium canned chicken broth

This recipe for this rich and earthy classic sauce was inspired by Rick Bayless, author, restaurateur, and leading exponent of Mexican cooking. Traditionally it is part of a dish and cooked along with it, rather than separately dolloped over, like a salsa, but when cooked elements like roasted garlic and charred tomatoes and onions are incorporated, it works very well that way. The amount of sauce made is generous; freeze any not used immediately and use it later over other types of fish, poultry (especially turkey and duck), or pork, whether grilled or cooked more conventionally.

1. Position a rack in the middle of the oven and preheat to 375°F.

2. Remove the outer papery peels from the garlic. Cut off the top one-quarter of the garlic bulbs, exposing the cloves within. Partially enclose each head in a piece of foil. Drizzle each head with 1 tablespoon sherry and 1 tablespoon olive oil. Enclose the garlic tightly in the foil and bake until very soft, about 1 hour.

3. Meanwhile, in a shallow pan, like a cake tin, toast the pumpkin seeds until crisp, brown, and beginning to pop, about 10 minutes. Remove the pumpkin seeds and transfer to a bowl.

4. Cool the garlic to room temperature in the foil packets.

5. Position a rack about 6 inches from the heat source and preheat the broiler. In a shallow metal pan, like a cake tin, broil the tomatoes and onion, turning once, until soft and charred, 12 to 14 minutes total. Remove and cool, then roughly chop.

6. Stem and seed the anchos and tear them into small pieces. In a small bowl, cover the anchos with boiling water and let soak for 30 minutes. Drain the anchos.

7. Squeeze the softened garlic out of the peels into a food processor. Add the tomatoes, onion, anchos, bread, peanuts, chipotle, allspice, cinnamon, pepper, thyme, cloves, sugar, and ¼ teaspoon salt. Process with a few bursts of power. Add 1½ cups broth and process, stopping several times to scrape down the sides of the work bowl, until the sauce is fairly smooth.

8. In a heavy medium saucepan over moderate heat, warm the remaining 1 tablespoon olive oil. Add the puree (it may spatter) and cook, stirring constantly, for 5 minutes; the puree will thicken. Gradually whisk in the remaining 3 cups broth. Bring to a simmer, decrease the heat, partially cover and cook, stirring often, until the pipian has thickened to the texture of heavy cream, about 45 minutes. Adjust the seasoning.

9. You can use the sauce immediately, but the flavor will be better if the sauce is allowed to rest overnight in the refrigerator. Rewarm gently over low heat before using.

Chipotle Cream Sauce

This elegantly creamy, slightly fiery sauce is particularly good over grilled seafood (salmon and shrimp in particular), but it will also add company panache to plain old chicken breasts. Resist the temptation to increase the chipotle level—it can easily overwhelm more subtle foods.

1. In a small heavy nonreactive saucepan over medium heat, whisk together the cream, broth, honey mustard, chiles, garlic, and ½ teaspoon of the salt. Bring to a simmer and cook partially covered, stirring occasionally, until reduced by about one-third, about 15 minutes.

2. Remove from the heat. Stir in the lemon juice and season generously with pepper. Taste and add more salt if necessary.

3. Serve at once, or cover and refrigerate for several hours. Rewarm over low heat just before serving.

MAKES ABOUT 1¼ CUPS
(4 SERVINGS)

¾ cup whipping cream
¾ cup reduced-sodium canned chicken broth
5 tablespoons honey mustard
2 canned chipotle chiles en adobo, minced
1 garlic clove, crushed through a press
Salt
1 teaspoon fresh lemon juice
Freshly ground black pepper

Bourbon-Mustard Sauce

MAKES ABOUT 1⅓ CUPS
(4 SERVINGS)

1½ tablespoons unsalted
  butter
¼ cup finely chopped
  shallots
1 garlic clove, minced
½ cup good-quality
  bourbon (Maker's Mark
  is recommended)
¾ cup whipping cream
¾ cup beef stock
3 tablespoons grainy
  mustard
Salt
Freshly ground black
  pepper

Sweet, smoky bourbon gets a kick from mustard and shallots, and all are smoothed by the judicious use of heavy cream—great stuff, almost good enough to drink, but better on a piece of good grilled beef. If you have no access to good beef stock (there is a nationally available frozen brand), use reduced-sodium canned chicken broth instead. Canned beef broth is better avoided.

1. In a small heavy saucepan over low heat, melt the butter. Add the shallots and garlic, cover and cook without browning, stirring occasionally, for 3 minutes. Uncover, add the bourbon, and increase the heat to high. Simmer briskly, stirring often, until the bourbon is reduced to half, 2 to 3 minutes.

2. Decrease the heat and whisk in the cream, stock, mustard, and ½ teaspoon of the salt. Bring to a brisk simmer, partially cover, and cook, stirring occasionally, until the sauce is reduced to by about one-third and has thickened slightly, 12 to 15 minutes. Add black pepper to taste.

3. Serve immediately, or cool, cover, and refrigerate for up to 1 day. Rewarm over low heat just until simmering. Serve hot.

Coffee Barbecue Sauce

There are a lot of coffee-based barbecue sauces around these days, but the first recipe I ever remember seeing came from Mark Miller's book, *Coyote's Pantry*. This recipe began life as Mark's, but it has undergone enough revisions for me to now claim it as my own. I think of it as an haute chuck wagon kind of sauce, the creation of a frugal cowpoke who hates to throw anything away. It's thin and on the sweet side, but with a hit of heat that builds and builds. Best on beef, I think, but the sauce also goes well with poultry, pork, or even lamb.

1. In a heavy nonreactive saucepan over low heat, warm the oil. Add the onion, garlic, cumin, oregano, red pepper, and cinnamon. Cover and cook, stirring once or twice, for 5 minutes.

2. Stir in the coffee, ketchup, chile puree, vinegar, orange juice, sugar, and soy sauce and bring to a brisk simmer. Cook, uncovered, stirring occasionally, until reduced by about one-quarter and thickened slightly, about 20 minutes. Remove from the heat and cool.

3. For a smoother, slightly thicker sauce, transfer to a food processor and puree.

4. Use the sauce immediately or cover and refrigerate for up to 3 days or freeze for up to 3 months. Return to room temperature before using.

MAKES ABOUT 3½ CUPS

2 tablespoons olive oil
⅓ cup finely chopped onion
3 garlic cloves, finely chopped
1¼ teaspoons ground cumin (preferably freshly ground from toasted seeds)
¾ teaspoon dried oregano, crumbled
¼ teaspoon crushed red pepper
Pinch ground cinnamon
1¼ cups strong brewed French roast coffee
1 cup ketchup
1 cup Mixed Dried Red Chile Puree (page 305) or purchased red chile puree
½ cup sherry wine vinegar
½ cup fresh orange juice
½ cup packed dark brown sugar
4 teaspoons soy sauce

Chipotle-Peanut Barbecue Sauce

MAKES ABOUT 2½ CUPS
(SAUCING AT LEAST 4 POUNDS OF
PORK, POULTRY, OR SEAFOOD)

1 cup Mixed Dried Red
   Chile Puree (page 305)
   or purchased red chile
   puree
1 cup ketchup
¼ cup smooth or chunky
   peanut butter (any
   supermarket brand)
4 chipotle chiles en
   adobo, with clinging
   sauce, minced
2 tablespoons packed
   dark brown sugar
2 tablespoons sherry wine
   vinegar
1 tablespoon soy sauce
1 tablespoon Dijon
   mustard
½ teaspoon onion powder
¼ teaspoon garlic powder

Suavely nutty and quite fiery, this sauce is loosely based on one from Huntley Dent's *Feast of Santa Fe*, still one of the best books written on the food of the Southwest. In addition to being delicious, it's quick, and you can literally mix it up while the grill is heating. I love it on pork, and its satay-like flavor is also terrific on poultry and seafood (especially shrimp).

1. In a heavy nonreactive saucepan over low heat, combine the chile puree, ketchup, peanut butter, chipotles, sugar, vinegar, soy sauce, mustard, onion powder, and garlic powder. Heat, stirring often, just until the peanut butter is melted and the sauce is smooth.

2. Cool to room temperature.

3. Use the sauce immediately or refrigerate it for up to 3 days or freeze for up to 3 months. Bring to room temperature before serving.

Mexican Barbecue Sauce (Adobo)

This is one of the great sauces of Mexico, but its essential flavors are equally at home in the American Southwest. Versions vary dramatically, so determining an "authentic" one wasn't easy and in the long run wasn't all that important. The product of this recipe tastes good and tastes Mexican, and that's really all that matters. Adobo is used full strength as a marinade or wet rub, or thinned with an appropriate liquid (red wine, orange juice, tequila) to function more like a traditional American barbecue basting sauce. Since it's a bit of a project to make, the recipe yields a generous quantity. The sauce freezes well, and it's so versatile you'll never want to be without it.

1. Position the rack about 6 inches from the heat source and preheat the oven to 400°F.

2. Remove the loose, papery outside peels of the garlic bulb. With a sharp knife, cut off the top one-quarter of the garlic, exposing the cloves within. Partially enclose the garlic in a packet of heavy-duty foil. Drizzle evenly with the sherry and olive oil. Seal the packet tightly, set it on the oven rack and bake until the garlic is fragrant and very tender, about 1 hour. Cool, then squeeze or scoop the softened garlic out of the peel.

3. Position a rack about 6 inches from the heat source and preheat the broiler. In a shallow metal pan, like a cake tin, broil the tomatoes and the onion half, turning them once, until well-charred, about 15 minutes total. Remove from the broiler and cool. Coarsely chop (do not peel) the tomatoes and the onion half.

4. In a food processor, combine the chile puree, tomatoes, onion, garlic, vinegar, sugar, salt, oregano, cinnamon, cumin, pepper, thyme, and cloves.

MAKES ABOUT 3 CUPS

1 large bulb regular (not elephant) garlic
1 tablespoon dry sherry
1 tablespoon olive oil
4 plum tomatoes (about 12 ounces)
½ small onion
1⅓ cups Mixed Dried Red Chile Puree (page 305) (see Note)
⅓ cup sherry wine vinegar
2 tablespoons packed dark brown sugar
1 tablespoon salt
1¼ teaspoons dried oregano, crumbled
½ teaspoon ground cinnamon
½ teaspoon freshly ground cumin (preferably from toasted seeds)
½ teaspoon freshly ground black pepper
¼ teaspoon dried thyme, crumbled
Pinch ground cloves

Process, stopping once or twice to scrape down the sides of the work bowl, until the adobo is smooth.

5. You can use the adobo immediately, but it will develop more flavor if you cover it and refrigerate it overnight. The adobo can be frozen for up to 2 months. (Consider freezing it in the compartments of an ice cube tray, then storing the cubes in a plastic freezer bag, so you can conveniently defrost a few tablespoons as needed.)

Note: For a smokier, chipotle-flavored adobo, omit the chiles de árbol when making the dried red chile puree and add canned chipotle chiles, along with some of the sauce from their can, when pureeing the tomatoes, garlic, and other ingredients. Three to four chipotles will make a fairly spicy adobo.

Using Liquid Smoke

If you're grilling with wood chips, liquid mesquite flavoring in a sauce is probably redundant, but to many people, it just isn't barbecue sauce with the tang of smoke. (Of course, if you're using the sauce on oven-barbecued chicken or a meatloaf, the smoky taste will be welcome.) In any case, liquid smoke is a pure flavoring, distilled from real smoke. It's pungent, though, so don't use more that what's called for, or your sauce may taste bitter. The unused portion of the bottle of smoke flavoring will keep, refrigerated, virtually forever.

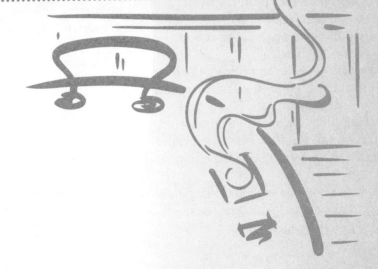

Branding Iron Barbecue Sauce

Here is a terrific and fairly hot but otherwise traditional barbecue sauce that tastes as if it could have inspired the entire genre. It's familiar, you understand, but better in every way than what we get from those supermarket bottles. It is good both brushed onto food as it grills and as a drizzle or dip at the table afterward. The quantity is large, since the sauce freezes well. And despite the long ingredient list, it's easy to make and it's very nice to have around. In addition to the obvious uses of this on grilled chicken, shrimp, pork, and so on, you'll find it very good as the replacement for the ketchup in your next batch of meatloaf.

1. In a heavy nonreactive saucepan over low heat, warm the olive oil. Add the onion, garlic, and jalapeño. Cover and cook, stirring occasionally, for 10 minutes. Add the tomatoes, tomato juice, ketchup, picante sauce, wine, chipotles, molasses, vinegar, sugar, soy sauce, and liquid smoke. Bring to a simmer, then partially cover and cook, stirring occasionally, until slightly thickened, about 30 minutes.

2. Cool to room temperature. For a smooth sauce, puree in a food processor.

3. Use the sauce immediately or cover tightly and refrigerate for up to 2 weeks or freeze for up to 2 months.

MAKES ABOUT 7 CUPS

3 tablespoons olive oil
1 cup finely chopped onion
4 garlic cloves, chopped
1 large fresh jalapeño, stemmed and minced
1 (28-ounce) can crushed tomatoes with added puree
1½ cups tomato juice
1 cup ketchup
½ cup prepared picante sauce (Pace is a recommended brand)
½ cup dry red wine
⅓ cup finely chopped canned chipotle chiles en adobo
⅓ cup unsulphured molasses
3 tablespoons cider vinegar
2 tablespoons packed dark brown sugar
5 teaspoons soy sauce
½ teaspoon liquid mesquite or hickory smoke flavoring (optional)

Grilled Three-Chile Salsa with Black Beans and Corn

3 large garlic cloves
1 fresh jalapeño
1 large ear sweet corn,
  husks and silks removed
2 ripe tomatoes (about 1
  pound total)
1 tablespoon olive oil
3 long green chiles, such
  as Anaheim or New
  Mexico
2 poblano chiles
⅓ cup chopped onion
3 tablespoons fresh lime
  juice
2 tablespoons tequila
Salt
¾ cup cooked black beans,
  well drained
⅓ cup finely chopped
  cilantro
⅓ cup finely diced red
  onion

SMOKING CHIP OPTION: MESQUITE

H ere is a salsa packing nearly every weapon in the modern southwestern culinary armory. Multiple smoky grilled chiles, charred tomatoes, a splash of tequila, plenty of cilantro, plus fundamental corn and fashionable black beans—all conspire to deliver a bold load of flavor, texture, and color. This is not some anonymous, mousy little salsa to enjoy on a corn chip. It's a major player on the plate and a festive partner to everything from quesadillas to chicken, beef, and lamb.

1. Light a direct-heat charcoal fire and let it burn down to medium-hot (5 seconds to "ouch") or preheat a gas grill to medium-high. Position the grill rack about 6 inches above the heat source.
2. Meanwhile, slide the garlic cloves and jalapeño onto a flat metal skewer. Brush the corn with the olive oil.
3. When the grill is ready, lay the skewer, the corn, tomatoes, long green chiles, and poblanos on the rack. Cover and grill, turning occasionally, until the chile peels are lightly but evenly charred, the garlic and corn are lightly browned, and the tomato peels are well charred, 8 to 12 minutes. Remove the chiles as they are ready, transfer to a closed paper bag, and steam until cool. Transfer the corn, tomatoes, and skewer with the garlic and jalapeño to a plate and cool.
4. Rub away the burnt peels from the long green and poblano chiles. Stem, seed, and finely chop the chiles. Core the tomatoes. Cut the corn kernels off the cob and reserve. Chop the garlic. Stem the jalapeño but leave the charred peel on; chop the jalapeño.

5. In a food processor, combine the tomatoes (leave the charred peels on), yellow onion, garlic, jalapeño, lime juice, tequila, and ¾ teaspoon of the salt. Process until fairly smooth. Transfer to a bowl. Stir in the chopped chiles, corn, beans, cilantro, and red onion.

6. Taste and adjust the seasoning. Cover and hold at room temperature. For best flavor and texture serve the salsa within a few hours of making it.

Mango Pico de Gallo

I first encountered the chunky and very fiery salsa called pico de gallo ("rooster's beak") in El Paso, where it is especially popular. (A similarly named chile-dusted jicama-and-orange salad/snack is a specialty of the Mexican state of Jalisco.) Whether it's the repetitive pecking action eating it requires, or the sharp bite it inflicts, the moniker is apt. In El Paso, the chile of choice is the *güero* (blond), a yellow chile about the same size, shape, and heat level as the jalapeño, a suitable substitute. The mango is my addition, and makes the salsa a fine accompaniment to queso fundido (pages 29 through 32), as well as to seafood, poultry, and some pork dishes. Like most raw, fresh salsas, this is best eaten shortly after completion.

1. In a bowl, combine the green chiles, mango, tomato, onion, jalapeños, lime juice, and salt.

2. Cover and refrigerate for up to 1 hour, to blend the flavors. Just before serving, stir in the cilantro and adjust the seasoning.

MAKES ABOUT 3½ CUPS

*6 mild long green chiles,
such as Anaheim or
New Mexican, roasted,
steamed, peeled, and
chopped (about 1 cup)*

*1 large, firm but juicy-ripe
mango, peeled and
cubed*

*1 large, firm but juicy-ripe
tomato (about 12
ounces) cored, seeded,
and coarsely chopped*

¾ cup diced red onion

*1 to 2 fresh jalapeños,
stemmed and minced*

*3 tablespoons fresh lime
juice*

¾ teaspoon salt

*⅓ cup finely chopped
cilantro*

Café Pasqual's Cucumber Salsa

MAKES ABOUT 2 CUPS

1 large English or hot-
house cucumber, seeded
and diced
1 large red bell pepper,
stemmed, seeded and
diced
½ cup diced red onion
1 to 2 small fresh
jalapeños, stemmed and
minced
2 tablespoons olive oil
1 tablespoon red wine
vinegar
Salt
½ cup finely chopped
cilantro

Though designed for use on the restaurant's signature Grilled Salmon Burritos (page 62), this
colorful, crunchy salsa can also be used on
other plain or chile-rubbed seafood—particularly
salmon, for which it has a great and natural affinity.

1. In a bowl, combine the cucumber, bell
pepper, onion, jalapeño, olive oil, vinegar, and ½
teaspoon of salt.
2. Cover and let stand at room temperature,
stirring once or twice, for at least 30 minutes and
up to an hour. Add the cilantro and adjust the
seasoning just before serving.

Blackberry Salsa

MAKES ABOUT 3½ CUPS

2 large bell peppers,
preferably yellow
6 tablespoons fresh
orange juice
1 cup roughly mashed
fresh blackberries
⅔ cup finely chopped
onion
¼ cup fresh lime juice
1 fresh habanero chile,
stemmed and minced
¾ teaspoon salt

This may be a modern concoction, but at least
it comes from Mexico, discovered there in
Michoacan by photographer-author Nancy
Zaslavsky and described in her wonderful book, *A
Cook's Tour of Mexico*. As long as you are okay
with fruit and meat, try this on otherwise unsauced
grilled chicken, pork, or even seafood (especially
shrimp or lobster). It's also good on quesadillas
made with fairly sharp cheese.

1. In the open flame of a gas burner, under a
preheated broiler, or on a preheated grill, roast the
bell pepper, turning it occasionally, until the peel
is lightly but evenly charred. Transfer to a closed

paper bag and steam until cool. Rub away the burned peel, stem and core the pepper, and chop the flesh.

2. In a medium bowl, combine the chopped pepper, orange juice, blackberries, onion, lime juice, habanero, and the salt.

3. Cover and let stand at room temperature to blend the flavors for 2 hours. Adjust the seasoning before serving.

Salsa Verde with Pineapple

Tomatillo-based salsas have a tart and herbal briskness that makes them especially appropriate with seafood and with rich dishes, such as those with a lot of cheese. If you have eaten throughout the Southwest and Mexico, you will probably welcome this zippy quality; if you have not, it may take some getting used to. Persevere, since the more salsas you have in your repertoire, the happier you'll be in the long run. As a middle ground, begin with this salsa verde, its bite tempered with a bit of sweet, juicy pineapple.

1. Bring a saucepan of water to a boil. Add the tomatillos and cook, stirring once or twice, until they are soft and tender, about 10 minutes. Drain and cool.

2. In a food processor, combine the tomatillos, yellow onion, ¼ cup of the cilantro, the serranos, garlic, and salt. Process, scraping down the sides of the work bowl once or twice, until fairly smooth.

3. Transfer the tomatillo mixture to a bowl. Stir in the red onion, pineapple, and remaining ¼ cup cilantro. Cover and hold at room temperature for up to 1 hour or refrigerate for up to 24 hours. Return to room temperature and thin the salsa with water if necessary before serving.

MAKES ABOUT 2½ CUPS

1 pound (about 20 medium) tomatillos, husked
⅓ cup chopped onion
½ cup finely chopped cilantro
2 medium serrano chiles, stemmed and chopped
1 garlic clove, peeled and chopped
¾ teaspoon salt
⅓ cup diced red onion
⅓ cup diced fresh pineapple
3 to 4 tablespoons water (optional)

Avocado-Tomatillo Salsa

MAKES ABOUT 1 CUP

2 large tomatillos, husked
⅓ cup finely chopped
 cilantro
1 serrano chile, stemmed
 and coarsely chopped
 (seeds and ribs
 included)
1 green onion, tender top
 included, trimmed and
 chopped
1 medium-large, perfectly
 ripe black-skinned
 (Hass) avocado
½ teaspoon salt

This relish is a close cousin to guacamole, made tarter and lighter by the inclusion of tomatillos. Their berrylike acidity adds a fresh note that makes the salsa especially good with cheese dishes like queso fundido or quesadillas, as well as on grilled seafood or pork. Doubled or tripled, it can be served just like guacamole, with tortilla chips for scooping. For convenience, the tomatillo seasoning puree can be prepared up to an hour in advance, but the salsa should be finished no more than a few minutes before serving.

1. Set a small saucepan of water over high heat and bring to a boil. Add the tomatillos and cook until tender, about 10 minutes. Drain and cool.

2. In a small food processor, combine the tomatillos, cilantro, serrano, and green onion. Process until fairly smooth.

3. Halve the avocado and remove the pit. With a large spoon, scoop the flesh into a bowl. With a fork, roughly mash the avocado. Stir in the tomatillo mixture and the salt.

4. Cover tightly with plastic wrap and hold at room temperature for no more than 30 minutes before using.

Cascabel–Roasted Garlic Salsa

Sweaty fears to the contrary, not all southwestern salsas are fire-engine hot. A good case in point is this mellow, deeply flavorful but only moderately picante condiment, one that is just as good on grilled meats (particularly beef) and seafood as it is on melted cheeses (goat cheese especially) or plain old tortilla chips. Medium-hot cascabels have a flavor that experts describe as smoky, woodsy, and nutty, a description that fits the salsa as well.

MAKES ABOUT 2½ CUPS

3 ounces (about 18) dried cascabel chiles, stemmed, seeded, and broken into pieces (see Note)
2 cups boiling water
1 large head bulb regular (not elephant) garlic
1 tablespoon dry sherry
1 tablespoon olive oil
2 large ripe tomatoes (about 1½ pounds total)
⅔ cup diced onion
2½ tablespoons sherry wine vinegar
1 teaspoon salt
½ teaspoon freshly ground black pepper

1. In a medium, heatproof bowl, combine the chiles and boiling water. Cover and let stand, stirring occasionally, until the water is cool and the chiles have softened, about 2 hours.

2. Position a rack in the middle of the oven and preheat to 375°F.

3. Remove the loose, papery outside peels from the garlic bulbs. With a sharp knife, slice off the upper one-quarter of the garlic bulb, exposing the cloves within. Partially enclose the garlic in a packet of heavy-duty foil. Drizzle with the sherry and the olive oil. Tightly seal the packet, set it on the oven rack, and bake until the garlic is very tender, about 1 hour. Let the garlic cool to room temperature in the foil. Open the packet and squeeze or scoop the softened garlic out of the peels.

4. Position a rack 6 inches from the broiler and preheat. Set the tomatoes in a shallow pan, like a cake tin, and broil, turning them once, until the peels are well blackened and the tomatoes have softened, 15 to 20 minutes total. Cool to room temperature.

5. Drain the cascabels, reserving the soaking water. Transfer the chiles to a food processor and blend, stopping several times to scrape down the sides of the work bowl, until a rough puree forms. Add ⅓ cup of the reserved chile soaking water and process again, until fairly smooth. Transfer to a sieve set over a bowl. With a rubber scraper, force the chile puree through the sieve into the bowl. Discard the tough peels remaining in the sieve. You should have about ⅓ cup cascabel puree.

6. Core, but do not peel, the tomatoes and coarsely chop them. In a food processor, combine the tomatoes, garlic, cascabel puree, half the onion, the vinegar, salt, and pepper. Process, stopping several times to scrape down the sides of the work bowl, until the ingredients are well blended; leave some texture. Transfer to a bowl, stir in the remaining onion and adjust the seasoning.

7. Use immediately or store, tightly covered and refrigerated, for up to 3 days. Return to room temperature before serving.

Note: There will be less depth of flavor (but also less work) if commercially prepared frozen hot red chile puree is substituted—use the same quantity—for the cascabel puree.

Yucatan Habanero Salsa (Xnipec)

MAKES ABOUT 2½ CUPS

2 medium-large, dead-ripe
tomatoes (about 1¼
pounds total), cored,
seeded, and coarsely
chopped
⅔ cup diced onion
3 tablespoons fresh
orange juice
3 tablespoons finely
chopped cilantro
2 fresh habanero chiles,
stemmed and minced
1 tablespoon fresh lime
juice
1 garlic clove, crushed
through a press
Salt

This fresh, crunchy, and fiercely hot salsa is one of those dishes that I can't stop eating, despite the pain. (The name translates from the Mayan as "dog's nose," the damp condition of which your own will soon emulate if you eat too much *xnipec*.) Reminiscent of pico de gallo, but with a different kind of heat and with a citrus tang, it goes together in minutes. In tropical Mexico, it would be made with sour or Seville oranges; here a combination of sweet orange and regular lime juices works fine. Xnipec is particularly suited to simple grilled fish dishes, like Yucatan Shark "Bread," page 66, which it enlivens in the most remarkable way. Since it's quick to make, try to serve it freshly made, with all its texture intact.

1. On a cutting board with a long knife or in a food processor with short bursts of power, evenly chop the tomatoes, leaving plenty of texture. Transfer to a bowl.

2. Stir in the onion, orange juice, cilantro, habaneros, lime juice, garlic, and ½ teaspoon salt. Stir. Adjust the seasoning.

3. Cover and hold at room temperature. For best flavor and texture, serve the salsa within an hour or so of making it.

Golden Tomato Salsa Borracha

Sweet yellow tomatoes make a delicious and beautiful salsa and seem the natural partners for gold tequila, which is what makes this relish *"borracha,"* or drunken. Sweetly hot and complex, with a potent tequila kick, it's good on dishes with cheese, like quesadillas, and great on grilled chicken or seafood. The best places to find the necessary big yellow tomatoes are a farmers' market or your own garden, though they do occasionally turn up for sale in specialty produce stores. Red tomatoes, can, of course, be substituted; the salsa will taste good but will not be as distinctive-looking.

1. In a medium bowl, stir together the tomatoes, onion, jalapeños, lime juice, orange juice, tequila and salt. Let stand at room temperature, stirring once or twice, for 30 minutes.

2. Stir in the cilantro and adjust the seasoning.

3. For best flavor, serve the salsa within a few minutes of making it.

MAKES ABOUT 3½ CUPS

2¼ pounds (5 large) yellow tomatoes, cored, seeded, and coarsely chopped

⅓ cup finely diced red onion

2 to 3 fresh jalapeños, stemmed and minced

2 tablespoons fresh lime juice

2 tablespoons fresh orange juice

2 tablespoons tequila

¾ teaspoon salt

⅓ cup finely chopped cilantro

Salsas, Sauces, and Condiments

Chile de Arbol Salsa
with Rosemary and Orange

MAKES ABOUT 2½ CUPS

10 chiles de árbol,
  stemmed
2 medium-large tomatoes
  (about 1¼ pounds total),
  cored, seeded, and
  chopped
¼ cup fresh orange juice
2 tablespoons fresh lime
  juice
2 garlic cloves, chopped
Salt
½ cup finely diced onion
2 teaspoons minced fresh
  rosemary
2 teaspoons minced
  orange zest

Chiles, like many cooking ingredients, go through fashionable upswings and downturns. Chipotles will no doubt remain the flavor of the month for some years to come, but chiles de árbol are also showing increasing signs of becoming what can only be called hot. Small dried red chiles, usually sold with their woody stems attached, they have both heat and an acidic flavor that makes them particularly good at firing up salsas. Here chiles de árbol, orange juice and zest, plus the unexpected addition of minced fresh rosemary, combine to produce a tasty and offbeat salsa. This is good on chips, but even better on full-flavored fish and robust grilled meats.

1. In a heatproof bowl, combine the chiles and 1 cup boiling water. Cover and let stand, stirring occasionally, until cool. Drain. Chop the chiles.

2. In a food processor, combine the tomatoes, chopped chiles, orange juice, lime juice, garlic, and salt to taste. Process until fairly smooth. Transfer to a bowl.

3. Stir in the onion, rosemary, and orange zest.

4. Cover and let stand at room temperature for 30 minutes to blend the flavors. For best flavor and texture, serve within an hour or so of making the salsa. Adjust the seasoning before serving.

Fast and Bumpy Salsa Ketchup

This is an easy stir-together that tastes great anywhere you want ketchup with a little attitude. Various salsas make for differing final results. I generally reach for something hot and chunky but otherwise on the thin side, like Pace Picante Sauce. Good on burgers, transforming on onion rings and French-fries.

MAKES 1½ CUPS

¾ cup high-quality
  ketchup
¾ cup hot salsa

1. In a small bowl, stir together the ketchup and salsa.

2. Use immediately or cover tightly and refrigerate indefinitely.

Hot Pepper Jelly Dipping Sauce

This tangy concoction, the perfect meatball dip (see page 52) is derived from that all-too-familiar fifties chafing dish specialty that combined grape jelly and barbecue sauce. I've taken it several steps further along the *picante* line, so that the results, while still sweet, also pack more than a little fiery heat. In addition to meatballs, try it on plain grilled chicken wings or spareribs. Look for red pepper jelly; the bright green kind makes the sauce look grotesque.

MAKES ABOUT 1½ CUPS

½ cup hot and smoky
  prepared barbecue sauce
⅓ cup peach or pineapple
  preserves or orange
  marmalade
⅓ cup hot pepper jelly
2 tablespoons prepared
  cream-style horseradish
1 tablespoon honey
  mustard
1 tablespoon fresh lime
  juice

1. In a heavy, medium, nonreactive saucepan over low heat, combine the barbecue sauce, preserves, jelly, horseradish, honey mustard, and lime juice. Cook, stirring often, just until the preserves and jelly have melted.

2. Use immediately or cool, cover, and refrigerate for up to 7 days. Rewarm over low heat before serving.

Salsas, Sauces, and Condiments

Cantina Red Table Sauce

MAKES ABOUT 4 CUPS

1 (28-ounce) can crushed
    tomatoes with added
    puree
¾ cup water
½ cup finely chopped
    onion
2 tablespoons olive oil
¼ cup fresh lime juice
1 tablespoon cider vinegar
4 garlic cloves, crushed
    through a press
2½ teaspoons dried
    oregano, crumbled
¾ teaspoon salt
1 teaspoon crushed red
    pepper flakes

Sometime you just want a plain old, ultra-hot, garlicky, bright red table sauce into which to dip your tostaditas while you drink margaritas and wait for something or other to finish grilling. Quickly prepared in bulk, nearly always without benefit of fresh tomatoes (let alone charred ones or yellow ones or sun-dried ones) and yet completely habit-forming, such salsas are staples in modest southwestern restaurants everywhere. To enjoy that same uncomplicated pleasure at home, mix up a batch of this, based upon the one served at Tucson's El Charro restaurants. It's among the best and surely is one of the easiest.

1. In a medium, nonreactive saucepan, combine the crushed tomatoes, water, onion, olive oil, lime juice, vinegar, garlic, oregano, salt, and red pepper. Bring just to a boil over medium heat. Remove from the heat and cool.

2. Cover and, for best flavor, refrigerate overnight. (The sauce can be prepared in advance and held in the refrigerator for up to 1 week.)

3. Return the salsa to room temperature and adjust the seasoning before serving.

Red Chile–Peanut Sauce

This satay sauce gets a special touch of sweet heat from the pureed red chiles. Frozen, jarred, or homemade chile paste can be used, with each producing a different-tasting sauce. For the deepest, richest flavor (and a little more heat), use your own homemade dried chile puree. It's worth the kitchen time.

MAKES ABOUT 1½ CUPS

¾ cup smooth or chunky peanut butter (any supermarket brand)
6 tablespoons Mixed Dried Red Chile Puree (page 305) or frozen red chile puree
⅓ cup reduced-sodium canned chicken broth
3 tablespoons fresh lime juice
2 tablespoons soy sauce
3 garlic cloves, chopped

1. In a food processor, combine the peanut butter, chile puree, broth, lime juice, soy sauce, and garlic. Process, stopping twice to scrape down the sides of the work bowl, until smooth.
2. Use immediately or cover tightly and refrigerate for at least 1 week. Return to room temperature before serving.

Cool Green Dipping Sauce

This simple cilantro-and-sour cream dip was the complementary bar snack at the chili restaurant I helped found in Greenwich Village many years ago. That it was a freebie says a lot about how easy it is to make (even in quantity, if you're throwing a party). At the bar, customers dunked corn chips into it, and why not, but it's also good as a dip for chicken wings, pork or chicken satays, grilled shrimp, and raw or grilled vegetables. It keeps well, but never lasts long, and gets a little spicier on standing.

MAKES ABOUT 2½ CUPS

3 cups roughly chopped clean cilantro leaves and tender stems
2 to 4 fresh jalapeños, stemmed and roughly chopped
1 cup sliced green onions, tender tops included
1 tablespoon salt
1 pound (about 2 cups) sour cream

1. In a food processor, combine the cilantro, jalapeños, green onions, and salt. Process, stopping once or twice to scrape down the sides of the work bowl, until fairly smooth.

2. In a medium bowl, whisk the sour cream until smooth. Add the cilantro mixture and blend. Adjust the seasoning.

3. Serve immediately, or refrigerate the sauce for up to 5 days. Bring almost to room temperature before serving.

Salsa Mayonnaise

MAKES ABOUT 1 CUP

¾ cup mayonnaise
¼ cup finely chopped
* oil-packed sun-dried*
* tomatoes*
1 green onion, trimmed
* and finely chopped*
1 tablespoon minced
* pickled jalapeños*
1 teaspoon fresh lime
* juice*

Various salsa-type ingredients are pureed into prepared mayonnaise, creating a ruddy, fiery, and very tasty condiment for all sorts of grilled food. In addition to the portobello mushroom burger on page 59, try this on any of the red meat or poultry burgers, or as a dip for grilled shrimp or chicken wings. Given the small quantity called for, this seems a good place to use purchased, rather than homemade, chile paste, though if you have some on hand in the freezer, by all means use it.

1. In a small food processor, combine the mayonnaise, tomatoes, onion, jalapenos, and lime juice. Process, scraping down the sides of the work bowl once or twice, until fairly smooth. Adjust the seasoning.

2. Serve immediately or cover tightly and refrigerate for up to 3 days. Bring almost to room temperature before serving.

Chipotle Mayonnaise

A rich sauce like mayonnaise transforms chipotles from something sharp and biting into something mellower but still plenty spicy. This is great on a hamburger (beef or otherwise), on a grilled chicken breast sandwich, and it makes a fine dressing for potato salad and a great dip for grilled shrimp or vegetables.

MAKES ABOUT 1 CUP

1 cup mayonnaise
2 canned chipotle chiles en adobo with clinging sauce
½ teaspoon fresh lime juice
Pinch salt
Freshly ground black pepper

1. In a small food processor, combine the mayonnaise, chiles, lime juice, salt, and a generous grinding of pepper. Process, stopping once to scrape down the sides of the work bowl, until smooth. Alternately, you can mince the chipotles on a cutting board, then stir them, along with a bit of the adobo and the remaining ingredients, into the mayonnaise.

2. Serve immediately or cover tightly and refrigerate for up to 1 week. Bring to room temperature before serving.

Avocado Mayonnaise

Wherever plain mayonnaise is good, this cool celadon variation is better. Particularly suited to leaner grilled fish and chicken (dollop it on after the food comes off the grill), it adds seductive flavor and color to what might otherwise be disappointingly dry. It makes a nice dip for raw or grilled vegetables as well. It's not a successful keeper, so indulge yourself: Slather away and try to use it up the day you've made it.

MAKES ABOUT 1½ CUPS

1½ medium-large perfectly-ripe black-skinned (Hass) avocados
⅓ cup mayonnaise
1 tablespoon fresh lime juice
¾ teaspoon hot pepper sauce, such as Tabasco
¼ teaspoon salt

1. In a small food processor, combine the avocados, mayonnaise, lime juice, pepper sauce, and salt. Process, scraping down the sides of the work bowl once or twice, until smooth.

Salsas, Sauces, and Condiments

2. Serve immediately for best results, but the mayonnaise can also be covered tightly and refrigerated for up to 2 hours. Return it to room temperature before using.

Roasted Garlic Aioli

*2 very large bulbs regular
(not elephant) garlic
(about ½ pound total)*
2 tablespoons dry sherry
2 tablespoons olive oil
1 cup mayonnaise
*3 tablespoons fresh lemon
juice*
*½ teaspoon hot pepper
sauce, such as Tabasco*
¼ teaspoon salt

It says a lot about the successful fusion of southwestern flavors with those of other cuisines that a French-derived roasted garlic mayonnaise makes such a fine addition to so many dishes in this book. Brilliant as a dressing for potato salad (page 206), the mayo is also good on lean fish or chicken (dollop on after grilling), or as a dip for raw or grilled vegetables, satays, or plain grilled seafood, like shrimp. Good on a burger, too.

1. Position a rack in the middle of the oven and preheat to 375°F.

2. Remove the loose, papery outside peels of the garlic bulbs. With a sharp knife, cut off the top one-quarter of the garlic heads, exposing the cloves inside the peels. Partially enclose each garlic bulb in a packet of heavy-duty foil. Drizzle the garlic heads evenly with the sherry and olive oil. Seal the packets tightly, set them on the oven rack and bake until the garlic is fragrant and tender enough to pierce easily with a paring knife, about 1 hour. Cool, then squeeze or scoop the softened garlic out of the peels.

3. In a food processor, combine the garlic, mayonnaise, lemon juice, pepper sauce, and salt. Process, stopping once or twice to scrape down the sides of the work bowl, until smooth. Adjust the seasoning.

4. Serve immediately or cover tightly and refrigerate for up to 3 days. Bring to room temperature before serving.

Grill-Roasted Green Chile Tartar Sauce

Some newcomers to southwestern cooking think its practitioners mad, tossing hot chiles into everything from martinis to ice cream. It's true we sometimes get a little carried away, but the heat and flavor of these fiery pods are as fundamental to us as salt, pepper, or sugar, and there are few dishes to which they don't contribute something special. This tartar sauce, especially when it's to be used on something hot and smoky off the grill, is a fine example of how chiles can transform a familiar food. Try it on fish, shellfish, or even chicken.

MAKES ABOUT 1½ CUPS

3 fresh hot long green chiles
1 cup mayonnaise
3 green onions, tender tops included, trimmed and minced
2 tablespoons drained small (nonpareil) capers
1 tablespoon drained diced dill pickle
½ teaspoon Dijon mustard
½ teaspoon fresh lime juice
Hot pepper sauce
Pinch salt

SMOKING CHIP OPTION: MESQUITE

1. Light a direct-heat charcoal fire and let it burn down to medium-high (5 seconds to "ouch") or preheat a gas grill to medium-high. Position the rack about 6 inches above the heat source.

2. When the grill is ready, lay the chiles on the rack. Cover and grill, turning them several times, until the peels are lightly but evenly charred, 6 to 8 minutes. Transfer the chiles to a closed paper bag and let them steam until cool. Rub away the burned peel, stem and seed the chiles, and chop the flesh. There should be about ⅓ cup.

3. In a medium bowl, whisk together the chopped chiles, mayonnaise, onion, capers, pickle, mustard, lime juice, a few drops of hot pepper sauce, and salt.

4. Serve immediately or cover tightly and refrigerate the sauce for up to 3 days (it will get hotter). Let it return almost to room temperature before serving.

About the Chiles

The most common long green chile, the Anaheim, doesn't have enough heat to contribute much difference to this sauce. If you have no hot New Mexico chiles, substitute 2 good-sized poblanos instead. I'm not hassled by lighting the gas grill to grill-smoke the chiles for the tartar sauce, since it's quick and easy. I wouldn't light a charcoal grill for that, however, but you can always roast some chiles on one night for use later on or grill the chiles while the coals are burning down for the entrée and throw the tartar sauce together at the last minute.

Goat Cheese Cream

MAKES ABOUT 1⅓ CUPS

5 ounces fresh mild goat
   cheese, at room
   temperature
⅔ cup sour cream
¼ cup buttermilk
Pinch salt

This is a sort of fantasy sauce for me—it has the smooth richness of sour cream and the tang of goat cheese, an irresistible combination. Use a squeeze bottle to drizzle it over grilled seafood, lamb, or vegetables.

1. In a food processor, combine the goat cheese, sour cream, buttermilk, and salt. Process, stopping twice to scrape down the sides of the work bowl, until smooth.

2. Transfer to a squeeze bottle and use at once or store in the refrigerator, tightly covered, for up to 1 week. Bring it to room temperature before using.

Lime Cream

MAKES ABOUT ¾ CUP

6 tablespoons sour cream
6 tablespoons mayonnaise
2½ tablespoons fresh lime
   juice
1 garlic clove, crushed
   through a press
   (optional)
Pinch salt

This *crema* adds moisture, color, and a pleasantly acidic citrus shock to various grilled foods, particularly fish and shellfish. It keeps well, so make a quantity, store it in the refrigerator (right in the squeeze bottle if desired), and use it often.

1. In a small bowl, whisk together the sour cream, mayonnaise, lime juice, the garlic if you are using it, and salt. Adjust the seasoning; the cream should be tangy.

2. Transfer to a squeeze bottle and refrigerate. Return to room temperature before using.

Lime Caesar Dressing

Traditional Caesar salad is made from a vinaigrette-like dressing, thickened with half-cooked eggs. This version begins with purchased mayonnaise, which eliminates salmonella worries and makes the dressing quicker to prepare. Use whatever cheese you are using in the salad; I recommend the mellow Spanish sheep's milk cheese Manchego. Don't limit the dressing to the Warm Chicken Caesar Salad on page 94. It makes a fine dip for grilled shrimp and for raw or grilled vegetables.

1. In a small food processor, combine the mayonnaise, anchovy, cheese, lime juice, zest, garlic, mustard, and Worcestershire sauce. Process until smooth. Season generously with pepper and process to blend.

2. Use immediately or cover tightly and refrigerate for up to 3 days. Return it to room temperature before serving.

Makes about 1 cup

¾ cup mayonnaise
5 oil-packed anchovy fillets, drained and chopped
2 tablespoons grated cheese (preferably Manchego)
1½ tablespoons fresh lime juice
1 tablespoon minced lime zest
2 garlic cloves, chopped
1 teaspoon Dijon mustard
1 teaspoon Worcestershire sauce
Freshly ground black pepper

Salsas, Sauces, and Condiments

Chipotle Vinaigrette

MAKES ABOUT 1 CUP

*3 tablespoons sherry wine
vinegar*
*1 tablespoon balsamic
vinegar*
2 garlic cloves, chopped
*2 canned chipotle chiles
en adobo, chopped*
*2 tablespoons adobo
sauce from the chipotle
can*
½ teaspoon salt
⅔ cup olive oil
*Freshly ground black
pepper*

This smoky and seductive dressing is not too fiery hot and so can be used on salads ranging from plain (though not delicate) greens to main-dish salads featuring meat, poultry or sea-food. It only takes minutes to prepare.

1. In a food processor or blender, combine the sherry vinegar, balsamic vinegar, garlic, chipotles, adobo and its sauce, and salt. Process until smooth. With the motor running, gradually add the oil through the hole in the lid; the dressing will thicken. Season with pepper and pulse to blend. Adjust the seasoning and pulse again just before using.

2. Use immediately or cover tightly and refrigerate for up to 3 days. The dressing may separate; return to room temperature, then rewhisk to blend.

Cilantro-Parsley Vinaigrette

MAKES ABOUT ⅔ CUP

*½ cup lightly packed
roughly chopped
cilantro leaves and
tender stems*
*½ cup lightly packed
roughly chopped
flat-leaf parsley*
4 garlic cloves, chopped
*4 teaspoons sherry wine
vinegar*
½ teaspoon salt
*Freshly ground black
pepper*
½ cup olive oil

Fresh, green, and zippy, this is best the same day it's made. Use it to sauce warm grilled meats, seafood, or vegetables rather than salad greens. A little minced fresh jalapeño or serrano chile is a nice addition.

1. In a blender, combine the cilantro, parsley, garlic, vinegar, and salt. Pulse a few times, and then with the motor running, gradually add the oil through the hole in the blender lid. Stop once or twice to scrape down the sides of the blender jar, then blend again briefly on high speed. The dressing will thicken.

2. Transfer to a bowl and season generously with pepper. Adjust the salt. Use within an hour or so of making.

Southwestern Herb and Spice Butter

Boldly colored and flavored, this is a highly versatile compound butter. Not only is it good on red meat, it complements seafood, poultry, and vegetables (especially grilled corn on the cob) as well. And it's an essential part of my nontraditional grilled Texas Toast (page 217)—bruschetta of a very different sort. If you like the idea, grilled green onions can be added to this butter for an extra boost of flavor.

1. In a medium bowl, cream the butter until light. Add the cilantro, garlic, chile powder, lime zest, cumin, oregano, salt, pepper, and cinnamon and mix well.

2. Use immediately or cover tightly and refrigerate for up to 3 days or freeze for up to 1 month. Soften at room temperature before using.

MAKES ABOUT ⅔ CUP
(ENOUGH FOR 2 POUNDS MEAT,
SEAFOOD, POULTRY, OR VEGETABLES)

8 tablespoons unsalted
  butter, softened
3 tablespoons minced
  cilantro
1 garlic clove, crushed
  through a press
1 teaspoon medium-hot
  unblended chile powder,
  preferably Chimayo
1 teaspoon minced lime
  zest
½ teaspoon freshly ground
  cumin (preferably from
  toasted seeds)
¼ teaspoon dried oregano,
  crumbled
¼ teaspoon salt
¼ teaspoon freshly ground
  black pepper
Pinch cinnamon

Green Chile–Cheese Butter

MAKES ABOUT ½ CUP

1 large hot long green
  chile
5 tablespoons unsalted
  butter, softened
2 tablespoons grated fresh
  (not aged) Romano
  cheese
Salt and freshly ground
  black pepper

Among the tastiest of compound butters, this one, combining hot green chiles and tangy Romano cheese, is also one of the most versatile. Though designed for use on corn on the cob (page 193), it's equally at home melting over grilled chicken, beef, shrimp, or full-flavored fish like salmon, it's wonderful on hot cornbread, and it makes great Texas Toast (page 217). If you can't locate a hot green chile (Anaheims just won't do), substitute a good-sized poblano.

1. In the open flame of a gas burner, under a preheated broiler, or on the grill if desired, roast the chile, turning it occasionally, until the peel is lightly but evenly charred, 6 to 8 minutes. Transfer to a paper bag, seal the bag, and steam the chile until cool. Rub away the burnt peel, stem and core the chile, and finely chop it.

2. In a bowl, thoroughly cream together the chile, butter, and cheese. Season with a pinch of salt and pepper and mix again. Use immediately or cover and refrigerate for up to 3 days or freeze for up to 1 month. Soften to room temperature before using, if chilled.

Compound Butters

Seasoned butters are one of the easiest and most attractive ways of adding extra color, flavor, and gloss to grilled foods. Compound butters keep well in the refrigerator or freezer, and are a convenient way to add last-minute flair to an otherwise simple grilled entrée. Bold but logical combinations of ingredients are the secret to good compound butters, and don't stint on quantity—you need to pack enough intense taste into a couple tablespoons of butter to flavor an entire entrée portion. (Don't stint on the quality of the butter, either; use the freshest, tastiest unsalted butter you can find and afford.) Be sure to return chilled or frozen butter almost to room temperature before using. Restaurant chefs like to form their compound butters into logs about 1-inch in diameter. The butter log is sliced into thin disks, two or three of which look nice overlapped atop the steak, fish, or whatever. At home, you can be less fussy and just slather a generous amount of the butter evenly over the hot entrée.

Habanero-Pineapple Butter

The habanero—world's hottest chile—comes from tropical climates (it's named for Havana) and has a uniquely fruity quality that makes a natural partner for tropical fruit. This butter, not really all that spicy, adds a sweet heat when melting over salmon, shrimp, and lobster in particular, though it's also good on pork and chicken. Mango can replace the pineapple, just don't chop it quite as fine.

1. In a small bowl, combine the butter, pineapple, habanero, green onion, and salt. Mix thoroughly.

2. Use immediately or cover tightly and refrigerate for up to 3 days or freeze for up to 1 month. Return chilled or frozen butter to room temperature before using.

MAKES ABOUT ½ CUP (4 SERVINGS)

6 tablespoons unsalted
  butter, softened to room
  temperature
3 tablespoons minced
  drained pineapple
1 fresh habanero chile,
  stemmed and minced
1 green onion, tender top
  included, trimmed and
  minced
Pinch salt

Roquefort–Toasted Pecan Butter

MAKES ABOUT ⅔ CUP
(ENOUGH FOR 2 POUNDS MEAT
OR POULTRY)

⅓ cup pecans
2½ ounces trimmed
   good-quality Roquefort
   cheese, at room
   temperature
5 tablespoons unsalted
   butter, at room
   temperature
Hot pepper sauce, such
   as Tabasco
Freshly ground black
   pepper

Here's a butter that can stand up to the assertive flavor of beef, or it can be used on poultry, which can always use a little flavor-boosting. (It's also fantastic melted into a baked potato, in place of plain butter.) Unlike most compound butters, this one doesn't freeze all that well—the nuts get soggy. Plan to use it the same day you make it.

1. Position a rack in the middle of the oven and preheat to 375°F. In a shallow metal pan, like a cake tin, toast the pecans, stirring them occasionally, until they are crisp and lightly browned, about 8 minutes. Remove from the heat, cool, and chop.

2. In a medium bowl, cream together the cheese and butter. Add the pecans, a few drops hot pepper sauce, and a generous grinding of pepper (no extra salt is needed) and mix well.

3. Use within an hour or two of making.

Chile de Arbol, Grilled Green Onion, and Sun-Dried Tomato Butter

This is a robust, all-purpose butter with a nice kick of heat. Chiles de árbol can be found already powdered, or you can grind your own in a spice mill. If you do, leave some coarse flecks of chile for color and a less-homogenized texture. Melt the butter over beef, lamb, chicken, or seafood—it will complement them all.

1. In a small bowl, cream the butter until light. Chop the green onions. Add the onions, tomatoes, garlic, powdered chile, and salt to the butter and mix well.

2. Use immediately, or cover tightly and refrigerate for up to 3 days or freeze for up to 1 month. Soften almost to room temperature before using.

MAKES ABOUT $\frac{2}{3}$ CUP BUTTER (ENOUGH FOR 2 POUNDS MEAT, CHICKEN, OR SEAFOOD)

6 tablespoons unsalted butter, softened
4 green onions, preferably grilled
3 tablespoon finely chopped drained oil-packed sun-dried tomatoes
2 garlic cloves, crushed through a press
1 teaspoon chile de árbol powder
¼ teaspoon salt

Grilling Green Onions

Since the butter freezes successfully, you don't need to light the grill just for the onions. Grill them whenever it's convenient, then make up and freeze the butter; you'll be glad you have it on hand. Select large, fat green onions for grilling. Trim to leave about 3 inches of green top. Brush with oil and grill until lightly marked, 3 to 4 minutes.

Dried Apricot and Green Chile Chutney

MAKES ABOUT 4 CUPS

12 ounces dried apricots,
  chopped
1½ cups sugar
1⅓ cups cider vinegar
1 cup chopped roasted hot
  green chiles
½ cup dried sweet cherries
½ cup chopped red onion
3-inch piece cinnamon
  stick
1½ teaspoons whole
  yellow mustard seeds
¾ teaspoon salt

The adventurous modern southwestern cook recognizes that chiles are fruits, and that they have an affinity for other, more traditional fruits. This chutney is a fine example of that adventurous spirit, a fusion of several cuisines that, in the end, manages to taste completely southwestern. The recipe produces a modest yield and the chutney keeps well in the refrigerator, so it is not canned. Serve with the Sweet Hickory Whole Smoked Chicken on page 145, any good ham of your choice, or as an accompaniment to the Grill-Smoked Pork Loin on page 163. The chutney is good on sandwiches of smoked turkey and so on, and right at home among the garnishes for a traditional Indian curry dish.

1. In a large, heavy, nonreactive saucepan over medium heat, combine the apricots, sugar, vinegar, green chiles, cherries, onion, cinnamon stick, mustard seeds, and salt. Bring to a simmer, partially cover, and cook, stirring occasionally, until the apricots are tender and the chutney is thick, 20 to 25 minutes.

2. Remove from the heat and cool completely.

3. Cover and refrigerate for at least 24 hours before serving. Leftovers, covered airtight, will keep indefinitely.

Mixed Dried Red Chile Puree

Many southwestern recipes begin with the directions to soak and puree dried red chiles. Like a lot of kitchen chores, making this puree soon becomes second nature, but it's still a rather messy project. If you've mail-ordered in your chiles, it's also one you'll want to undertake while they're at their freshest, then freeze for future convenience. This all-purpose puree incorporates chocolaty, medium-hot anchos, berry-sweet, medium-hot guajillos, and tart and fiery chiles de árbol. Other combinations can be tried (chipotle-lovers, for example, will already know what to do) so that you can personalize your cooking. Freeze the finished puree in the compartments of ice cube trays, and then store the cubes in the freezer in a plastic bag, so that you can defrost a few spoonfuls now and again, as needed.

MAKES ABOUT 1¾ CUPS

4 ounces dried ancho
    chiles
3 ounces dried guajillo
    chiles
5 dried chiles de árbol,
    stemmed, seeded, and
    crumbled
4 cups boiling water

1. In a large heavy skillet over medium heat, and working in batches, toast the ancho and guajillo chiles, turning once or twice, until the chiles are limber and fragrant, 1 to 2 minutes per side. Let cool to room temperature, then stem, seed, and cut into small pieces with a kitchen scissors.

2. Transfer to a medium-large heatproof bowl. Add the chiles de árbol and boiling water. Cover and let stand, stirring occasionally, until the water is cool and the chiles are softened and reconstituted, at least 1 hour or longer, if convenient.

3. Drain the chiles, reserving ¾ cup of the soaking water. Transfer the chiles to a food processor and blend, stopping once or twice to scrape down the sides of the work bowl, until the chiles are roughly pureed. Add the reserved soaking water to loosen the blades and facilitate the pureeing.

4. Transfer the pureed chiles to a coarse sieve set over a bowl. With a flexible rubber scraper, force the puree through the sieve into the bowl. Also scrape puree clinging to the bottom of the sieve into the bowl. Discard the tough bits of peel in the sieve.

5. Use immediately or cover and refrigerate for up to 3 days or freeze for up to 2 months.

The Southwestern Pantry

In an increasingly homogenized world, where things look and taste more alike every day, insisting on using genuine ingredients is not a culinary affectation, but an essential part of getting the food right. Of all the regional cuisines of America, that of the Southwest remains the most "foreign," and thus the most dependent on building blocks that are the real thing.

In order to reproduce the authentic flavors of the Southwest, here are some chiles, spices and other ingredients you just won't want to do without. Most will be found in well-stocked supermarkets; many neighborhoods now boast ethnic food specialty shops, founded to supply the needs of the country's growing Latino population. Ordering by mail, both conventionally and through the Internet, remains a reliable alternative (see page 321). Please make the effort to get the authentic ingredients—you'll be glad you did.

Achiote Paste

One of a generous number of recados, or seasoning pastes, of the Yucatan region of Mexico, this brick-red mixture, based upon the hard seeds of the annatto (also called achiote) tree, can be made from scratch or purchased. The seeds themselves are difficult to locate, but the commercial paste made from them is fairly common. It is quite plain, with little more than garlic, salt, and pepper augmenting annatto's rather medicinal flavor. When combined with other ingredients (citrus juices, chiles, sweet spices), it adds unique flavor to marinades and sauces. It is sold in small bricks in some supermarkets and in stores specializing in Latin American ingredients. Once the package is unwrapped, any unused achiote paste should be stored in an airtight container and used up within a month or two.

Avocados

Mexico has a whole repertoire of avocados from which to choose. In the U.S., however, we chiefly get two kinds—the black-skinned, pear-shaped California type and the large, smooth-skinned one from Florida. For my taste, the buttery, high-fat, California avocados (Hass and Fuerte are the two best varieties, though produce stores usually don't label them as such) are preferable to the Florida ones, which can sometimes be bland, watery, and stringy. Rarely are supermarket avocados handled properly, so plan ahead, buy hard green specimens, and ripen them yourself at room temperature for four to five days (enclosing the avocados in a paper bag with a ripe banana can speed things up by a day or two). Do not refrigerate the avocados and when ripe—the skin will turn black while the flesh will yield to gentle pressure on the stem end—eat them more or less immediately. Buy an extra avocado or two. You will want to discard any that show excessive bruising when cut open.

Beans

One of the Southwest's great indigenous food sources, dried beans have now become nutritional darlings as well, providing considerable protein with almost no fat. From the cook's point of view, they store indefinitely, take willingly to any number of zesty seasonings, are good hot or cold, and, with some exceptions, cost only pennies per serving. In the Southwest, pinto beans are the most widely cooked; black beans, which are long-time staples in central Mexico, are newly fashionable on this side of the border, while chickpeas (garbanzo beans), kidney beans, and black-eyed peas appear occasionally. Dried beans should be picked over for stones and twigs, rinsed, and then, except for beans in a few unique recipes and for

black-eyed peas always, soaked overnight (really 12 hours and up to 24) at room temperature. Discard the soaking water (which contains some of the elements that cause gas), cover with fresh cold water, and simmer, partially covered, until tender. The age of the beans and the altitude of your kitchen will have something to do with the cooking time, so monitor the beans closely until they reach creamy, tender perfection.

One old wives' tale can be dispensed with here: Salting beans at the beginning of their cooking time does not render them tough, and, in fact, contributes to their overall tastiness. On the other hand, if you have hard water, soak and cook the beans in filtered bottled water instead, and your cooking times will be remarkably shorter. Quick-soaking beans works well, also. For this speeded up process, cover dried beans in a heavy pot with water, set over medium heat, and bring to a boil. Remove from the heat, partially cover, and let stand in the water until cool, about two hours. Drain and proceed as if the beans had been soaked overnight.

The quality of canned beans varies with type and brand, but when good, they are a great pantry convenience. For a discussion of heirloom beans— rare varieties brought back from virtual extinction by boutique growers—see page 204.

Cajeta de Leche

Cajeta is a caramelized dessert sauce, resembling butterscotch, based on goat's or cow's milk. A number of fundamental Mexican cookbooks give recipes for making your own; for the purposes of this book, the commercial variety is more than acceptable. Brands made with goat's milk are, naturally, more flavorful and are worth seeking out. In addition to using it in the Cajeta Caramel-Pecan Bars on page 232, use cajeta as a topping for raw or grilled fruit, dessert crepes, plain cakes, or ice cream.

Canela

Canela (or Ceylon cinnamon) is best bought in stick form. Softer and shaggier than conventional cinnamon or cassia sticks, which come primarily from Vietnam, canela sticks can be easily ground in a home spice mill or (less successfully—you may have to sieve out some unground pieces) in a blender. Fresh canela is at once more delicate and more intensely sweet-smelling than the Saigon sort and is preferred in Mexico. In recipes in this book, except for the Canela–Black Pepper Ice Cream on page 237, which is an ideal dish in which to discover the pleasures of canela, I rely on the convenience of regular cinnamon, commonly used throughout the Southwest.

Cheese

Among increasingly available southwestern and Mexican ingredients, authentic cheeses—many of them fairly perishable—are less widely found away from the border. Even in the American Southwest, substitutes—chiefly plain or jalapeño Monterey Jack, Colby, and sharp cheddar—are far more common, and so are called for exclusively in this book. Goat cheese, with some historical validity, shows up in many of my recipes, its robust flavor right at home among the Southwest's assertive seasonings. In a recipe or two, grated fresh feta is used in place of a tangier Mexican alternative.

Chiles

Chiles are the fruits of a variety of plants indigenous to the New World. Their assorted flavors and the sensation of heat that eating them creates have made them indispensable seasonings in both hemispheres. In this country, due to the popularity of southwestern and Asian cooking, chiles are celebrated and are more widely available, in their various fresh and preserved forms, than ever before.

Chiles Frescas

Fresh chiles, in modest variety, are found in many supermarkets these days; specialty stores will stock a wider array. The Southwest, unlike Mexico and Central America, has traditionally cooked with a fairly limited list of chiles, but that has changed here, as it has everywhere, and adventurous cooks have welcomed the new abundance. Like bell peppers, chiles go through stages of color change, most commonly from green to red, and flavor changes, from vegetal to sweet, as they ripen, inevitably approaching the point at which they spoil. Though cooking with a fully ripe red chile can produce a slight boost of sweet flavor (and a welcome touch of color), green chiles are perfectly fine, and can be used wherever red chiles can.

Buy specimens that are firm, glossy, and free of soft spots. Store them loosely wrapped in the vegetable compartment of your refrigerator and use them as soon as possible, though some varieties will remain good for a week or more. For many recipes, chiles must be fire-roasted. This loosens the tough, indigestible peels for easy removal, partially cooks the flesh, and can contribute a smoky flavor edge. As with bell peppers that are roasted, chiles are turned in the open flame of a gas burner, under a preheated broiler, or outdoors on the grill (nice with a quantity of hotter chiles since indoors the fumes can cause stinging eyes and coughing), until the peels are lightly but evenly charred, than steamed until cool in a closed paper bag or under an inverted bowl on the kitchen counter. The burnt peels then rub away (use your fingers or a paper towel). Avoid rinsing the burnt peels off with water, which can wash away smoky flavor. Some chiles, like roasted tomatoes or onions, are pureed with their charred peels intact, fully incorporating the deep smoky flavor into a sauce or salsa.

Some people find that their hands are sensitive to capsaicin, the substance that makes chiles feel hot. Such cooks should use rubber gloves when handling any fresh or dried chiles, being correspondingly careful when handling knives, since most gloves are cumbersome. Others can work on chiles with glove-less impunity, needing only a brisk hand-washing with lots of soapy hot water when done, to prevent transferring the capsaicin to eyes and other sensitive tissues, and thus avoiding discomfort to which no one is immune.

COMMON FRESH CHILES

SERRANOS. Small, narrow chiles, green or ripening to red, very hot. Slice, chop, or puree them for use in marinades, salsas, guacamole, salads, and salad dressings. A couple of serranos can be used in place of one fresh jalapeño, if necessary.

JALAPEÑOS. A chubby, blunt, slightly larger chile, bright green with black touches, sometimes seen ripening to red. Widely available, jalapeños are the workhorse chile of the Southwest. But these days jalapeños are sometimes represented by varieties bred to be mild. Why? There's little point to a mild jalapeño except exasperating the cook who wants it hot. I have better luck with mid-sized jalapeños; the big, beautiful ones seem to generate less heat. If push comes to shove, break one open in the store and taste (or at least smell) it, to be sure of what you're getting. Recipes in this book are written to use hot jalapeños.

NEW MEXICO LONG GREEN OR ANAHEIM CHILES. Six to nine inches long, the tapering New Mexico or long green chile is the premier cooking chile of the Southwest. There are a number of varietals, most hybridized for commercial production, in a variety of heat levels and sizes, some fairly gnarled, others straight and symmetrical, designed for stuffing. Grown primarily in the southern and central parts of the state, the New Mexico long green is roasted, often in quantity, in the fall, in open, rotating, propane grilling contraptions, producing a seasonal fragrance every bit as distinctive as, but much more mouth-watering than, that of burning leaves. The largest cash crop of New Mexico, much of the chile (despite the tonnage produced, it is always referred to by natives in the singular) is frozen and is widely available year-round, chopped or whole, mild, hot, or extra hot. The milder Anaheim, developed to be canned, is named for the California town where the Ortega Company's factory was located. Anaheims are found fresh as well, pretty much coast to coast, and, with the addition of a little jalapeño for heat, can be made to serve in place of long greens in some recipes. It's rare, confined mostly to chile-growing regions, but both these chiles can also be found fully ripened to red. (Good southwestern cooks know to grab the sweet-hot beauties and use them immediately, preferably as battered, cheese-stuffed, deep-fried chiles rellenos.) Long green chiles are used whole, for stuffing, cut into strips (rajas) for use in salads and on sandwiches, or chopped and added to salsas and sauces.

POBLANOS. Pointed at the tip but broad at the shoulder, meaty, glossy, medium-hot to hotter poblanos have a complex flavor that makes them among the most satisfying of chiles to cook. (Since the heat level varies, sniff or taste a few in any batch and adjust the quantity called for in the recipe accordingly.) As with long greens, these 5- to 6-inch chiles are nearly always roasted and peeled before use. Whole poblanos can be stuffed or cut into strips or chopped for use as rajas or in salads, salsas, and sauces.

HABANEROS. Among those who drop the names of chiles, the habanero gets dropped more often than most these days. Hardly anyone interested in anything even slightly spicy doesn't know that the habanero (often grouped with its cousin, the tam o'shanter-shaped Scotch bonnet) is the hottest chile known, ranging, it is said, fifty to sixty times hotter than the jalapeño. Mostly found ripened to red, orange, or yellow, these tropical chiles, originally grown in the Caribbean and Central America, have an almost fruity sweetness and a fierce, compelling (some say psychedelic) heat that is, fortunately, of short duration. They are mostly used raw in salsas, sauces, and chutneys and are essential in the Jamaican grilled meat dish called jerk.

Chiles Secos

Chiles are ripe fruits, perishable in nature and with a brief growing season, conditions which long ago created the culture of the dried chile, best exemplified by the long strings or ristras of chiles used both as quintessential southwestern ornament and as practical storage. (Hanging them prevents broken chiles, lets the cook take instant inventory, and, in the Southwest's dry climate, keeps them in peak condition). Most chiles for drying are fully red-ripe (there are also some dried long green chiles and jalapeños around these days) and left whole, even on the stem. The best are slowly and naturally sun-dried, while others are dried on conveyor belts in kilns, darkening their bright colors slightly and producing a caramelized flavor that is a little less than completely desirable, at least to the connoisseur.

Even the meatiest of chiles, when dried, are impossible to peel whole. Instead, dried chiles are broken up, sometimes after being briefly toasted on a dry skillet or griddle for a flavor boost, then soaked until softened. Drained of their soaking water, the chiles are pureed, then sieved, removing any tough bits of peel and producing a smooth puree of red flesh that is the very essence of the chile. It's messy (rubber scrapers and dish towels inevitably will be permanently colored by contact with the puree) but low-tech, and a crucial technique to experience if you want to understand handling chiles. The puree can be prepared well in advance and frozen in ice cube tray compartments or in larger quantities, for use when needed.

Dried chiles can become infested with insects, especially in humid climates. Store them in the freezer to be absolutely certain they maintain their original condition and use them up within a year, thus freeing you to take advantage of the next season's fresh crop just arriving in the market, just as any good southwestern cook would. (Chiles, like any spices, fade with time and exposure to light and should be used when fresh and discarded when stale.)

COMMON DRIED CHILES

NEW MEXICO RED OR COLORADO CHILE. Also called ristra chiles, these are the dried red versions of the long green or Anaheim chile. It is said that in the old days, when ristra chiles were hung in the fall to be used in cooking until the next season's crop became available, the amount of chile needed to last that long was determined by figuring one ristra per family member, each as correspondingly long as the family member in question was tall—a charming, if apocryphal, story that nevertheless illustrates the importance of this all-purpose chile in southwestern cooking.

ANCHO. The poblano, when dried, becomes the ancho, a wrinkly and dark reddish-brown dried chile. Like all dried chiles, the best are soft, flexible, almost leathery, not brittle, with a strong jammy fragrance. Their flavor is sweet-hot and almost chocolaty. This is a very delicious and desirable chile, great in purees, which can be used to flavor barbecue sauces and salsas.

GUAJILLO. A long, reddish-brown chile, similar to the ristra chile but slightly smaller, guajillos are common in Mexico, less so here. This is a chile whose sweet, berrylike heat makes important contributions to barbecue sauces and salsas.

CASCABEL. Round chiles, like small reddish-brown golf balls, cascabels are full of seeds that rattle when the chiles are shaken, hence the name, which means rattle. Increasingly common on this side of the border, cascabels are medium-hot, with a tart, smoky flavor—great in salsas and barbecue sauces.

CHILES DE ARBOL. Small, thin chiles de árbol (the name means "treelike"), a cayenne relative, grow on a woody bush and are usually sold with their stems intact. They can be crushed or powdered, for use in chili, sauces, or salsas or as a sprinkled-on table seasoning, or soaked and blended with other dried chiles, contributing their zippy tart heat to mixed chile purees.

CHIPOTLES. Chipotles are red-ripe jalapeños which have been smoked, creating a flavor that New Mexico chef Mark Miller describes as "smoky, sweet, with chocolate and tobacco tones and a Brazil nut finish." Wow! Moras and moritas are similar, though less common, smoked jalapeños. Dried chipotles, which are fairly hard to soften, even with extended soaking, seem less useful to me than powdered or canned chipotles (see below). That smoky taste makes them a natural flavor booster in many southwestern grill dishes.

Powdered Chiles

Another way of dealing with the un-peelable nature of dried chiles is to grind or crush them, discarding none of the precious, spicy pod. This is the chile form American cooks are most familiar with, whether as chile caribe in the Southwest (crushed red pepper flakes in the rest of the country's spice racks, actually a misnomer—they're chiles, not peppers), or as cayenne and the blended seasoning mix intended for use in chili con carne. Southwestern cooks, as well as anyone with an independent spirit and a modicum of curiosity, find pure, unblended powdered chiles a better choice, adding seasonings such as cumin, oregano, and garlic to the dish separately. Such pure powders are infinitely more useful, since the cook is not locked into one formula. Commonly available chile powders include plain red (some are designated by their area of growth, a mark of quality, such as Chimayo, a northern New Mexico village famed for its chiles), ancho, chipotle, de árbol, habanero, red and green jalapeno, and others even more exotic. To experience them at their best, store these powders airtight, away from extreme heat or sunlight and use them up within a few months.

Canned Chiles

Chiles are also preserved in more modern and more familiar ways. Jalapeños and fairly mild long greens are canned—in strips, chopped, or whole—with just a little packing liquid, yielding rather soft and tinny-tasting chiles that, when rinsed and well-drained, can be used where a firmer texture is not important. Pickled jalapeños, sold whole or in nacho slices, in cans or jars, and in a range of heat levels, are crisper than regular canned chiles and can be used where the tart, pickled taste does not intrude on the dish (they are not acceptable in subtle, nutty guacamole, for example). Frozen chiles, the green ones chopped or whole, in a range of heat levels and the red in pureed form, also in a range of heat levels, are commonly found throughout the Southwest. The easy convenience and high quality of these products have a lot to do with all the various ways they get tossed into so many different dishes here (tuna salad, macaroni and cheese, meat loaf). Their distribution is chiefly limited to the region, but they are available by mail order. Soft, smoky chipotles, canned in a simplified version of the Mexican barbecue sauce known as adobo, are easily minced or pureed into sauces, or even used whole on sandwiches, for those who like it real hot. The thickness and flavor of the adobo vary with various brands; nearly all are good, just different. Sample a few until you find a brand you like. Unused chipotles can be transferred to an airtight, non-reactive container and refrigerated. They keep for several months, and a steady diet will eventually grow into a relentless craving.

Chorizo

Chorizo in the southwestern U.S. is a highly seasoned fresh sausage, not the firm, dried chorizo of Spain (the sort that turns up in good paella). Made from ingredients one would rather not contemplate, chorizo, with a lot of spices and garlic and typically with a dash of vinegar, comes in bulk or in casings, frequently of plastic, from which it is removed for cooking. Sautéed to render out its considerable fat, the resulting crumble of zesty well-drained bits is used more as a seasoning than as a meat product to be eaten on its own, and is at its best added to scrambled eggs, sprinkled onto quesadillas and pizzas, or stirred into bean and cheese dishes.

Cilantro

The most widely used herb in the world according to some food authorities, this pungent flavor-maker has taken the Southwest by storm. Now used in greater quantity and in more varied dishes here than it is in Mexico proper, the great irony is that there is not much, if any, traditional cilantro use in the region, parts of which, even today, remain too cold and too dry for it to grow easily. Recent popularity aside, there are still plenty of diners who detest its strong, "soapy" taste, and there are dishes (one tortellini salad comes to mind) where it doesn't belong. Anyone who has eaten much food in Mexico, however, knows how crucial it is to that country's authentic cuisine, and how welcome it is (in moderation and with a sense of what is appropriate) in the relatively herb-less cookery of the Southwest.

Cilantro is a fragile green, best bought very fresh, ideally with the roots on. The tender leaves should be free from mushy brown spots and although individually floppy should look perky on their stems. Store cilantro refrigerated upright in a glass of water, like cut flowers in a vase, loosely covered with a plastic bag, and use it up within a day or two. If the cilantro is to be pureed, the tender stems can be included.

Corn

Corn is a New World native plant that has enormous significance in the southwest, both as a food and as a religious object. The latter use derives from the former, corn's nutritional importance in keeping man alive easily coming to symbolize a greater power. Of course it all just tastes good, too, and in the modern southwestern kitchen, newly hybridized tender sweet corn joins a host of other corn products in bringing savor to the table. In this book, aside from those sweet, tender ears, which get grilled a couple of ways (pages 193 and 194), blue and yellow cornmeal are also found. The former, from a strain of corn with dark blue kernels, has, along with its pollen,

particular religious significance to the Pueblo Indians. It grinds up rather blue-gray and has an intensely corny flavor and gritty texture that make it distinctively delicious. Masa harina, the lye-treated cornmeal intended for use in tortilla-making, supplies a unique flavor as a thickener for chili con carne. Yellow cornmeal, the kind you find in your supermarket or, better yet, the stone-ground sort from a health food store, is used plenty, too, in this book as the main ingredient in several cornbread recipes. The transition to cornbread from mush, tortillas, and unleavened griddlecakes was an easy, though fairly recent one, brought about by the availability of commercial leaveners, and influenced by the close proximity of the deep South. There is no distinctive cornbread style in the Southwest, as people choose white, yellow, or blue meal and sugar the bread according to personal taste, though there is a tradition of adding plenty of rich embellishment—grated cheese, hot chiles, corn kernels, sour cream and so on.

Cumin

Another seasoning that has taken the food world by storm, cumin, used around the world, has a vital place in the cooking of the Southwest. Especially in Tex-Mex dishes, it is used with a very heavy hand indeed, one that shocks Mexican cooks, used to that country's more subtle approach. Chili just wouldn't be chili without it, and it's indispensable in all sorts of barbecue sauces, salsas, and particularly in dry rubs, for food to be grilled.

Cumin is best dry toasted. Buy whole seeds—a jar or even two—and spread them in a small, heavy skillet. Set over medium heat and toast, stirring often, until the seeds begin to pop and turn a rich brown. Do not overtoast, or the cumin will become bitter. Remove the seeds from the hot skillet immediately, cool them to room temperature and store airtight, well away from sunlight or heat. Grind the seeds, in an electric spice mill, or in a mortar with a pestle, just before using.

Epazote

A pungently flavored herb of Southwest, epazote (also called pigweed), actually grows wild in much of the U.S. Its traditional Mexican use (aside from being brewed into a tea that is said to cure stomach ailments), is in the cooking of black beans. Not used in an amount that one can taste, it nevertheless has a vanillalike effect on the beans, making them even more delicious than they would be without it. If you have no fresh epazote growing behind your garage in the alley, or no Central Park in which to forage (it is said to grow abundantly there), the dried herb can be found in spice shops or in health food stores, loose or in tea bags. The rule of epazote: A little goes a long way.

Garlic

G arlic is nearly as universal a seasoning as salt, certainly in the modern Southwest. In Mexico proper, garlic is sometimes charred on a dry griddle before being incorporated in a dish. The equivalent of that technique in my kitchen is roasted garlic, wrapped in foil and baked until soft, nutty, and sweet. Various garlic varieties come into the market throughout the year, so being specific about one kind is not possible. Look for firm, heavy heads that show no signs of sprouting. Personally, I pick large heads (but not elephant garlic), both for roasting and for using raw, just to save kitchen time and frustration. Store garlic in a cool, dark place and use it up before it dries out or begins to sprout.

Jicama

T his large, tan vegetable (which resembles a root but is, in fact, a legume), when peeled, reveals a crisp white flesh that, at its best, is juicy and almost apple-sweet. Prized mostly for its crunch when shaved or julienned into salads, jicama also can be sliced, the slices sprinkled with powdered chile and served as a snack on its own, or in place of tostaditas with guacamole.

Widely available, if not widely understood, jicama can be found in many produce sections these days. Buy firm, heavy-seeming specimens, store them unwrapped in the vegetable compartment of your refrigerator and peel and slice them just before using. An uncut jicama in good condition will last at least a week, maybe longer.

Limes

Limes in Mexico, called *limones*, are the same as those known as the Key lime. Small, yellow-skinned, and bursting with an intensely limey fragrance and mellow tartness, they are unique. In the Southwest proper, they are not very common (until a few years ago, they were not even allowed over the border), and the common large green supermarket (or Persian) lime has been made to do. One way of getting the same intense effect out of Persian lime juice is to include plenty of its grated or minced peel (zest) to any dish. The recipes in this book have been tested with Persian limes, but anyone who locates limones should not hesitate to substitute them.

Mangoes

Luscious golden tropical fruits, mangoes are increasingly available in this country almost year-round. They add a sweet note to a variety of inventive southwestern dishes. See the box on mangoes (page 44) for more information.

Nopales

Nopales are the pads or leaves of prickly pear cacti. When peeled, cut into strips, and parboiled, they are called nopalitos. The flavor calls to mind green beans and they are good in salads and salsas. Read more about them and their fruits in the boxes on pages 25 and 252.

Oregano

There are many oreganos in Mexico, more than a few of them pungently resinous and very tasty. It used to be a little precious for me to call for Mexican oregano in a recipe, but at least one national dried herb and spice company now markets it, so there's little reason not to experience this intense herb, and the authentic flavor it creates. If it remains unavailable in your area, a good substitution is a 50/50 combination of regular oregano and marjoram. Always crumble dried herbs thoroughly before adding them to a dish, for maximum flavor.

Pine Nuts

Pine nuts come from the pinecones of a common southwestern evergreen tree, the piñon. The tiny, high-fat nuts are hand-harvested in the fall, after a hard freeze pops open the cones. Foragers must necessarily work quickly, since birds and squirrels, storing fat for the winter, are fierce competitors for the tasty morsels. The abundance of the crop varies with the season, but large, rough brown local pine nuts are usually a bargain, even in lean years. At other times, or in other parts of the country, pine nuts from China and other places can be found. Cheaper in bulk, pricier in jars, these imported nuts work just as well in traditional and modern recipes as the southwestern sort. Store them airtight at room temperature for the short term, or freeze them if you won't be using them up within a month or so.

Toasting pine nuts adds another dimension to their resinous taste: Spread them in a shallow pan, like a cake tin, and bake in a 375° oven, stirring once or twice, until lightly browned, about 10 minutes. I usually keep toasted pine nuts on hand, saving time when I need them in desserts or savory dishes, not necessarily southwestern.

Prickly Pear Fruit

Also called tunas, these oval red fruits have a light berry flavor and a stunning ruby color. They often find their way, pureed, into cocktails and desserts. Read more about them on page 252.

Rosemary

Rosemary may seem like an Italian or French herb to you, but the rugged shrub grows well in the Southwest and finds its way into our modern cookery fairly often. Naturally, the things it goes well with in Europe, it goes well with here (lamb, pork, chicken), but its sharp, piney taste is also good in salsas, marinades, and seasoning pastes. For those with hillsides covered with the stuff, it also makes a fine addition to a grill fire: Near the end of the cooking period (the flavor is fleeting), toss several handfuls over the coals. Be generous, but avoid smothering the fire. The fragrant smoke that results will add additional savor to the food. (It's also said to be a good mosquito repellent.)

Sherry Wine Vinegar

This brown, robust, and nutty-flavored vinegar is from Spain. While it has no particular southwestern association (other than Spain's exploration and settlement of much of the region), its unique flavor complements the area's other bold ingredients wonderfully. Not usually found in supermarkets, but common in gourmet shops, a little of it goes a long way and creates a big effect. For this casual, spicy cooking, the really pricey brands are not necessary. If you fail to locate it at all, substitute a good quality red wine or malt vinegar.

Squash Blossoms

Squash in various forms is another ancient and traditional food of the Southwest. As in Europe, the decorative blossoms are eaten as well. (They also show up in Native American silver jewelry as a decorative motif.) Sautéed and used in quesadillas (page 35), stuffed and deep-fried, or used raw in green salads, their bright color makes them a natural part of this region's cookery. Read more about them on page 36.

Tamarind

Tamarind is another ingredient from tropical parts that has found its way into modern southwestern American cooking. The tart, sticky pulp that surrounds the seeds inside the tamarind pod is thinned with water, then usually sweetened or otherwise flavored to make it a tasty addition to everything from barbecue sauce to cocktails. Read the box on tamarind on page 270 for more information.

Tequila

The fiery national spirit of Mexico, tequila is enjoying newfound appreciation throughout the Southwest. The array and quality of the brands available has grown dramatically, and tequila, like single-malt scotch before it, is being sipped, analyzed, and enjoyed by a new group of connoisseurs. See the box on tequila on page 250 for more information.

Tomatillos

Related to the ground cherry and the Cape gooseberry, not the common tomato, these tart green fruits, enclosed in paper-lantern-type husks, are extensively used in Mexican sauces and salsas, broiled, briefly cooked in simmering salted water, and occasionally raw. There are also canned tomatillos, but they are rather bland and soggy, tasting nothing like the fresh thing, which has a welcome, berrylike tartness and, especially when raw, a sparkling, gem-like color. Now more widely available than ever, fresh tomatillos keep well, so stock up when you see prime specimens (inside the papery husk, the sticky green fruits should be firm and shiny; choose medium-sized rather than large), then store them loosely wrapped (in a paper bag is ideal) in the vegetable compartment of your refrigerator until you are ready to use them.

Tortillas

Once painstakingly prepared by hand, these flatbreads of the Southwest are now rarely found in that rustic way except in some private homes and a few dedicated restaurants. The machine-made sort are good enough, trading reliability and convenience for the freshness, texture variations, and boost of flavor the handmade kind deliver. There are corn and flour tortillas, the former of white, blue, or yellow, the latter of white or wheat flour and nowadays made with vegetable shortening in place of lard, or, even more radically, fat-free. Commercial tortillas have preservatives and keep in the refrigerator about as long as commercial loaf bread will. They should be reheated to recall them in their fresh state: Wrap 4 or 6 corn or flour tortillas tightly in foil and heat in a 400°F oven until steamy, about 10 minutes. When feeding a crowd, make up several packets rather than one large one and set them in the oven at staggered intervals, so that you can keep pulling out freshly heated tortillas throughout the meal.

Mail-Order Sources

BUENO FOODS
2001 4th Street SW
Albuquerque,
    New Mexico 87102
800-952-4453
www.buenofoods.com
Frozen green and red chile products.

THE CHILE SHOP
109 East Water Street
Santa Fe, New Mexico
    87501
505-983-6080
Dried whole and powdered chiles and other south-western ingredients.

COYOTE CAFÉ GENERAL STORE
132 West Water Street
Santa Fe, New Mexico
    87501
800-866-4695
www.coyote-cafe.com
A wide array of southwest-ern ingredients.

D'ARTAGNAN
280 Wilson Avenue
Newark, New Jersey
    07105
800-327-8246 ext. 118
www.dartagnan.com
Foie gras, moulard duck breasts, and game meats.

EL PASO CHILE COMPANY
909 Texas Avenue
El Paso, Texas 79901
800-274-7468
www.elpasochile.com
Wood chips, barbecue sauces, chiles, and other southwestern ingredients.

FRIEDA'S, INC.
4465 Corporate Center
    Drive
Los Alamitos, California
    90720
800-241-1771
www.friedas.com
Fresh and dried chiles and other specialty produce.

LOS CHILEROS
P.O. Box 6215
Santa Fe, New Mexico
    87502
505-471-6967
Dried chiles.

MELISSA'S SPECIALTY FOODS
P.O. Box 21127
Los Angeles, California
    90021
800-588-0151
www.melissas.com
Fresh and dried chiles and a wide assortment of fruits.

PENDERY'S, INC.
1221 Manufacturing
    Street
Dallas, Texas 75207
800-533-1870
www.penderys.com
Chiles and spices.

PENZEYS SPICES
P.O. Box 933
Muskego, Wisconsin
    53150
800-741-7787
www.penzeys.com
Dried whole and powdered chiles, herbs, and spices.

PEOPLES WOODS/ NATURE'S OWN
75 Mill Street
Cumberland, Rhode
    Island 02864
800-729-5800
www.peopleswoods.com
Real charcoal, smoking chunks, and smoking chips.

RONNIGER'S ORGANIC FARM
HCR 62 Box 332A
Moyie Springs, Idaho
    83845
888-267-7079
Elizabeth Berry's heirloom beans.

**SANTA FE SCHOOL OF
COOKING AND MARKET**
116 West San Francisco
Street
Santa Fe, New Mexico
87501
800-982-4688
www.santafeschoolof-
cooking.com
*Specialty chiles, prepared
foods, and mixes.*

**SAYERSBROOK
AMERICAN GOURMET**
SayersBrook Bison
Ranch
P.O. Box 10
Potosi, Missouri 63664
888-472-9377
www.sayersbrook.com
*Buffalo, venison, and other
game meats.*

Index

Index